MW00443866

COLLEGE ATHLETES'
Rights and Well-Being

COLLEGE ATHLETES'

Rights and Well-Being

Critical Perspectives on Policy and Practice

Edited by
EDDIE COMEAUX

Johns Hopkins University Press ▪ Baltimore

© 2017 Johns Hopkins University Press
All rights reserved. Published 2017
Printed in the United States of America on acid-free paper
9 8 7 6 5 4 3 2 1

Johns Hopkins University Press
2715 North Charles Street
Baltimore, Maryland 21218-4363
www.press.jhu.edu

Library of Congress Cataloging-in-Publication Data

Names: Comeaux, Eddie, 1973– editor.
Title: College Athletes' Rights and Well-Being : Critical Perspectives on
    Policy and Practice / Edited by Eddie Comeaux.
Description: Baltimore : Johns Hopkins University Press, 2017. | Includes
    bibliographical references and index.
Identifiers: LCCN 2017008836| ISBN 9781421423852 (pbk. : alk. paper) | ISBN
    1421423855 (pbk. : alk. paper) | ISBN 9781421423869 (electronic) | ISBN
    1421423863 (electronic)
Subjects: LCSH: College athletes—United States. | College
    athletes—Education—United States. | College sports—Social
    aspects—United States. | College sports—Moral and ethical
    aspects—United States. | National Collegiate Athletic Association—Rules
    and practice. | Well-being—United States.
Classification: LCC GV351 .C63 2017 | DDC 796.043—dc23
    LC record available at https://lccn.loc.gov/2017008836

A catalog record for this book is available from the British Library.

*Special discounts are available for bulk purchases of this book. For more information,
please contact Special Sales at 410-516-6936 or specialsales@press.jhu.edu.*

Johns Hopkins University Press uses environmentally friendly book materials,
including recycled text paper that is composed of at least 30 percent post-consumer
waste, whenever possible.

Contents

Preface

The Division I college athlete experience is extraordinarily complex and compelling and has generated myriad critical questions for educators and social scientists. At the core of these analyses are growing concerns about underlying issues of equity, fairness, and inclusion. For college athletes, these issues emerge as early as their binding agreement with a college or university—the National Letter of Intent (NLI).

In 2014–15, it was estimated that more than 24,000 Division I freshman athletes agreed to compete in intercollegiate athletics on behalf of colleges and universities in exchange for partial or full athletic scholarships. The contractual relationship between these athletes and their institutions principally comprises the NLI and a financial aid agreement (FAA). By signing the NLI, these athletes have agreed to attend their respective schools to pursue a program of study and participate in intercollegiate athletics. As well, an FAA formalizes their college or university's commitment to providing athletic grants-in-aid in exchange for their commitment to playing college sports.

An athletic scholarship affords athletes an opportunity to pursue both their athletic and academic dreams. Nevertheless, the inherent value of a formal college education relative to the revenue generated by athletes in big-time collegiate sports and the ever-increasing salaries of head coaches has been highly debated. Many critics of college athletics, in fact, argue that the contractual relationship between athletes and their institutions is rarely a fair exchange. For instance, as commercial interests in college sports continue to grow, there are more extensive game schedules, more travel, and increased "special admit" athletes who do not meet the admission standards of their institutions. It is increasingly difficult to ignore the effects of these circumstances on the quality of educational experiences for college athletes.

Brown (2011) reported that athletes at Division I football subdivision schools spend 43.3 hours per week on sport-related activities, and men's and women's basketball players miss the most classes—2.4 and 2.5 per week, respectively. Missed classes are largely the result of coaches' demands and television networks' dictation of schedules and times for games. Moreover, some athletes are restricted to certain academic majors because of scheduling conflicts (Fountain & Finley, 2009). And studies have shown low graduation rates among Division I athletes in high-profile sports, particularly Black, male athletes (Harper, Williams, & Blackman, 2013). Unfortunately, economic and commercial interests create an organizational culture where academic goals and obligations, as well as the overall well-being of athletes, are less of a priority among coaches and other stakeholders of athletics.

Many critics of college athletics have also argued that this contractual relationship is disproportionately unfavorable to athletes because they are not receiving basic rights and protections, including (but not limited to) guaranteed multiyear athletic scholarships to help them complete their degrees, guaranteed medical benefits if they are injured during sport participation, health and safety rules to reduce the types of injuries that cause brain trauma, and, because of NCAA amateurism ideals, the ability to profit from their own names, images, and likenesses.

Meanwhile, power brokers who determine the rules of engagement for college athletics continue to benefit quite handsomely from the multibillion-dollar college sports enterprise. For the fiscal year ending in 2015, the revenue of the National Collegiate Athletic Association (NCAA) exceeded $1 billion. A significant portion of this revenue is the result of a 14-year, $10.8 billion agreement with CBS and Turner Sports for the television and marketing rights to the Division I men's basketball tournament. Further, head coaching salaries in big-time football and men's basketball are rapidly rising—on average, they now exceed $1 million— and salaries for athletic directors and NCAA conference commissioners are also steadily climbing.

Despite the argument that the current intercollegiate athletics enterprise is not a fair exchange for athletes, current athletes and their advocates have incredible power in their political and social voices. Rarely have these voices been exercised, however, because support systems and reasonable protections within athletic departments and their institutions are absent. As such, many athletes agree to contractual relationships and conform to current policies and practices of intercollegiate athletics rather than challenge them.

Nonetheless, a growing number of current and former college athletes across the country are finding their way and choosing their battles in the name of fairness, basic rights, and well-being. The Missouri players' protest against racism, the Grambling State players' boycott for better playing conditions, and the Northwestern University football players' union bid are all examples of athletes' activism and of their ability to participate in the transformation of the present intercollegiate athletics enterprise. These actions, coupled with several court rulings in recent years and a pending antitrust claim, do indeed demonstrate college athletes' power and authority in effecting change. And, as Paulo Freire (2000) reminds us, actions can become "the practice of freedom" (p. 34).

Until now, there has been no supplemental text for the study of college athletes' rights or their personal and academic well-being. These will be among the most critical issues facing athletics in higher education over the next decade. Both of these issues—the absence of a comprehensive teaching tool to consolidate baseline knowledge in this area and the heightened enthusiasm for the study of athletes' rights and well-being—created the need for this important and timely anthology.

■ ■ ■

THIS IS A PRACTICAL TEXT, particularly suitable for those who seek to enhance their understanding of the intercollegiate athletics landscape. The textbook is primarily intended for upper-level undergraduate and graduate students, though scholars, teachers, practitioners, policy makers, athletic administrators, and advocates of college athletes will also find it essential. The book is arranged into 16 individual chapters that cover diverse topics on college athletes' rights and well-being. It is not exhaustive, but the current concerns, challenges, and themes of relevance to the college athlete experience are well addressed.

The chapters are organized into four parts that describe in depth: (1) the historical foundations that have shaped student rights and well-being in intercollegiate athletics; (2) the formal policies and principles established by the NCAA and member institutions that influence how college athletes experience life on campus; (3) the highly commercialized business enterprise of college sports; and (4) the overarching structures and conditions that influence the quality of experiences and well-being of college athletes.

The 16 chapters provide distinctive expert voices from a range of fields. Each offers reasonable policy and practice recommendations that, when implemented, will ensure a more inclusive future for college athletes and protect their rights and improve their well-being. Each chapter also includes guided discussion questions that are ideal to spark further conversation in the classroom and beyond. In all, adopters of this text will find that this timely content sheds new insight and presents unique opportunities for the study and protection of college athletes' rights and well-being in American higher education.

References

Brown, G. (2011). *Second GOALS study emphasizes coach influence.* Indianapolis, IN: NCAA. Retrieved from http://www.ncaa.org/wps/wcm/connect/public/NCAA /Resources/Latest+News/2011/January/Second+GOALS+study+emphasizes+coach +influence

Fountain, J., & Finley, P. (2009). Academic majors of upperclassmen football players in the Atlantic Coast Conference: An analysis of academic clustering comparing White and minority players. *Journal of Issues in Intercollegiate Athletics, 2,* 1–13.

Harper, S. R., Williams, C. D., Jr., & Blackman, H. W. (2013). *Black male student-athletes and racial inequities in NCAA Division I college sports.* Philadelphia, PA: University of Pennsylvania Center for the Study of Race and Equity in Education. Retrieved from https://www.gse.upenn.edu/equity/sites/gse.upenn.edu.equity/files/publications /Harper_Williams_and_Blackman_%282013%29.pdf

Freire, P. (2000). *Pedagogy of the oppressed.* New York: Bloomsbury Publishing.

Acknowledgments

The development and advancement of my understanding of college athletes' rights and well-being is a process in which many pioneering scholars and activists have played an important role and to whom I am incredibly indebted. In particular, I wish to thank sociologist and civic activist Dr. Harry Edwards for introducing me to this area of study as an undergraduate student and for his continued mentorship. I am also most grateful to all the contributors of this volume for providing attentive insights and fresh ideas, not least for meeting chapter submission deadlines, which has enabled me to deliver the manuscript in a timely manner. I have an awesome editorial team at Johns Hopkins University Press, and I thank them for their support and inspiration throughout the development and production of this text. Finally, I continue to learn and be energized my family, friends, students, and colleagues and thank them for helping to shape this volume.

A Whole New Ball Game for College Athletes?

John R. Thelin

A glance at the calendar suggests that the college football season starts with games in late August then continues with the bowl games throughout December and finally ends in January. Well, perhaps so. But football quickly resumes. Or, put another way, for American colleges and universities the football season never really ends. Each year in mid-February local television station crews and newspaper reporters gather at high school gymnasia for a press conference hosted by the principal and head football coach, joined by parents and classmates. It's National Signing Day. Stalwart young players who have finished their senior year of scholastic football are hosted and toasted as they announce their plans for going to college—and, most important, commitments for playing college football. It forms a seamless web, as four years later a handful of these same energetic, optimistic players will have completed their college varsity competition for the National Collegiate Athletic Association (NCAA) and then are ready to be applauded and introduced when they are drafted by professional teams in the National Football League (NFL).

But what happens between the end points of those happy media events marked by the NCAA and NFL Signing Day press conferences? This is a rich, complex American drama—perhaps at times an American tragedy (Branch, 2011). For starters, the pyramid of success in high-profile American sports, such as football and men's basketball, is defined by a steep slope. It's exhilarating for those who persist and prevail—but often a trail of tears down the mountain for those who fall short (Nocera & Strauss, 2016). The pressing current issues about college athletes and their rights and welfare have acquired a visibility and urgency that is undeniable. Equally striking is how the present and past are fused. The characters and issues have been intertwined for a long time. It's a story that has been evolving for at least 150 years.

There's a complication in this snapshot. First, although football and men's basketball are dominant, we must keep in mind that some universities offer as many as 39 varsity sports. Second, does serious commitment to extending the rights and well-being of college athletes include NCAA Divisions II and III along with, for example, NCAA Division I? Furthermore, any analysis of college athletes should and must include women as well as men. It's hard for a single picture to cover the panorama and make good generalizations about athletes across all college sports.

Although the college athlete has been a fixture in American higher education and in our literature and popular culture for more than a century, a focus on the rights and well-being of collegiate athletes is relatively new. This ignorance or neglect, however, is changing. The momentum shifts toward scrutiny and advocacy from a variety of places. This anthology is timely, because each chapter is written by an established researcher and influential leader representing a distinctive discipline. This collective effort results in a comprehensive assembly of participants-observers in the fledgling topic of college athlete rights that is not going to go away.

What fair and reasonable person could be opposed to providing and then protecting the rights and well-being of intercollegiate athletes? Who agrees on how to operationalize and define these rights and well-beings? The answer to *both* questions is "no one"—and that is a problem that a flourishing body of new research, policy proposals, campus incidents, and court cases is gradually and painfully trying to achieve. It is going to be slow and contentious, in some ways because of partisan and even selfish interests who may lose revenues and power if college athletes eventually were to achieve legitimate rights. But also, building a structure and culture of athlete rights will be tough sledding, in part, because the concepts and their fulfillment of a college student are fraught with contradictions.

To bring a measure of coherence to analyzing college athlete rights and well-being, there are some conspicuous themes and landmark episodes that have surfaced as part of the history of American colleges and universities since about 1850. Foremost is that of the college athlete as both a campus hero and as an icon in popular culture and national media. Sports pages, Hollywood movies, popular songs, sheet music, fashion advertisements, and college brochures have long heralded the champion athlete as an "All American." Future presidents of the United States, including Dwight D. Eisenhower, Richard Nixon, Gerald Ford, and Ronald Reagan played college football and invoked its lessons of leadership, character building, and teamwork. President George H. W. Bush was the captain and first baseman for the Yale University baseball team, which played in the first College World Series in 1947. Ronald Reagan doubled the deal in the acting role that vaulted him to Hollywood stardom in the early 1940s as Notre Dame's legendary halfback, George Gipp. His melodramatic hospital deathbed scene in which he implored his famous coach, Knute Rockne, to tell Notre Dame players to "Win one for the Gipper" endures as a staple of American lessons and lore. Politics and college sports remain closely joined, as each year the president of the United States invites the national championship college football squad for a reception and press conference salute at the White House.

The flip side of this adulation is the equally strong image over time of a college figure that is conspicuous as the butt of jokes or as an object of either shame or pity. This is, of course, the omnipresent "dumb jock." Starting in the 1890s, the caricature draws from a succession of minority groups, many of whom were recent immigrants, whose talent on the athletic field was accompanied by problems in the classroom. James Thurber, one of the most successful and famous writers ever in American literature, wrote in his memoir about undergraduate days at Ohio State University in 1919 and included a profile of "Bolenciecwcz"—the star lineman on the football team who struggles through an introductory economics class as classmates and instructor keep rooting for him, giving him easier and easier questions to try to answer so that he can be academically eligible for the big game on Saturday (Thurber, 1933).

Closely related to the dumb jock figure is that of the college star athlete who receives perks and privileges. Hugh McIlhenny, an All American halfback at the University of Washington who went on to be an all-pro halfback for the San Francisco 49ers in the early 1950s, gained fame and infamy for his observation that he had to take a cut in pay when he left college football to play in the NFL (Thelin, 1994). The irony was that his quip was not a wisecrack. It was less a reference to his lavish living as a college athlete and more a puzzled surprise at how low the salaries were for professional athletes in the 1950s and 1960s.

Official concerns between 1900 and 1970 were less about student athlete rights than they were about student athletes doing things right. And usually this meant doing what they were told to do by coaches and athletics directors. This ranged from the young NCAA imposing sanctions on illegal, dangerous play on the field, which had resulted in a barrage of deaths and serious injuries; and in 1948 the NCAA's passing the so-called Sanity Code attempted to mandate regulations and restrictions on compensation for athletes, ranging from summer jobs to the award of scholarship monies.

The common denominator in all these images and episodes, whether celebratory or critical, stemmed from the concept of the *amateur athlete. Amateurism* was at the heart of the ideal of the college athlete—and always with varying gaps between the ideal and reality. This schism was compounded by the fact that, although everyone invoked and ostensibly believed in amateurism as the defining code of college sports, the meaning of the term "amateur" varied from one governing body to another—and even within a college conference or the NCAA or the American Olympics Committee, the term had multiple and fluctuating meanings. At the very least, what constituted an "amateur" in one era could change formally and legally in another. It also varied from sport to sport. This was the harsh lesson learned by Jim Thorpe, considered the great American athlete of the first half of the twentieth century, who was an All American in football for the Carlisle School and a multiple gold medalist in track and field in the Olympics. All this was for naught, as he naïvely and honestly played summer league baseball and got subsistence pay, all using his own name. Meanwhile, numerous other college players also played summer ball for pay—but escaped scrutiny because they were sufficiently clever and devious to play under aliases.

Monitoring the academic good standing and the financial amateur status of college athletes became a regulatory battleground between colleges and conferences—and in the early 1950s pitted colleges against the US Congress (Thelin, 1994). The stalemate was that intercollegiate sports, by definition, cross campus boundaries—but many college presidents, board and athletic directors resented and resisted the right of some larger collective body setting standards that infringed on a university's right of autonomy and self-determination. It was one thing to agree that every college football field would be standardized as a playing field 100 yards long appended by end zones. It was quite another for the NCAA to dictate and enforce how much a college could award to a student in the form of an athletic scholarship—or what grade point average allowed a student to be eligible to play in a varsity game.

This historical survey provides good, necessary background. But by now it should also lead readers to ask, "What is wrong with this picture?" The answer is that, although the college athlete is the center of attention, one searches in vain for any allowance for athletes to gain a voice or a seat at the table in shaping their own educational experience and professional futures. Although active on the field, for years they had been blocked out, essentially passive in policy and programs. An important sign of change started to surface in the late 1960s and continued in the 1970s with the initiative and publicity surrounding a group that had been used and often abused: namely, African American athletes. It came to be known as the Revolt of the Black Athletes (Edwards, 1969). In some ways, even though their message was strong, it was too little, too late. For example, Jesse Owens was long hailed as an American hero for his four gold medals in the Berlin Olympics—and as the nemesis of Adolf Hitler's Aryan racial superiority claims. But look again—in those same years Jesse Owens as an undergraduate student and track star at Ohio State University was prohibited from eating in campus dining halls or living in campus dormitories.

If the revolt of the Black athletes represented heightened consciousness for some student athletes starting in the late 1960s, then the next landmark event was Title IX, the federal legislation passed in 1972. It brought rights and protections to women as students and as athletes. Slowly this led to inclusion in the NCAA and, sadly, triggered the demise of the long-established Association for Intercollegiate Athletics for Women. In this same era one finds athlete accounts of their campus experience as being treated by some legendary coaches as expendable "meat on the hoof" (Shaw, 1972). These accounts gradually opened the door to some reforms and demands for changes which now were undeniable and could not be revoked. The cumulative result of these reforms and research is that we inherit the question, in connecting the past and present, whether such bodies as the NCAA have gone from allegedly protecting to later exploiting college athletes (Leitch, 2016; Nocera & Strauss, 2016).

A recurrent, stock feature article in popular magazines and newspapers deals with the saga of the highly recruited high school athlete who is wooed by college coaches, boosters, donors, and alumni. Then, after signing with a particular college, the star athlete faces problems involving some combination of low grades, which threaten academic eligibility, allegations of criminal charges involving misconduct, and/or use of prohibited monies. Typically, the story has a bad and sad ending. Often the athlete is required to drop out of college without a degree and an uncertain professional future. Meanwhile, even when the college officials—including coaches, the athletic director, the president, and the board—may face some reprimand or self-imposed penalty, the university and its sports program come back to play another day (Michener, 1976).

A dilemma for an earnest reader is how to best make good sense out of this ritualized story of woe. At some point the succession of these stories over time lessens their dramatic impact, because they tend to saturate and then desensitize even an attentive, concerned audience. What is one to do? Who is to blame? What are the solutions? A complication is that, in one case covered prominently in 2016, an athlete recruited to play men's basketball at Southern Methodist University was used and abused (Powell, 2016). But the detailed story left open the question: Does he bear any responsibility? Is he completely victimized? His mother cooperated and collaborated on deliberations for changing high schools and working with various youth league basketball representatives, as did his high school coach, his school principal, and a long roster of university officials. The university admissions committee gave him special consideration and decided to offer admission based on a "holistic" appraisal of his activities and record. So, sorting out heroes and villains and victims gets bogged down in nuances and complexities. What responsibility does the university president, for example, bear? Interesting to note is that in this case, the president was a longtime member of the Knight Commission on Intercollegiate Athletics.

A major source of tension, even among advocates for college athletes, will be the distinction between rights and well-being versus compensation. Providing support services for academics, health insurance, medical treatment, career planning, nutrition, time management, and other dimensions of a balanced life might be accomplished while still being silent on the matter of salary and compensation beyond the customary scholarships and grants-in-aid. A further complication is that some athletes and their representatives essentially want things "both ways"—to be treated as "normal students" but perhaps at the same time wanting special treatment and perks as valuable "athletes." Such logical binds are going to usher in long discussions.

The answers and reforms will become less obvious when one incorporates the findings of such systematic studies as William G. Bowen's co-authored books, *The Game of Life: College Sports and Educational Values* (Shulman & Bowen, 2001) and *Reclaiming the Game: College Sports and Educational Values* (Bowen & Levin, 2003). One provocative finding in these studies is that college athletes are not the only ones who devote a great deal of time to extracurricular activities. Editors of the campus newspaper and performing artists such as musicians, dancers, and actors also balance a demanding schedule of excellence in their activities as well as their studies—often with far less in terms of institutional support services and systems than do athletes. Furthermore, systematic studies of college students indicate widespread stress of having to work long hours at low-paying jobs while also going into deep debt with student loans in order to pay bills to stay enrolled. Is the plight of college athletes any more difficult than these? So, if the concern is with athletes as part of the category of rights as *students,* these larger spheres of campus life warrant consideration. Otherwise, the risk is a partial gain and a Pyrrhic victory for genuine reform of college life and activities.

In 1991 the Knight Foundation's Commission on Intercollegiate Athletics released its report, *Keeping Faith with the Student-Athletes,* which set forth a new model for intercollegiate athletics. Ironically many of the excesses it criticized have become accepted practices. For example, even conferences and the NCAA note without outrage that typically a college athlete devotes about 40 hours per week to her or his varsity sport in some form or another. A critical response to these time demands is that college athletes now are mentioned in terms of such descriptors as "indentured" (Nocera & Strauss, 2016), "plantations" (Branch, 2011) , "exploitation" (Leitch, 2016), and "unpaid professionals" (Zimbalist, 2001). Whether the promises and pledges of the Knight Commission's 1991 "new model" will be fulfilled remain unclear in light of these more recent characterizations of a new generation of widespread practices, which are not in the best interests of college athletes. But it is at the very least a work in progress. Fortunately for the health and future of American higher education and its athletes, some good answers and explorations of these questions are forthcoming in this timely, provocative anthology.

References

Bowen, W. G., and Levin, S. A. (2003). *Reclaiming the game: College sports and educational values.* Princeton, NJ: Princeton University Press.

Branch, T. (2011, October). The shame of college sports. *The Atlantic.*

Edwards, H. (1969). *The revolt of the Black athlete.* New York: Free Press.

Leitch, W. (2016, February 23). March to madness: How the N.C.A.A. went from protecting student-athletes to exploiting them. *New York Times Book Review.*

Michener, J. (1976). *Sports in America.* New York: Random House.

Nocera, J., & Strauss, B. (2016). *Indentured: The inside story of the rebellion against the NCAA.* New York: Portfolio/Penguin.

Powell, M. (2016, March 6). The tragedy of a hall of fame coach and his star recruit. *New York Times.*

Shaw, G. (1972). *Meat on the hoof.* New York: St. Martin's Press.

Shulman, J. L., & Bowen, W. G. (2001). *The game of life: College sports and educational values.* Princeton, NJ: Princeton University Press.

Thelin, J. R. (1994). *Games colleges play: Scandal and reform in intercollegiate athletics.* Baltimore, MD: Johns Hopkins University Press.

Thurber, J. (1933). *My life and hard times.* New York: Harper and Brothers.

Zimbalist, A. (2001). *Unpaid professionals: Commercialism and conflict in big-time college sports.* Princeton, NJ: Princeton University Press.

PART ONE

Historical Perspective

There is a long history of athlete protests on college campuses and attempts to establish player advocacy groups in order to challenge existing athletics structures and practices that too often do not favor college athletes. In chapter 1, Valyncia Raphael and J. P. Abercrumbie offer an historical account of the college athlete voice, as well as describe past and present student-led movements and advocacy groups. As such, part one sets the stage for a broader understanding of college athletes' rights and well-being, providing an important context for the sections that follow. ■

The Muzzle and the Megaphone

Enlisting the College Athlete Voice for Meaningful Reform

Valyncia C. Raphael and J. P. Abercrumbie

March 2014 saw Peter Sung Ohr, regional director of the National Labor Relations Board (NLRB) (Region 13), deem a class of Northwestern football players eligible to unionize. Ohr reasoned that college players were sufficiently compensated and controlled by their schools to enjoy the same statutory labor law protections afforded to employees. Distinguishing college athletes from graduate students, Ohr opined that Northwestern athletes have a primarily economic relationship with their institutions, while graduate students enjoy a primarily academic relationship, based on the time athletes spend in their athletic pursuits relative to their studies (NLRB, 2014).

> **KEY TERMS**
>
> ▶ College sports reform
>
> ▶ College athlete voice
>
> ▶ Athlete advocacy
>
> ▶ Social movements
>
> ▶ Radical flank effects

   Following Ohr's 2014 decision, Northwestern football scholarship athletes were allowed to vote on whether to unionize (Strauss, 2014). The results from the vote, however, were sealed and impounded, pending the outcome of Northwestern's appeal of Ohr's decision to the NLRB (Strauss, 2014). In August 2015, the NLRB reviewed Northwestern's appeal and explicitly declined to answer whether the Northwestern football players who received scholarships were employees (NLRB, 2015). Instead, the board declined to exercise its jurisdiction, halting the Northwestern players,' and in effect other college athletes,' ability to form a union—at least for the time being (NLRB, 2015).

   Although the ability of college players to form a union is on hold for now, this case highlights the fact that issues concerning college athletes, such as athletic time commitment and health and safety concerns—for example, concussions and long-term care for lingering injuries—can no longer be dismissed as rare or isolated incidents (USHCEW, 2014a). Accordingly, the decision acknowledges a need for a mechanism for college athlete self-advocacy.

Some avenues for this advocacy already exist, both internal and external to the National Collegiate Athletic Association (NCAA). The National College Players Association (NCPA), the College Athletes Players Association (CAPA), and the Student-Athlete Human Rights Project (SAHRP) all exist externally to advocate for college athletes' rights and protection against abuse and economic exploitation. Within the NCAA, the Student-Athlete Advisory Committee (SAAC) has become an advocacy staple at the national, conference, and campus levels. This chapter discusses the means athletes have used to organize reform in collegiate athletics. Using radical flank effect analysis, we surmise that through coordination, internal and external college athlete advocacy organizations can create positive radical flank effects that may yield meaningful reform in intercollegiate athletics. At the close of this chapter, recommendations best suited to incite and implement such reform are provided.

COLLEGE ATHLETE SELF-ADVOCACY

Before the NCPA, CAPA, the SAHRP, and the SAAC worked to protect athletes from physical, mental, emotional, and economic harm, college athletes organized themselves to protest mistreatment. During the Civil Rights era, Black students across the country revolted against egregious racism and residual second-class treatment of the school's Black community (Edwards, 1969). Recent waves of state budget cuts have inspired athletes to speak out as well. Here, two revolts are highlighted.

During the late 1960s at San José State University (SJS), current and former college athletes organized the United Black Students for Action (UBSA) alongside their non-athlete peers to secure racial equality on campus. The organization demanded equal access to campus housing and student organizations as well as fair treatment for prospective and current athletes from the athletics department. Initiating the revolt, UBSA approached the campus administration; failing to spark change internally, they made a public appeal, holding an equality rally.

After the rally, UBSA recognized the power of athletics and threatened to prevent SJS's opening football game against the University of Texas, El Paso, if the administration refused to meet demands. True to their word, the football game did not occur, costing the university community $100,000 (Edwards, 1969). Accounting for inflation, the costs would be equivalent to over $670,000 today, about three times the amount an average Pac-12 school spent on each scholarship football player in 2013 (Knight Commission, 2015; US Department of Labor, 2015). With time and persistence, many of the Black college athletes' demands were met, and the revolt was a success. Similar revolts occurred at 37 major college campuses during the 1967–68 school year (Edwards, 1969).

More recently, athletes motivated by safety and well-being concerns have resurrected the activist spirit of the 1960s. In October 2013, football college athletes at Grambling State University boycotted practice and a game to expose unanswered complaints about their unsafe practice facilities, unreasonable travel and summer camp accommodations, and their coach's suspect use of alumni funds (Zirin, 2013a). The team's refusal to play against Jackson State University (JSU) cost Grambling as much as $300,000 (Brandt, 2013; Demby, 2013; Dumlao, 2014; Ware, 2013; Zirin, 2013a). This figure includes neither the damages JSU sought nor conference fines, a sum valued at over $600,000 (Watkins, 2014). The final settlement resulted in an undisclosed amount to be paid over three years (Associated Press, 2014).

Another recent example of this occurred in November 2015 at the University of Missouri (Mizzou). When 30 Black football athletes refused to play until the university president and the chancellor resigned (Tracy & Southall, 2015). This revolt was in solidarity with a Mizzou graduate student's hunger strike and other student protests of the university president's and the chancellor's neglect of the campus's increasingly hostile racial climate (Tracy & Southall, 2015). Via several social media posts, the athletes' stance was expressly supported by their white teammates and head coach Gary Pinkel (Fernandez, 2015; Tracy & Southall, 2015). With national media attention on the protests and estimated financial losses of over $1 million for an unplayed game, both the president and the chancellor resigned within a week of the threatened strike (ESPN.com News Services, 2015; Tracy & Southall, 2015). Moreover, in December 2015, the Missouri State Legislature proposed a bill that would allow a state school to revoke a college scholarship should an athlete protest (ESPN.com News Services, 2015; Visser, 2015). The resignations and the proposed legislation illustrate the profound impact college athletes can have when they successfully leverage their social and political capital through activism.

Beyond San José State, Grambling State University, and Mizzou, other protests against mistreatment have been executed at institutions like the University of Washington, Howard University, and the University of Notre Dame (Zirin, 2013b).While such protests have not been widely publicized by mass media, they provide examples of successful efforts of athletes' voices sparking reform. Moreover, these revolts were successful because athletes and students worked together to push for reform, seeking to alter the status quo. The next section uses social movement theoretical concepts to discuss current organizational reform efforts with an emphasis on the locus and influence of their voices.

RADICAL FLANK EFFECTS AND THE COLLEGE ATHLETE'S VOICE

History shows campus-level revolts are often successful, but widespread reform and culture change within the NCAA will require a marked social movement. Social movements occur when conscious groups make "socially shared demands for change" (Oberschall, 1973, p. 15) and often occur through radical flank effects. Radical flank effects are interactive processes involving groups (radical factions) that offer an understanding of the problem they seek to solve, often with drastic change as a solution (Den Hond & De Bakker, 2007; Haines, 1984; Snow, Della Porta, Klandermans, & McAdam, 2013).

With such diverse perspectives, different groups may form, with actions and agendas altering the success of one another. These results can be referred to as positive or negative flank effects. A positive flank effect occurs when the presence of one group bolsters the leveraging capacity of another; alternatively, negative flank effects result when one group undermines the position, goals, activities, or legitimacy of another (Haines, 1984). Radical flank effects provide an understanding of how the college athlete voice may challenge the status quo within and external to the NCAA. The following sections refer to the external voices as megaphones, a symbol of more radical voices amplifying the grievances of vulnerable or exploited parties; in contrast, the muzzle represents the internal college athlete voice: the Student-Athlete Advisory Committee.

THE MEGAPHONES

The National College Player Association

Recent congressional stances criticize athletes' self-advocacy outside of the NCAA, stating it "will do more harm than good" but challenges "all institutions to step up and . . . help ensure the real challenges [college athletes] face are resolved" (USHCEW, 2014b, para. 2). Formed by former University of California, Los Angeles (UCLA) football player Ramogi Huma, the NCPA evolved from the College Athlete Coalition (CAC)—a UCLA student group independent from athletic administration that allowed college athletes to voice their opinions, address their concerns, and influence NCAA rules and regulations (Aguirre, 2004). Since 2001 the NCPA, a California-based advocacy organization, has worked to be an extra voice for athletes.

Through state and federal lobbying, among other advocacy campaigning, the NCPA has worked to resolve issues faced by college athletes, particularly those competing in revenue-generating programs. These issues include: lifting athlete transfer and employment restrictions, protecting athlete eligibility interests, and raising scholarship award amounts (NCPA, 2015). Over the years, the NCPA has been pivotal in bringing forth such reforms as: securing a $10 million fund to assist former athletes to either complete their undergraduate degree or attend a graduate or professional program; sponsoring the Student-Athlete Bill of Rights in California;[1] and increasing amounts athletes can receive in scholarship awards, part-time jobs, and other health and safety protections (NCPA, 2015).

With a successful track record of advocacy, the NCPA may provide a radical flank mechanism to spark widespread reform. While it remains to be seen whether college athletes can be defined as employees under the National Labor Relations Act (NLRA), the NCPA could set a revolution-focused strategic plan and communicate the plan's objectives with other college athlete advocacy groups (positive flank effects). Where revolutionary action reaches an impasse from outside the NCAA, conferences, and member institutions, other groups, such as the SAAC or SAHRP could work in tandem to influence reform. With this shared or coordinated agenda, the groups could work together to move NCAA, conference, and institutional-level policy forward with respect to matters related to college athlete well-being. In this way, the NCPA may be able to supplement advocacy efforts and influence the NCAA and its membership to reform the college athlete experience in conjunction with other advocacy groups.

College Athletes Players Association

CAPA, a labor organization co-founded in January 2014 by former college football athletes Ramogi Huma and Kain Colter, and former college and professional basketball player Luke Bonner (CAPA, 2015a), exists to protect the various interests of college players. Aiming to allow players to collectively bargain for rights, CAPA filed the Northwestern petition[2] with the NLRB and is supported by the United Steelworkers Union. Together, the partnership advocates for sports-related medical expenses for current and former players, concussion reform in game play and practice, academic and time-to-degree reforms, increased athletic scholarships, ability for college player endorsement deals, and an increase in due process rights for athletes facing NCAA infractions charges.

Similar to the NCPA, CAPA has the potential to be another catalyst for college sports reform. As it stands, "CAPA intends to represent FBS football players and Division I men's basketball players" (CAPA, 2015b, para. 16), but the variety in state labor laws across the country may be an obstacle. This legal diversity may prevent CAPA from uniformly representing athletes across the country, as other national unions would. Additionally, without a partnership, the work of CAPA and the NCPA might produce negative flank effects, especially for revenue-sport college athletes and their interests, because of the overlapping leadership. While CAPA may be instrumental in reform, the organization's future is uncertain, since the question remains as to whether college football scholarship athletes are employees under the NLRA.

College Athlete Human Rights Project

The College Athlete Human Rights Project (the Project) is a 501 (c)(4) organization formed to "end the exploitation of college athletes while promoting their development and overall well-being" (SAHRP, 2015, para. 1). The Project, partnering with philanthropists, activists, and social justice champions, "provides real time advocacy and activism for college athletes in cases where they are treated unjustly" (SAHRP, 2015, para. 2). To execute their advocacy when injustice is reported, volunteer members discuss the issues and decide whether to contact the institution at which the incident occurred. If the institution is contacted, the Project either meets with administrators or discusses the situation with administration as an athlete advocate.

Using this strategy, the Project has been helpful for current athletes and their parents seeking assistance when they feel as though they have nowhere else to turn. The Project is composed of an array of academics with desires to protect the interests of college athletes. The service is free to the affected athletes, but the Project accepts donations from those interested in college athlete advocacy. This advocacy ranges from drafting letters to athletic departments, communicating with the NCAA leadership, filing Office for Civil Rights complaints, and providing resources to college athletes and their parents when incidents of mistreatment arise. Considering incidents of alleged college athlete abuse, such as what occurred at Rutgers[3] and Illinois,[4] where public exposure led to improved college treatment, the Project aims to intervene, expose, and ameliorate injustices on college athletes' behalf. In this way, the Project seeks to be an ombudsman for college athletes to neutralize the ability of athletic departments to exploit their athletes' vulnerability, especially when their eligibility is at stake and/or when there are accusations of abuse.

Although the Project is not an organization led by college athletes, its purpose is to advocate for and intervene on behalf of college athletes. As an unofficial ombudsman, it has been included in this discussion, since it provides an important service that CAPA and the NCPA do not. In this position, the SAHRP is poised to be a radical faction, able to intervene on behalf of college athletes when individual institutions cannot be trusted to address student-athlete concerns. This intervention can undermine an institution's ability to protect athletes, placing pressure on conferences or the NCAA to address concerns of college athlete welfare.

The NCPA, CAPA, and the SAHRP each provide examples of organizations external to the NCAA that provide large-scale advocacy for college athletes' well-being. Although they are external to the NCAA, their membership may include current students bound by NCAA rules. These external organizations provide distance from the NCAA's grasp but offer attenuated help, as most current athletes are insulated from getting assistance from less egregious mistreatment while they compete. To address more benign or rule-related reform, internal advocacy is better suited. To understand internal advocacy, we turn to the sole form of sanctioned college athlete voice, the Student-Athlete Advisory Committee.

THE MUZZLE

Student-Athlete Advisory Committee

Proposal 77 of the 1989 NCAA convention created the SAAC as a student governance body to allow a college athlete voice within the NCAA. The SAAC was tasked with addressing the educational, athletic, and other needs of all college athletes across all divisions. Many describe the SAAC's evolution as increasingly effective, becoming a body to work beyond airing grievances but offering athlete advocacy (NCAA, 2014). Today, separate forums exist for each of the three divisions, composed of both male and female representatives from the sports sponsored by that division, who provide insight on matters concerning proposed and existing NCAA legislation, governance structure, programs, activities, and other subjects of interest to college athletes (NCAA, 2004).[5]

In 1995, member institutions adopted legislation mandating a SAAC at each institution. Although it was an NCAA mandate, bylaws do not specify whether the organization should function as a recognized student organization—with access to greater campus resources, provisions, and peer-group recognition—or if it should exist informally—solely under athletic administration. There are no suggested guidelines for how members are selected, but it is noted that the composition and overall function warrant special attention.[6] The campus committee should serve as a voice among college athletes, coaches, and administrators addressing issues of college athlete welfare. Through campus SAACs, college athletes have the opportunity to improve the college athlete experience and promote educational growth through sports participation (NCAA, 2004).

As Van Rheenen and colleagues note (2011), college athletes are already lacking secure and protective mechanisms in this world of intercollegiate athletics, because it is built on a profit-based market. By giving the college athletes a "voice," the NCAA claims to give some power and authority back to the college athletes whose lives are being affected by the decisions of NCAA officers. However, lack of specificity in the rules that govern SAACs alludes to the depth of concern for student voice. When altering the only (sanctioned) way college athletes voice their concerns, "these key stakeholders are seldom invited to offer their critical perspectives about . . . important decisions" that affect the student-athlete experience (Van Rheenen, et al., 2011, p. 162).

At the 2014 NCAA convention, Melissa Minton, a then Division I SAAC member, shared her sentiments on the association's policies muzzling college athlete voice on important issues. Citing the NCAA's necessary approval for any "position of advocacy" SAAC representatives may take, Minton's points are hard to ignore. She states, "They want to filter any and everything we say/do . . . They want us to have a voice, but they put a muzzle on us" (Wolverton, 2014, para. 5). Despite the constraints placed upon the college athlete leaders who represent the hundreds of thousands competing nationwide, Minton remains hopeful that change will come for the future, noting, "We [college athletes] have the potential to impact things a lot . . . [and] we want our voice to be heard" (Wolverton, 2014, para. 13).

RECOMMENDATIONS

For athletes seeking self-advocacy and reform, we advance the following recommendations. First, whether from an internal or external organization, members need to communicate, enabling the formation of a broader, more cohesive plan of action. Similarly, students wishing to incite reform must establish an agenda so that there are clear objectives and timelines. The agenda will help each organization understand the issues, perspective, and progresses of the other(s). This communication and policy setting can take place at an annual meeting conference, via newsletter, or even through social media platforms.

In addition to communication, the external and internal organizations should collaborate to advance their strategies. Because some external groups have overlapping leadership and goals, joining forces will help concentrate efforts to further their cause. Additionally, when current and former athletes band together, presenting multiple perspectives on the issues, cross-collaboration enables members to access additional resources and knowledge and create positive radical flank effects. Without communication and collaboration, the reform movements will be perceived as adversarial (negative flank effects) rather than complementary and may cancel each other out; for meaningful intercollegiate athletics reform there is greater strength in numbers and coordination.

We also note that protecting college athlete well-being requires more campus administrators to view college athletes beyond objects in a corporate enterprise. We recommend that athletics administrators employ principles of self-authorship and student development to ensure that college athlete voices and perspectives are heard and their developmental needs and welfare met. This strategy enables athletes to succeed during and beyond collegiate sport participation.

Finally, we also advocate for an examination of the legislation, implementation, and relevance of the bylaws mandating the organization and integration of college athlete voice in athletics administration. Administrators and students alike should critically understand the state of NCAA legislation and how it impacts athletes, including more of the student voice in decisions that affect their collegiate experience. Seeing college athletes as consultants in their experience could yield unprecedented success (Cook-Sather, 2011) on and off the field, and such support and understanding ensures that college athlete welfare is safeguarded—the NCAA mission.

CONCLUSION

College athlete–led reform is possible from efforts external to or within the NCAA structure. After considering the attributes of each, however, we ponder which is best suited for athletes. While the question seems binary, the answer is complicated, warranting a more complex response. For this we propose that both the external and sanctioned voices are necessary to advance college athlete–led reform.

The SAAC, the NCAA-sanctioned voice, is better suited if it works in tandem with the external voice. The SAAC can offer NCAA leadership a chance to work collaboratively with students, which may yield seemingly less radical reform than revolutionary demands pushed by external radical factions. If coordinated with the external faction groups, the SAAC can offer a moderate approach while the megaphones amplify the grievances of vulnerable or exploited parties if the internal efforts are not legitimately met with concern. Standing united on similar issues, while approaching them from all sides, could make reforms more likely to be adopted by the NCAA.

Increasingly, college athletes have accessible platforms to organize and confront exploitation and mistreatment experienced during their NCAA sport participation. As Michael Aguirre (2004) notes, "[College athletes] can no longer afford to be manipulated, ignored or discounted" (p. 1469). Self-advocacy in social movements has proven to be worthwhile, especially when employing strategies geared toward successful organization and execution of change like those discussed in this chapter. Moving forward, college athletes should leverage the positive flank effects of both internal and external organizations that champion their story and voice. If the internal and external institutions communicate and collaborate for their interest where they align, former, current, and prospective college athletes, and their advocates, can influence revolutionary change in how the NCAA engages with and treats college athletes.

QUESTIONS FOR DISCUSSION

1. What are some potential negative flank effects of collaboration and communication between internal and external reform organizations?

2. How do these reform efforts conflict with the position of promise and opportunity, or the myth of meritocracy, afforded by collegiate sports participation?

3. What other strategies or tactics could be effective in promoting college sports reform across all NCAA-sponsored sports, regardless of profit potential? How would you go about implementing them?

Notes

1. A mandate that athletic programs provide scholarships for permanently injured athletes, sports-related medical coverage, scholarships for degree completion, and similar protections.

2. If unsealing the Northwestern votes reveals a vote in favor of unionization, then CAPA will become the organization that represents the athletes.

3. In 2013, men's basketball coach Mike Rice was exposed in a video physically and verbally abusing his players.

4. In 2015, current and former women's basketball players and former football players alleged abuse and mistreatment against their coaches at Illinois, citing verbal and emotional abuse, racist remarks, ignoring injuries, and threats to revoke scholarships.

5. This includes the college athlete's experience, well-being, and image.

6. National representatives are chosen from a pool of conference nominees favored if their sport/race/gender is underrepresented within the current committee. Student body size, access to media markets and public scrutiny, and financial equity concerns make the sociocultural factors a bigger concern for Division I than the other Divisions (Branch, 2011; Byers & Hammer, 1995; Smith, 2011).

References

Aguirre, M. (2004). From locker rooms to legislatures: College athletes turn outside the game to improve the score. *Arizona State Law Journal, 36*(4), 1141–1470.

Associated Press. (2014, March 23). JSU seeks legal action against Grambling, SWAC. *Washington Times*. Retrieved from http://www.washingtontimes.com

Branch, T. (2011). *The cartel: Inside the rise and imminent fall of the NCAA*. San Francisco, CA: Byliner.

Brandt, D. (2013, October 21). Grambling players end boycott, have no regrets. Armstrong Mywire. Retrieved from http://www.armstrongmywire.com/

Byers, W., & Hammer, C. (1995). *Unsportsmanlike conduct: Exploiting college athletes*. Ann Arbor: University of Michigan Press.

CAPA. (2015a). More information. Retrieved from http://www.collegeathletespa.org

CAPA. (2015b). Frequently asked questions. Retrieved from http://www.collegeathletespa.org

Cook-Sather, A. (2011). Teaching and learning together: College faculty and undergraduates co-create a professional development model. *To Improve the Academy, 29,* 219–232.

Demby, G. (2013, October 24). Football player boycott at Grambling highlights budget woes. NPR. Retrieved from http://www.npr.org

Den Hond, F., & De Bakker, F. G. (2007). Ideologically motivated activism: How activist groups influence corporate social change activities. *Academy of Management Review, 32,* 901–924.

Dumlao, R. (2014, November 14). SWAC tells Grambling State it's time to pay Jackson State. *USA Today*. Retrieved from http://www.usatoday.com

Edwards, H. (1969). *The revolt of the Black athlete*. New York: Free Press.

ESPN.com News Services. (2015, December15). Missouri bill would revoke scholarships if student-athletes strike. *Entertainment and Sports Programing Network (ESPN)*. Retrieved from http://espn.go.com/college-football/story/_/id/14369127/missouri -legislator-proposes-bill-revoke-student-athlete-scholarships-strike

Fernandez, E. (2015, November 8). Missouri football players won't play until university president resigns. Huffington Post. Retrieved from http://www.huffingtonpost.com /entry/missouri-football-players-strike-calling-for-university-presidents-resignation _563f4630e4b0411d30715897

Haines, H. H. (1984). Black radicalization and the funding of civil rights: 1957–1970. *Social Problems, 32,* 31–43.

Knight Commission on Intercollegiate Athletics. (2015). Football bowl subdivision spending. Retrieved from http://spendingdatabase.knightcommission.org/fbs

NCAA. (2004). College athlete advisory committee: Forming one on your campus. Retrieved from http://www.clariongoldeneagles.com/documents/2012/9/12/SAAC02 __2_.pdf

NCAA. (2013). 2013–2014 Division I Manual. Indianapolis, IN: NCAA.

NCAA. (2014, February 4). Finding their voice: Athletes are effective advocates, but success took time. Retrieved from www.NCAA.org

NCPA. (2015). NCPA Victories. Retrieved from http://www.ncpanow.org/about/ncpa -wins-victories-for-college-athletes

NLRB. (2014, March 26). Northwestern University, 2014 NLRB LEXIS 221, 198 L.R.R.M. 1837, 2014–15 NLRB Dec. (CCH) P15, 781, 2014 WL 1246914.

NLRB. (2015, August 17). Northwestern University, 2015 NLRB LEXIS 613; 204 L.R.R.M. 1001; 2014–15 NLRB Dec. (CCH) P15, 999; 362 NLRB No. 167. LexisNexis Academic. Web.

Oberschall, A. (1973). *Social conflict and social movements.* Englewood Cliffs, NJ: Prentice-Hall.

SAHRP. (2015). About. Retrieved from http://studentathleteshumanrights.com /about-us/

Smith, R. A. (2011). *Pay for play: A history of big-time college athletic reform.* Urbana: University of Illinois Press.

Snow, D. A., Della Porta, D., Klandermans, B., & McAdam, D. (2013). *The Wiley-Blackwell encyclopedia of social and political movements.* Malden, MA: Wiley-Blackwell.

Strauss, B. (2014, April 25). Waiting game follows union vote by Northwestern players. *New York Times.* Retrieved from http://www.nytimes.com/2014/04/26/sports /northwestern-football-players-cast-votes-on-union.html?_r=0

Tracy, M., & Southall, A. (2015, November 8). Black football players lend heft to protests at Missouri. *New York Times.* Retrieved from http://www.nytimes.com/2015/11/09/us /missouri-football-players-boycott-in-protest-of-university-president.html?_r=0

US Department of Labor. (2015, June 14). Consumer Price Index Inflation Calculator. Bureau of Labor Statistics. Retrieved from http://www.bls.gov/cpi/cpifact8.htm

USHCEW. (2014a). Big labor on college campuses: Examining the consequences of unionizing college athletes. Hearing (May 8, 2014). Video available at https://www .youtube.com/watch?v=3AbSGheR7Qc

USHCEW. (2014b). Committee examines troubling consequences of unionizing student athletes. Press Release. Retrieved from http://edworkforce.house.gov/news /documentsingle.aspx?DocumentID=379328

Van Rheenen, D., Minjares, V., McNeil, N., & Atwood, J. R. (2011). The elimination of varsity sports at a Division I institution: A college athlete perspective. *Journal for the Study of Sports and Athletes in Education, 5*(3), 161–180.

Visser, N. (2015, December 15). Missouri lawmaker wants to revoke scholarships if athletes protest. Huffington Post. Retrieved from http://www.huffingtonpost.com /entry/missouri-scholarships-athletes-protest_566f6c0ee4b0fccee16fa1a3

Ware, D. (2013, October 20). Grambling football: The aftermath: Players' boycott teaches a valuable Lesson. *JET.* Retrieved from http://www.jetmag.com/news/hbcu-game -time/grambling-football-aftermath/

Wolverton, B. (2014, January 16). They want us to have a voice, but they put a muzzle on us. *Chronicle of Higher Education.* Retrieved from http://chronicle.com

Zirin, D. (2013a, October 20). Why they refused to play: Read the grievance letter of the Grambling State Tigers football team. *The Nation.* Retrieved from http://www .thenation.com

Zirin, D. (2013b, October 21). ESPN is wrong: Grambling State isn't the first college team to fight back. *The Nation.* Retrieved from http://www.thenation.com

PART TWO

Formal NCAA and Member Institution Policies and Principles

The established policies and principles of the NCAA and its member institutions remain at the heart of ardent debates about athletes' rights and well-being, and this is the focus of part two. First, in chapter 2, Ellen J. Staurowsky examines the history of the National Letter of Intent and argues it is symbolic of the need for a college athlete players association. In chapter 3, Robert Scott Lemons addresses the NCAA amateur rule, arguing that the NCAA functions as the head of a cartel of colleges engaged in a sports-entertainment business and that amateurism rules protect the integrity of this cartel. Next, in chapter 4, Jennifer Lee Hoffman examines Title IX's gender-separate allowance, with special attention to underlying gendered and racialized discourses in the educational and commercial interests of college athletics reforms. In chapter 5, Whitney Griffin examines the evidence related to concussion definitions, assessment, management, and return to physical and cognitive activity. Chapter 6, by Gerald Gurney, provides a foundation for understanding the NCAA transfer rules, particularly for college athletes who have attended one four-year institution and wish to transfer to another. Chapter 7, by Steven J. Silver, covers due process in intercollegiate athletics. And in chapter 8, the final chapter in part two, Neal H. Hutchens and Kaitlin A. Quigley examine recent court rulings and the broader legal framework that governs collective bargaining at both public and private institutions. ■

The National Letter of Intent

A Symbol of the Need for an Independent College Athlete Players Association

Ellen J. Staurowsky

Kafkaesque: having a nightmarishly complex, bizarre, or illogical quality

(Merriam-Webster.com)

The first Wednesday in February marks a milestone in the recruitment of top high school football prospects. Known as National Signing Day (NSD), the widely covered event represents the opening of a window of time when a high school athlete can sign a binding agreement—a National Letter of Intent (NLI)—with a college or university that commits the athlete to that institution for at least one year and ensures a full athletic scholarship offer. While an athlete may take up to seven days to sign the NLI once issued, should an athlete delay beyond that seven-day period, he or she risks losing scholarship opportunities altogether as coaches move on to fill their classes and take athletes who are willing to sign. Thus, NSD usually follows a certain kind of script. Televised press conferences or signing shows feature athletes revealing news of their decisions, formalized with the signing of the NLI (Northeast Ohio Media Group, 2015).

> **KEY TERMS**
>
> ▶ **National letter of intent**
>
> ▶ **National Signing Day**
>
> ▶ **Commit**
>
> ▶ **Contract of adhesion**
>
> ▶ **Kafkaesque**

In February of 2015, four-star high school football recruit Roquan Smith interrupted that usual script when he verbally announced that he was going to the University of California, Los Angeles (UCLA) to play but declined to sign the NLI on Signing Day. While other athletes were signing with UCLA, Smith waited as word circulated that the coach responsible for sparking his interest, defensive coordinator Jeff Ulbrich, was contemplating a career move to the National Football League. Four days after Signing Day, Ulbrich's acceptance of a job offer from the Atlanta Falcons was confirmed. With Ulbrich's departure, Smith reopened his recruitment. Had Smith signed the NLI on Signing Day, he would have been bound by the provisions in the letter, which expressly state that the agreement "remains binding if the coach who recruited you leaves the institution with which you signed" (National Letter of Intent, 2015). His future would have been jeopardized, because he had no way of controlling who the new coach might be, what kind of defensive schemes that coach might run, and whether Smith would be seen as playing a key role under a new coach. And at a fundamental level, Smith's actions also point to the uncertain understandings recruits have about the agreements they are signing. Even with the letter's specified emphasis on the agreement being between the institution and the player, the relationship the player had was not with the institution but with the coach who had been tasked with getting the athlete to sign on the dotted line.

While Smith's refusal to sign the NLI, given what he was learning about the situation at UCLA, was novel, he was not alone. Detroit running back Mike Weber learned the day after he signed the NLI that the coach who recruited him to go to Ohio State University announced his departure for the professional ranks. Weber tweeted: "I'm hurt . . . I ain't gonna lie" (Helfand, 2015, para. 11). Du'Vonta Lumpkin, a player who had reached an agreement with the University of Texas, found out two days after signing that the position coach who had recruited him to become a Longhorn left for a job in Florida. Lumpkin observed, "Guess I've been lied to in my face" (Helfand, 2015, para. 12).

These cases illustrate the conundrum that big-time college athletes confront about their futures. On the surface, the NLI is presented as a document that neatly establishes a quid pro quo between an athlete and institution. As explained on the NLI website, when an athlete signs the NLI, the athlete agrees to attend the college or university he or she signs with for one academic year. In return, the athlete receives one year of athletics financial aid. A violation of the agreement on the part of the athlete results in the loss of one season of competition. The athlete must serve a one-year residency at another institution before being permitted to compete again ("What is the National Letter of Intent?," 2015).

The NLI does much more than simply codify that arrangement. In the vast majority of cases, it further binds athletes to National Collegiate Athletic Association (NCAA) rules at a time when they have had little to no training in what the rules mean and how the rules structure works. The absence of an independent players association or representational body that negotiates the terms and conditions under which they practice and work results in a situation where the interests of others—the NCAA, conference, institution, program, coaches—are protected while players' interests may be undermined, overlooked, manipulated, or ignored entirely.

In the aftermath of Roquan Smith's refusal to sign, writer Zach Helfand raised the question of whether the NLI was the worst contract in American sports. While that is a question worth contemplating, a more central question might be what or who do the athletes enter into an agreement with when they sign the NLI. This chapter examines the history of the National Letter of Intent, who or what is behind the NLI, perspectives on fairness of the NLI contract, and the implications of the NLI for rights of college athletes.

HISTORY OF THE NATIONAL LETTER OF INTENT

College recruits have been described as the lifeblood of college and university teams. From the mid-1850s to the present, competition for their talent has been keen (Stancil, 2014). Persuading a sought-after prospect to sign with one school over another has inspired generations of coaches to press the limits of the rules governing when the recruitment process commences and ends, how and when contact with recruits occurs, and what incentives a recruit is offered to play at a particular school. The pursuit of competitive advantage and pressures to win fuel creative strategies that exploit loopholes and unclear areas of the rules and provide fertile ground for suspicions regarding whether coaches or interested parties, such as boosters, are cheating, gaming the system, or just outhustling or outfoxing opponents (Staples, 2008).

In modern-day parlance, the tenuous nature of agreements struck between recruits, coaches, and programs is found in the language of the "commit" and "decommit." A recruit who has signed with a particular program becomes known as a commit, meaning that the recruit has signaled that the recruiting process is over and has made a commitment. A change of heart or attitude, a genuine misunderstanding, or personal circumstance may cause a recruit to decommit, to reverse course or back out of the deal in the hope of committing elsewhere. While current rules make such a reversal possible but difficult, it is the volatility within the player market that led to the creation of a document players sign called the National Letter of Intent.

The concept of the letter of intent emerged after World War II as the effects of the dawning television age, improvements in transportation systems, and means of communication influenced the scale and scope of college sport. Once reliant on players who could be found within the confines of a regional sweep of prospects, the expanse of territory coaches were willing to traverse in search of athletic talent expanded until it assumed national and international dimensions.

As that expansion occurred, some in the college sports community believed that programs and coaches should negotiate understandings among themselves so as to limit the amount of money schools were spending on recruiting and to establish times when recruiting would end. As a result, some conferences adopted an interconference letter of intent while others did not (Cozzillio, 1989). The oversight of those letters was based within individual conference offices.

By 1962, college football was in the midst of another evolution, one in which coaches were increasingly taking to the highways and byways of America in automobiles and by plane to find and court the best football talent the nation had to offer. J. William Davis, a faculty member at Texas Tech University, a member of the Southwest Conference, a conference that abided by a letter of intent, was on a mission to reign in the bidding wars that coaches engaged in that led to players switching schools after their initial commitments. University of Oklahoma head football coach, Barry Switzer (not bound by an NLI program), was a favorite target for frustration because of his penchant for getting athletes to sign with Oklahoma after signing with other schools (Sherrington, 2015).

After failed attempts to get support within the NCAA, Davis was successful in moving the Collegiate Commissioners Association (CCA) to create the voluntary National Letter of Intent Program (NLIP) (Sherrington, 2015). At the time the NLIP started in 1964, seven conferences and eight independent institutions agreed to participate ("Seven plus eight," 1964). By 2015, the program included 650 Division I and II participating institutions ("About the National Letter of Intent," 2015). Essentially, nearly all NCAA Division I and II institutions that award athletically related financial aid participate in the program. Responsibility for its administration eventually shifted out of individual conferences to the Southeastern Conference, where the NLIP was housed between 1995 through 2006 (Heitner, 2009).

WHO REALLY RUNS THE NLIP AND WHO ARE THE PARTIES TO THE LETTER OF INTENT?

For a recruit or average citizen, trying to determine who or what is behind the NLI is confusing to figure out. While the NCAA handles the daily operations of the NLIP, a role it assumed in 2007, when the association moved its headquarters from Overland Park, Kansas, to Indianapolis, it is the CCA that provides oversight for the program and is described as "the originating entity" ("A-Sun's Gumbart . . . ," 2015). In the 2014–15 NLI, the only mention of the role these entities play and the relationship between the two is found in the statement "Administered by the NCAA on behalf of the Collegiate Commissioners Association (CCA)" (letter on file with author).

Although the NLIP resides within the NCAA Eligibility Center and is administered as an office under that unit, something that is not explained on the NLI website,[1] the program itself is governed by the 34-member CCA through a group of four, five-member committees (the NLI Policy and Review Committee, DI Appeals Committee, DII Review Committee, and DII Appeals Committee) (Hosick, 2011; CCA, 2013). When the NCAA took over the operation of the program in 2007, then president of the NCAA, Dr. Myles Brand, was reported to have said, "We're just there to reconcile the books. We send out the letters, we collect the information and we turn it over to the schools. So we're doing the paperwork, we're not running it" (Davis, 2007). One might construe this to mean that the NCAA is running it . . . without running it.

There are scant traces of either the NCAA or the CCA on the National Letter of Intent website, a curious thing from the standpoint that typically the NCAA visibly brands everything it is associated with, including its subsidiaries. As a case in point, the Eligibility Center is clearly and obviously branded with the NCAA's recognizable blue disk and bears the NCAA's imprimatur in public representations, as in the "NCAA Eligibility Center."[2] No such references are made to the NLIP. There are even fewer traces of the CCA to be found on the website or in the public domain.

All of this apparatus is brought to bear in executing a voluntary agreement that is supposed to be between the athlete and the institution, with the consequence that the athlete, upon signing, is bound to the institution. But is the agreement really between the athlete and the institution? The agreement itself is branded with the logo of the National Letter of Intent, not of the institution. And it is invalid if the athlete does not have an NCAA ID issued from the NCAA Eligibility Center.

For an athlete who wishes to be released from the agreement, the request must be submitted through the NLIP website, although the institution makes the determination if a release will be granted and under what terms. In a video tutorial that appears under the question "Can I Be Released From My NLI?" (2015) on the NLI website, athletes are informed that institutions have "complete discretion" in granting releases and are advised that athletes may appeal release decisions if not granted by demonstrating "extenuating circumstances." The video advises that coaching changes are not extenuating circumstances.

An athlete is subject to one of three outcomes when seeking a release from the NLI agreement. He or she may be granted a *complete* release, which means that no penalty is assessed and the athlete is free to reopen the recruitment process. A *no release* means that the penalty for violating the agreement remains in effect and that athlete must serve a year in residence and lose a year of eligibility, barred from competing in any sport for a year, and unable to speak with coaches from other programs. A third alternative is that the *recruiting ban is lifted,* however, the athlete is not granted a release from the agreement. In this third scenario, the athlete pays the penalty but is given the opportunity to speak with coaches from other schools. Note, however, the institution's decision is subject to appeal to the NLI.

In the *Administrative Guidelines and Interpretations* (2015–16) for the NLI, institutions are reminded that by virtue of their membership in the program, they relinquish their right to legally challenge the NLIP and the CCA. Since they relinquish their autonomy as institutions in the cause of membership, what does this do to the foundational relationship between athlete and institution, the purported basis for the agreement to begin with? As a matter of due process, if the agreement was truly between the athlete and the institution, as the athlete is told to believe, one might think that the channel for due process would first go up through the institution itself rather than forwarded to the "originating entity." And if, in fact, the CCA is the originating entity with authority to overrule the institution, might the agreement then be with the CCA and not the institution? Further, if it is not clear who the parties are who are contracting with an athlete, can the contract be valid?

THE CONTRACTUAL NATURE OF THE NATIONAL LETTER OF INTENT

In *Sports Law: Governance and Regulation* (Mitten, Davis, Shropshire, Osborne, & Smith, 2013) the NLI is described as one of several documents that define the contours of a contractual relationship that exists between college athletes who receive athletic scholarships and their institutions. There is a requirement that the NLI be accompanied with an offer of athletically related financial assistance that outlines the terms, conditions, and amount of the award (National Letter of Intent, 2015). The NLI is not valid unless both the letter itself as well as the financial offer are signed and returned to the institution within seven days after the letter is issued. An athlete could still attend an institution that offered admission and an athletic aid award without signing the National Letter of Intent.

According to the "Quick Reference Guide to the NLI" (2015), 43,000 athletes (Division I and II) signed an NLI in 2014–15. Each year, approximately 2 percent of athletes who sign NLIs request releases. For the 2013–14 recruiting cycle, 1,056 athletes requested releases; 94 percent of those seeking releases were granted complete releases; and 70 percent of releases sought were filed by Division I athletes. The highest number of requests for release came from football and baseball players as well as women's basketball and soccer players. Of the 20 appeals filed by athletes contesting an institution's no release decision, three were eventually granted complete releases ("Status Report . . . ," 2015).

While the form itself includes a statement that the athlete understands that the agreement is with the institution and not a particular sport or coach and that the athlete is asked to acknowledge that he or she understands that it is not uncommon that coaches leave, a coaching change was listed as the top reason in 2014 for athletes being granted releases. There was a significant drop in the number of times that reason was invoked, however, between 2013 and 2014. In 2013, 154 athletes were granted releases because of coaching changes, compared to 110 athletes the following year. This may be due to efforts on the NLI website and in the NLI video that specifically note that coaching changes are not considered extenuating circumstances. Signees were also successful in obtaining releases citing these reasons: personal issues, financial hardship, desire to attend a different institution, and academic reasons.

The 2 percent who contested the agreement may not be reflective of the actual number who wished to pursue alternatives but were discouraged either by the process or concern about negative consequences if they sought a release and were unsuccessful. Such a scenario would have placed them at odds with a coaching staff and program that they would have to live with after disclosing this dissatisfaction.

The high participation rates in the NLIP should also not be construed to represent the preferences of athletes. The "benefit" of the program is said to be the cessation of recruiting and relief from the pressures of being sought after by coaches. As Tom Yeager, the commissioner of the Colonial Athletic Association opined, "Recruiting is a pressure-packed thing, and the NLI is a ceasefire on recruiting" (Schwarb, 2014). That said, being bound to terms and conditions of a contract when the athlete is not in a position to bargain seems to be a fairly high price to pay just to get coaches to stop calling and contacting them.

The letter itself is also suggestive that the document is weighted to the benefit of the athletic establishment, not the athlete. Once athletes receive the NLI, they confront two options—accepting the terms as they are and signing, or not signing. There is no opportunity for negotiation. As such, the NLI fits the definition of a contract of adhesion, a form of agreement drafted by one party to which another party is afforded no other alternatives apart from rejection or acceptance. As Doyle (2015) wrote, "The NLI's boilerplate language harms student-athletes due to the unequal bargaining power between the parties." Peter Rush, an attorney who represented former University of Colorado and world-class moguls skier Jeremy Bloom in a lawsuit against the NCAA, has argued that the NLI is not enforceable and could be challenged on the grounds of unconscionability (Davis, 2007). Citing a legal definition, Davis noted that "a contract is 'unconscionable' if it did not result from real bargaining between parties who had freedom of choice and understanding and ability to negotiate in a meaningful fashion" (para. 11).

CONCLUSION

The atmosphere of Signing Day contrasts sharply with the stark reality embodied in the National Letter of Intent. Michael Lee, a Michigan labor lawyer, observed, "Signing day is portrayed as Christmas morning, everyone opening their presents, everyone counting up what they brought in and then people ranking who had what. When in effect, many young people have just signed away their legal, if not constitutional rights" (Wetzel, 2001, para. 6).

The fact that the NCAA, the CCA, and the schools that are members of the NLIP are so willing to present a carefully constructed united front in their dealings with college athletes, offering them no opportunity to negotiate, is a lesson to consider when contemplating the rights of college athletes. The obvious exploitation of the power imbalance evident in the interlocking relationships that exist among the college sport entities (NCAA, CCA, schools, coaches) speaks to the value placed on college athletes and their humanity. The business practices employed are designed to control and bargain for college athletes as commodities who have no rights.

Roquan Smith's refusal to sign the NLI when he was being misled by the coaching staff at UCLA was a form of resistance, an assertion of personal agency, a push back against a system that would have comfortably moved on, trading in deception merely as a matter of business. Neither Smith nor Mike Weber nor Du'Vonta Lumpkin should have to fend for himself in trying to navigate this

Kafkaesque bureaucracy, which is "nightmarishly complex, bizarre, and illogical." Their treatment, which mirrors that of many college athletes, calls for representation, a players association independent of the college sport entities who have constructed the maze that college athletes attempt to survive. A players association external to the system would create a counterweight, offering the possibility for greater balance, greater leverage to effect change, and a source of advocacy to help athletes understand the forces that they are up against in accessing their rights.

QUESTIONS FOR DISCUSSION

1. If the NLI were truly voluntary, as NCAA and CCA officials assert, and if that was fully understood by athletes and their parents, why do the number of signees go up every year?

2. According to the NCAA's principle of amateurism, athlete participation is a matter of "avocation," meaning that it is done voluntarily and for fun. How does the encouragement to sign a letter of commitment that ultimately binds athletes to a set of rules that they did not negotiate and that they may feel they have no alternative but to sign (despite proclamations to the contrary) reconcile with that?

3. In your view, is the NLI the worst contract in American sports?

Notes

1. On the homepage of the National Letter of Intent website, there are links to the NCAA and to the NCAA Eligibility Center that appear discreetly at the bottom of a column on the right hand side of the page. There is no attempt, however, to explain that the NLI is an office under the Eligibility Center. A small, nondescript CCA logo appears on the homepage at the bottom of the lefthand column. See http://www.nationalletter .org/. Unless visitors go to the "About the National Letter of Intent" page, they would not be able to determine the connections between the NLIP, the CCA, and the NCAA.

2. The NCAA Eligibility Center can be accessed at http://www.ncaa.org/student -athletes/future/eligibility-center. The National Letter of Intent site can be accessed at http://www.nationalletter.org/

References

"About the National Letter of Intent." (2015). NCAA. Retrieved from http://www .nationalletter.org/aboutTheNli/index.html

Administrative guidelines and interpretations. (2015–16). NCAA. Retrieved from http:// www.nationalletter.org/documentLibrary/administrativeGuidelines.pdf

"A-Sun's Gumbart new president of Collegiate Commissioners Association." (2015, June 29). Press release. Atlantic Sun.org. Retrieved from http://atlanticsun.org/sports/bsb /2014-15/releases/20150629vowjzo

"Can I be released from my NLI?" (2015). NCAA. Retrieved from http://www
.nationalletter.org/

CCA. (2013). Federal tax form 990-EZ. Guidestar.org. Retrieved from http://www
.guidestar.org/FinDocuments/2014/300/189/2014-300189456-0b0f9f13-Z.pdf

Cozzillio, M. (1989, Summer). The athletic scholarship and the college national letter of
intent: A contract by any other name? *Wayne Law Review, 35*(4), 1277–1380.

Davis, S. (2007, November 13). National Letter of Intent. *Sports Illustrated.* Retrieved
from http://www.muscoop.com/index.php?topic=4512.0

Doyle, S. (2015, April 21). Revising the National Letter of Intent. *University of Cincinnati
Law Review.* Retrieved from http://uclawreview.org/2015/04/21/revising-the-national
-letter-of-intent/

Heitner, D. (2009). To sign or not to sign, that is the question. Sport Agent Blog. Retrieved
from http://sportsagentblog.com/2009/02/03/to-sign-or-not-to-sign-that-is-the
-question/

Helfand, Z. (2015, February 14). Is the college letter of intent "the worst contract in
sports"? *Los Angeles Times.* Retrieved from http://www.latimes.com/sports/la-sp-0214
-football-recruiting-lies-20150214-story.html

Hosick, M. B. (2011, February 2). History of the National Letter of Intent. NCAA News.
Retrieved from http://www.ncaa.com/news/ncaa/2011-02-02/history-national-letter
-intent

Mitten, M., Davis, T., Shropshire, K., Osborne, B., & Smith, R. (2013). *Sports law:
Governance and regulation.* Frederick, MD: Walters Kluwer.

National Letter of Intent. (2015). Binding agreement: FAQs. NCAA. Retrieved from
http://www.nationalletter.org/frequentlyAskedQuestions/bindingAgreement.html

Northeast Ohio Media Group. (2015, February 4). Watch live 9 a.m. video of Nordonia
football players signing, faxing Letters of Intent on National Signing Day 2015.
Cleveland.com. Retrieved from http://highschoolsports.cleveland.com/news/article
/-7330232118846288082/watch-live-9-am-video-of-nordonia-football-players-signing
-faxing-letters-of-intent-on-national-signing-day-2015/

"Quick reference guide to the NLI." (2015). Indianapolis, IN: NCAA.

Schwarb, A. W. (2014, November 19). Signing of the times. NCAA *News.* Retrieved from
http://www.ncaa.org/champion/signing-times

"Seven plus eight." (1964, May). *NCAA News, 1*(2), 3. Retrieved from http://fs.ncaa.org
/Docs/NCAANewsArchive/1964/19640501.pdf

Sherrington, K. (2015, February 7). Texas Tech official helped create National Letter of
Intent, ending raids. *Dallas Morning News.* Retrieved from http://www.dallasnews
.com/sports/columnists/kevin-sherrington/20150207-sherrington-texas-tech-official
-helped-create-national-letter-of-intent-ending-raids.ece

Stancil, B. (2014, February 6). Ninety years of college football recruiting, in one map.
Mode Analytics. Retrieved from http://blog.modeanalytics.com/niney-years-of
-college-football-recruiting/

Staples, A. (2008, June 23). A history of recruiting; how coaches have stayed one step
ahead. *Sports Illustrated.* Retrieved from http://www.si.com/more-sports/2008/06/23
/recruiting-main

"Status report: 2013–2014 signing year (2014–2015 enrollees)." (2015). Indianapolis, IN:
NCAA (document on file with author).

Wetzel, D. (2001). Letter of intent benefits schools, not student-athletes. SportsLine.
Retrieved from http://www.hsbaseballweb.com/letter_of_intent.htm

"What is the National Letter of Intent?" (2015). NCAA. Retrieved from http://www
.nationalletter.org/

Amateurism and the NCAA Cartel

Robert Scott Lemons

ECONOMICS OF THE CARTEL

The National Collegiate Athletic Association (NCAA) is the organizing body of a cartel comprising over 1,100 colleges and universities (NCAA, 2014a). Over the past 25 years, university presidents have largely taken over the administration of the NCAA (Igel & Boland, 2011).

KEY TERMS

▶ Amateur student athlete

▶ Collegiate athletics

▶ Cartel economics

▶ Monopsony/Monopoly

▶ Athletic scholarship

To understand the economics of college sports requires an analysis of the market power of the NCAA and its member schools. In essence, market power is the capacity to increase the market price over the marginal costs. In other words, firms with significant market power become "price makers," because they set the price. In contrast, firms in a competitive market act as "price takers," because they must take the price arrived at by the competitive market. In general, market power leads to socially undesirable results as price increases and quantity decreases. In economic terms, this would be called inefficiency or deadweight loss, resultant from excessive market power.

The NCAA member schools enjoy market power by controlling a large portion of the market. College sports, excluding junior colleges, are controlled by three distinct organizations: (1) the NCAA, (2) the National Association of Intercollegiate Athletics (NAIA), and (3) the United States Collegiate Athletic Association (USCAA). The NCAA claims 460,000 college athletes (NCAA, 2014a). The NAIA has 65,000 collegiate athletes ("About the NAIA," 2016). The USCAA probably has around 14,000 athletes. Thus, the NCAA controls 85 percent of the shares, with the NAIA and the USCAA controlling 12 percent and 3 percent,

This chapter includes revised versions of excerpts from a larger body of work: Robbie Lemons, "Amateurism and College Athletics" (Economics Honors Thesis, Stanford University, 2014).

respectively. Because the NCAA doesn't control the entire market, it cannot be described as a monopoly, but since they control 85 percent of the market, the NCAA schools can be described as having monopoly power. As the NCAA sells the product of college sports entertainment to various buyers, especially television networks, it acts as a monopolist, from the Greek "single seller." In his memoir entitled *Unsportsmanlike Conduct,* Walter Byers, the famed, first, full-time executive director of the NCAA, proclaimed, "Amateurism is not a moral issue; it is an economic camouflage for monopoly practice" (Huma & Staurowsky, 2012, p. 8).

The NCAA also behaves as a monopsonist (Greek for "one" and "purchasing food"). In contrast to a monopoly, where there is only one seller, monopsony describes a situation where there is a single buyer of a particular good or service in a given market. As the NCAA member schools acquire college athletes through the recruitment and scholarship process, they are effectively a single buyer of athletes. Any attempt to monopolize or monopsonize is illegal in the United States, according to section 2 of the Sherman Antitrust Act of 1890.

How do the NCAA member schools gain monopoly and monopsony power? The NCAA serves as a catalyst to foster collusion. Put another way, the NCAA operates as a collusive monopsony when "purchasing" athletes and a collusive monopoly when selling college sports. From an economic perspective, the NCAA promotes explicit collusion, because its members openly cooperate to make mutually beneficial pricing and production decisions. In many ways, the NCAA functions like OPEC (Organization of Petroleum Exporting Countries), as both collude, price-fix, and manipulate production (Nocera, 2011).

Judge Richard A. Posner, of the US Court of Appeals for the Seventh Circuit in Chicago and a leading antitrust scholar, agrees that the NCAA behaves monopsonistically. He says, "Although cartels, including monopsonistic ones, are generally deemed to be illegal per se under American antitrust law, the NCAA's monopsonistic behavior has thus far not been successfully challenged" (Posner, 2011, p. 1). Posner posits that colleges and the NCAA have avoided legal sanctions for their monopsonistic behavior for two reasons: 1) collegiate athletes are students, and their educational mission would be corrupted by compensation; 2) colleges and the NCAA are nonprofit institutions. Ironically, if colleges paid athletes, the schools would be engaged in a business unrelated to their academic mission and no longer immune from taxation.

Typically, cartels make agreements concerning prices, outputs, market areas, the use/construction of productive capacity, and advertising expenditures (Koch, 1973). The enterprise of college sports differs significantly from other cartel-driven industries; therefore, the cartel of NCAA member colleges functions differently from typical cartels. The NCAA functions as the head of a cartel in the following ways: (1) it fixes the compensation of college athletes; (2) it controls the supply of athletes; (3) it distributes profits in a fashion that satisfies its members; (4) it protects cartel rents; and (5) it enforces rules on athletes and member colleges (Miller, 2013).

THE NCAA FIXES THE COMPENSATION OF COLLEGE ATHLETES

The NCAA requires that collegiate athletes must compete without salary to maintain their amateur status. Any compromise to this amateur status disqualifies the athlete from all future collegiate competition. According to the NCAA, "No student shall represent a college or university in any intercollegiate game or contest . . . who has at any time received, either directly or indirectly, money, or any other consideration" (NCAA, 2013a, p. 1).

Amateurism mandates that athletic scholarships represent the sole remuneration to college athletes (Zola, 2013). Colleges cannot award to a college athlete financial aid that exceeds the "cost of attendance" (the amount calculated by a campus financial aid office, using federal regulations that include transportation and other expenses in addition to tuition and fees, room and board, and books) or the full "grant-in-aid" limit (defined by the NCAA as tuition and fees, room and board, and required textbooks), whichever is lower (Murray & Burton, 2003). These athletes are strictly prohibited from receiving compensation for non-athletic services that might be understood to reflect on their athletic ability. In essence, this represents a twofold restriction on player remuneration: (1) it caps the total amount of compensation; and (2) it restricts the form of remuneration, because scholarships can only purchase academic units.

College athletes differ from other scholarship students, who can use their talents to earn extra money while in school. For example, music students can play concerts and get paid, and science students can work in laboratories for a salary (Wharton, 2013). No similar options are made available to college athletes.

The NCAA effectively creates a price ceiling (compensation ceiling) for student-athletes by the limitations of their scholarships and by limitations on other compensation that student- athletes could receive. Price ceilings typically result in economic inefficiency, including deadweight loss. In figure 3.1, notice the disparity between the college (consumer) surplus and college athlete (producer) surplus, suggesting a significant advantage for the colleges from the price ceiling.

Beyond setting a price ceiling on scholarship compensation, the NCAA further fixes the compensation of college athletes by fixing their commercial rights at zero (O'Bannon, 2009). The NCAA accomplishes this by completely controlling the exposure of athletes in perpetuity. In essence, the NCAA controls if and when these college athletes will be exposed and retains all profits related to this exposure.

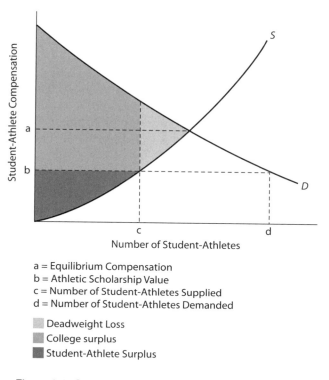

a = Equilibrium Compensation
b = Athletic Scholarship Value
c = Number of Student-Athletes Supplied
d = Number of Student-Athletes Demanded

▨ Deadweight Loss
▨ College surplus
▨ Student-Athlete Surplus

Figure 3.1. Comparison of College (Consumer) Surplus and College Athlete (Producer) Surplus

THE NCAA CONTROLS THE SUPPLY OF COLLEGE ATHLETES

Figure 3.1 also demonstrates that a price ceiling lowers the quantity of inputs, meaning fewer college students have the opportunity to participate in college sports. Thus, the price ceiling limits opportunities for potential college athletes, with too many talented/qualified athletes chasing too few athletic scholarships. If the NCAA allowed a progressively larger supply of athletes and events, the price of the events would decline. Therefore, the NCAA must control the quantity of athletes and competitions.

The NCAA limits the number of college athletes by limiting the number of scholarships per sport per college. In Division I basketball, each school is allowed just 13 scholarships. Football Bowl Subdivision (FBS) schools can award 85 football players with athletic scholarships.

The supply of college athletes is also controlled by the five-year eligibility rule, NCAA Bylaw 14.2.1 (NCAA, 2014b, p. 3). This rule mandates that college athletes only have five years of athletic eligibility to complete their four-year college athletic career. Simply put, they have just five years to play four seasons.

THE NCAA DISTRIBUTES PROFITS IN A FASHION THAT SATISFIES ITS MEMBERS

As with any cartel, the NCAA members expect that the NCAA revenue will be distributed to the membership, with the most successful members receiving the most revenue. In the 2012–13 school year, the NCAA revenue totaled $484,046,000 (NCAA, 2013c). In reality, the bulk of this revenue comes from the men's basketball tournament. March Madness captures almost 140 million viewers, and, according to NCAA president Mark Emmert, "Ninety percent of the revenue that flows into the NCAA comes from the media rights and ticket sales for the NCAA men's basketball tournament" (Bergman, 2011, p. 1). After the NCAA covers its overhead, all the remaining revenue is distributed to the member schools. The NCAA claims that 96 percent of all revenue collected returns to member colleges. As figure 3.2 demonstrates, the NCAA's largest distribution (39 percent of total revenue distributed) goes into the "basketball fund" (NCAA, 2014a). This fund "provides moneys to be distributed to Division I Men's Basketball Championships over a six-year rolling period. Independent institutions receive a full unit share based on their tournament participation over the same rolling six-year period . . . In 2012–2013, each basketball unit will be approximately $245,500" (NCAA, 2014a, p. 1). What does that mean? As an example, consider the tournament revenue generated by the University of Connecticut Huskies, who played in five tournament games in 2011 and seven tournament games over the previous five years. This gave Connecticut 12 "game units." In 2011, each game unit was worth $239,664 (Smith, 2012). Therefore, from 2006 to 2011, the university generated $2,875,968 ($239,664 × 12) for its Big East Conference (Smith, 2012).

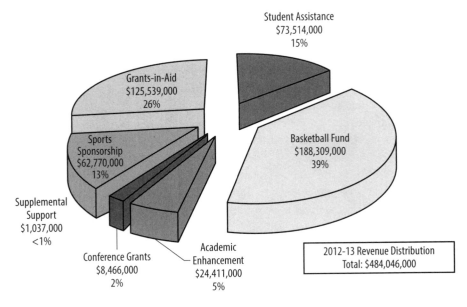

Figure 3.2. NCAA Revenue Distribution, 2012–13. *Source:* NCAA, 2013b

From the above, a couple of points become clear. First, it pays to be successful in college basketball, especially if the team qualifies for the NCAA tournament. Second, the revenue-distribution process seems complicated. Third, the member schools must be satisfied with the terms of the distribution process, as no schools have threatened to leave the NCAA cartel and no universities have filed public grievances against the NCAA's distribution process.

THE NCAA PROTECTS CARTEL RENTS

The actions taken by the NCAA to protect cartel rents represent another indicator that it functions as the head of a cartel. The NCAA has swallowed up any potential rivals. Consider how Walter Byers exploited the National Invitational Tournament (NIT) cheating scandal of 1951, elevating the NCAA basketball tournament into its premier position (Barra, 2012). Further consider how the NCAA eliminated the Association of Intercollegiate Athletics for Women (AIAW) in 1982 (Kahn, 2006). The NAIA may be the NCAA's next victim. Ever since the NCAA formed Division II and Division III levels of play in the mid-1970s, the NAIA's membership has steadily declined, with exiting members joining the NCAA ("The NAIA to NCAA," 2013, p. 2).

THE NCAA ENFORCES RULES ON ATHLETES AND MEMBER COLLEGES

Nobel laureate George Stigler described two challenges that successful cartels must overcome: (1) the cartel must be able to reach a consensus on its terms, and (2) the cartel must be able to police its collusive agents and punish those who have strayed from the agreed terms (Stigler, 1964). In the above section, the point was made that the NCAA member schools seem to have reached a consensus on arguably their most contentious term—revenue distribution.

Thus, the NCAA cartel seems to have overcome the first of Stigler's challenges.

Stigler claims that cheating represents the major threat to cartel stability. To understand how the NCAA overcomes Stigler's second challenge, it is important to understand how NCAA schools may stray from the cartel's rules. In a typical cartel, a firm may try to cheat the cartel by lowering the price to improve sales or lowering quality to decrease production costs. The NCAA members typically try to cheat the cartel in a different fashion: universities cheat to win football or men's basketball games. Winning conference titles, being invited to football bowl games, succeeding in March Madness, and being crowned national champion brings tremendous revenue, prestige, and media exposure. Therefore, the NCAA must police its collusive agents for trying to gain an unfair advantage over other cartel members.

Cartel behavior remains economically attractive as long as the expected cost of violating the agreement (rules violations) remains greater than the expected benefits from remaining in the cartel (additional revenue) (DeSchriver & Stotlar, 1996). With the establishment of the Committee on Infractions in 1951, the NCAA had a means of policing and punishing noncompliant members. Understand that this committee has no legal authority to either police or punish any university, yet the NCAA member schools voluntarily abide by NCAA rules, even when the punishment seems excessive. As a stark example consider the so-called death penalty imposed on Southern Methodist University in 1987 (Stahl, 2012).

Attorney Ian Ayres has argued that cartels can be identified by the pattern by which they punish alleged cartel members (Ayres, 1987). With that in mind, let's examine how the NCAA punishes its members. In other words, let's evaluate the rationale of the major infractions cited by the NCAA.

As table 3.1 demonstrates, the NCAA penalizes member schools most often for violations involving amateurism. Amateurism violations include outside compensation, inappropriate employment, improper accommodations, impermissible inducements and entertainment, travel expenses, and so on. Even though the NCAA owes its creation to safety concerns in college football a century ago, it now fails to police safety issues. Safety issues may include length/intensity of practice, equipment maintenance, water breaks, avoidance of hyperthermia, return-to-play guidelines after injury, and so on.

TABLE 3.1.

NCAA Major Infraction Cases (March 5, 1990–July 21, 2012)

Safety	Academic	Recruiting	Amateurism
0	11	21	24

Source: NCAA (2013b).

WHY DO UNIVERSITIES OBEY NCAA REGULATIONS?

Earlier in this chapter, it was brought out that the NCAA has no legal authority to regulate college sports. So why do universities capitulate to NCAA regulations? As already mentioned, the colleges benefit in multiple ways by the authority vested in the NCAA. It appears that there are five reasonable answers: (1) the NCAA organizes the cartel of college sports; (2) the NCAA obscures the school's academic mission with its athletic enterprises; (3) the NCAA employs a sophisticated and manipulative strategy that results in naïve, young athletes surrendering their financial rights in perpetuity for the benefit of universities; (4) the NCAA protects its member colleges from the medical consequences inherent to sports competition; and (5) the NCAA shields the universities from the absurdity of amateurism.

THE ACADEMIC EXPERIENCE OF THE COLLEGE ATHLETE

For students who would have attended college even without an athletic scholarship, the athletic scholarship offers no added value, except if the athlete gained acceptance to a higher-tiered college because of his or her athletic talents (Taha, 2011). For students who would not have attended college without an athletic scholarship, the indirect scholarship value represents the difference between the present value of their lifetime earnings as college graduates and the present value of their lifetime earnings if they had not graduated from college (Taha, 2011). This value should be considered in the range of hundreds of thousands of dollars (Taha, 2011). For college athletes who do not graduate, there is a modest, at best, increase in lifetime earnings capacity (Taha, 2011).

This brings up the overwhelmingly important issue of graduation rates for athletes. In 2003, Division I FBS football programs had a graduation rate of 69.2 percent, where Division I-A basketball programs graduated 66.4 percent of their athletes (Taha, 2011). At the Big 12 school Oklahoma, the football graduation rate was calculated at 38 percent by the federal calculation and 47 percent by the NCAA calculation. (For transfer-out players and those who leave school for the pros, the federal calculation assesses them as nongraduates, where the NCAA does not) (Gregory, 2013).

These athletic scholarships do not come without costs to the students. College athletes typically have a lower grade point average and class rank than other college students. Football and men's basketball players have a history of academic underperformance compared with nonrevenue athletes and the student body (Taha, 2011). As would be expected, these revenue-sports athletes probably face greater time pressures and other distractions than the rest of the student body.

With widespread academic failure and fraud involving college athletes, for those who actually graduate, what does that diploma represent? If that parchment represents little or no real education, what happens to the NCAA position that an athletic scholarship is sufficient compensation (Knight Commission on Intercollegiate Athletics, 2012)? As Billy Hawkins, an associate professor and athlete mentor at the University of Georgia, puts it, "To get a degree is one thing, to be functional with that degree is totally different" (Ganim, 2014, p. 5).

MEDICAL CONSEQUENCES FOR COLLEGE ATHLETES

In a variety of ways, the NCAA has limited the collegiate athletes' rights by way of the label "student-athlete." This became painfully obvious in the 1950s, when Ray Dennison died from a traumatic brain injury from college football. Ray's widow filed for worker's compensation death benefits (Branch, 2011). The case reached the Colorado Supreme Court, which ruled that colleges are "not in the football business" (Branch, 2011, p. 88). Since the college was not in the business of football, the college did not need to cover Mr. Dennison's death through worker's compensation. Walter Byers, former NCAA president, takes credit for coining the deliberately ambiguous term "student-athlete." When injured, the player is a student. When underperforming in the classroom, the player is an athlete.

Many college athletes suffer injuries from college sports, and many of these injuries linger after their college career ends. The NCAA requires universities to provide healthcare insurance during college participation but has not made clear standards for that coverage (O'Bannon, 2009). Each university can choose its own level of health insurance. Once the athlete leaves the college, the college has no responsibilities toward the athlete's ongoing healthcare.

CONCLUSION

The NCAA would do well to consider how the Olympics abolished the exploitative concept of amateurism. In 1978, President Jimmy Carter signed the bipartisan Amateur Sports Act, which ended Olympic amateurism (Branch, 2011). By 1986, the International Olympic Committee (IOC) had expunged the word "amateur" from its charter (Branch, 2011). The IOC simply lifted restrictions on Olympic competitors' commercial opportunities. In essence, the current Olympic model represents a restricted market model and has enjoyed tremendous success. The Olympics do not pay athletes; the IOC simply allows athletes to get paid (Hruby, 2012). Olympians can receive compensation from anyone, except the IOC, including corporations, personal donations, sponsorships, prize money, and even their home country. Despite much initial anguish about Olympic athletes being paid, the current IOC model represents a successful precedent for the professionalization of an amateur sports system (Branch, 2011). With the Olympic model translated into college sports, the universities would not pay their athletes; they would just let them pursue their commercial opportunities, such as endorsements, autograph signings, prize money, and so on (Nance-Nash, 2011).

Further, college athletes need a bill of rights. Stanley Eitzen (2000) proposed a bill of rights that included the following: (1) the right to transfer schools without penalty; (2) the right to a four-year scholarship guarantee; (3) the right to an open-ended scholarship until graduation if an athlete competes for a college for three or more years; (4) the right of athletes to be treated like other students—freedom of speech, privacy rights, fair redress of grievances, protection from physical/mental abuse; (5) the right to consult with agents; and (6) the right to endorsement revenue. I would add: (7) adequate health care; and (8) compensation for injuries with no statute of limitations.

QUESTIONS FOR DISCUSSION

1. What is the legal definition of amateurism? Could amateurism in college sports exist without the NCAA?

2. Assume that the NCAA adopts the IOC's compensation rules. Explore any residual shortcomings regarding college athlete welfare.

3. Assume that college athletes formed unions and negotiated contracts with universities. Explain potential negative consequences. Consider Title IX and tax consequences.

References

"About the NAIA." (2016). NAIA. Retrieved from http://www.naia.org/ViewArticle.dbml ?ATCLID=205323019

Ayres, I. (1987). How cartels punish: A structural theory of self-enforcingcollusion. *Columbia Law Review, 87,* 295–325.

Barra, A. (2012, March 6). How the NCAA basketball cartel seized its power. *The Atlantic.* Retrieved from http://www.theatlantic.com/entertainment/archive/2012/03/how-the -ncaa-basketball-cartel-seized-its-power/254612/

Bergman, L. (2011). Money and march madness. PBS. Retrieved from http://www.pbs.org /wgbh/pages/frontline/money-and-march-madness/

Branch, T. (2011, October). The shame of college sports. *The Atlantic,* 80–110.

DeSchriver, T., & Stotlar, D. (1996). An economic analysis of cartel behavior within the NCAA. *Journal of Sport Management, 10,* 388–400.

Eitzen, S. (2000, September 1). Slaves of big-time college sports. *USA Today.*

Ganim, S. (2014, January 8). CNN.com. Some college athletes play like adults, read like 5th-graders. Retrieved from http://edition.cnn.com/2014/01/07/us/ncaa-athletes -reading-scores/

Gregory, S. (2013, September 16). A cut for college athletes. *Time,* 36–42.

Hruby, P. (2012, July 25). The Olympics show why college sports should give up on amateurism. *The Atlantic.* Retrieved from http://www.theatlantic.com/entertainment /archive/2012/07/the-olympics-show-why-college-sports-should-give-up-on -amateurism/260275/

Huma, R., & Staurowsky, E. J. (2012). The $6 billion heist: Robbing college athletes under the guise of amateurism. A report collaboratively produced by the National College Players Association and Drexel University Sport Management. Retrieved from http:// www.ncpanow.org/news/articles/the-6-billion-heist-robbing-college-athletes-under -the-guise-of-amateurism

Igel, L., & Boland, R. (2011). National Collegiate Athletic Association. *Encyclopedia of Law and Higher Education.* Retrieved from http://sk.sagepub.com/reference /highereducation/n91.xml

Kahn, L. (2006). The economics of college sports: Cartel behavior vs. amateurism. IZA Discussion Paper No. 2186. Ithaca, NY: Cornell University Press.

Knight Commission on Intercollegiate Athletics. (2012). Retrieved from http://www .knightcommission.org

Koch, J. (1973). The troubled cartel: The NCAA. *Law and Contemporary Problems, 38*(1), 135–150.

Miller, A. (2013). NCAA Division I athletics: Amateurism and exploitation. *Sports Journal.* Retrieved from http://thesportjournal.org/article/ncaa-division-i-athletics-amateurism -and-exploitation/

Murray, K., & Burton, J. (2003). Senate Bill 193—Bill Analysis. Assembly Committee on Higher Education. *California State Senate Analysis,* prepared by Keith Nitta.

"The NAIA to NCAA." (2013). Retrieved from http://www.naiatoncaa.wordpress.com

Nance-Nash, S. (2011, September 13). NCAA rules trap many college athletes in poverty. *AOL.* Retrieved from http://www.dailyfinance.com/2011/09/13/ncaa-rules-trap-many -college-athletes-in-poverty/

NCAA. (2013a). Amateurism. Retrieved from http://www.ncaa.org/amateurism

NCAA. (2013b). NCAA rules violation. Retrieved from http://www.ncaa.org

NCAA. (2013c). Revenue. Retrieved from http://www.ncaa.org

NCAA. (2014a). 2012–13 Division I revenue distribution plan. Retrieved from http:// www.ncaa.com

NCAA. (2014b). Eligibility Rules. Retrieved from http://www.ncaa.org

Nocera, J. (2011, December 30). The college sports cartel. *New York Times.* Retrieved from http://www.nytimes.com/2011/12/31/opinion/nocera-the-college-sports-cartel .html?r=0

O'Bannon, Edward, Jr. vs. National College Athletic Association and Collegiate Licensing Company. (2009). Class Action Complaint. US District Court Northern District of California.

Posner, R. (2011, April 3). Monopsony in college athletics. *The Becker-Posner Blog.* Retrieved from http://www.becker-posner-blog.com

Smith, C. (2012). March madness: A trip to the final four is worth $9.5 million. Forbes. Retrieved from https://www.forbes.com/sites/chrissmith/2012/03/14/march-madness -a-trip-to-the-final-four-is-worth-9-5-million/

Stahl, L. (2012, July 17). NCAA death penalty for SMU a blow for decades; Should Penn State suffer same fate? *Washington Post.* Retrieved fromhttps://www.washingtonpost .com/blogs/she-the-people/post/ncaa-death-penalty-for-smu-a-blow-for-decades /2012/07/17/gJQA1t5pqW_blog.html

Stigler, G. (1964). A theory of oligopoly. *Journal of Political Economy, 72*(1), 44–61.

Taha, A. (2011). Are college athletes economically exploited? *Wake Forest Journal of Law & Policy, 2*(1), 69–94.

Wharton, D. (2013, June 20). O'Bannon vs. NCAA: Judge Weighing Class-Action Certification. *LA Times.* Retrieved from http://articles.latimes.com/2013/jun/20/sports/la -sp-obannon-vs-ncaa-20130620

Zola, W. (2013, February 11). The illusion of amateurism in college athletics. Huffington Post. Retrieved from http://www.huffingtonpost.com/warren-k-zola/college-athletes -pay-to-play_b_2663003.html

Title IX's Gender-Separate Allowance in the Context of College Athlete Rights and Intercollegiate Athletics Reform

Jennifer Lee Hoffman

In higher education, American colleges and universities survive despite limited federal oversight or aid, but they prosper because of their ability to sell themselves to the public (Smith, 2001). The limited federal intervention in higher education is a unique feature of US institutions. Independence from governmental coordination that makes US higher education institutions unique also contributes to the challenges in providing equity in educational settings.

Title IX introduces a federal policy to promote gender equity in higher education. Passed in 1972, this law has had an enormous impact across all of education, giving girls and women equal access to every educational opportunity from admissions to access to math and science. In every aspect of education, it is against the law to discriminate or treat women students differently based on their gender. Where this policy applies to athletics, it allows for gender-separate athletic opportunities, so long as several criteria are met. This differentiation based on gender requires that whatever the men's athletics teams have, the women's teams are entitled to as well. Under this gender-separate context of college sports opportunities, there has been varying success. Some institutions have gone beyond compliance with the law and offer elite-level athletic opportunities to women athletes on par with the most sophisticated football programs. Other institutions have resisted compliance or struggled to provide equitable resources and opportunities for all women (National Women's Law Center, n.d., Check it out).

While there is still work to be done to bring participation opportunities and financial aid in proportion with the overall women's student population, in the context of college athletics reforms, much of the dialogue on Title IX highlights

KEY TERMS

▶ Title IX

▶ Gendered discourses

▶ Women's sport

▶ Amateurism

▶ Commercialization

the ways in which we designate sports as educational in light of today's financial realities. The issue is not whether college sports should be educational or commercial. College sports are embedded in colleges and universities, which are both educational and entrepreneurial (Bok, 2003). That is, institutions offer academic programs, but they emulate business practices in teaching, research, and service through a wide range of activities. These include growth in some science majors, focusing on student career interests, hiring of more adjunct faculty, and the ways in which CEOs or branding language pervade the higher education leadership discourse. Reconciling how much educational values and entrepreneurial values can coexist in educational institutions is challenging enough. Layer on the unique context of a gender-separate system in athletics built on a financial foundation that requires high-level performance without university support (Smith, 2001), and the ways to introduce more equity for any athlete subgroup often exceed what the current system can support. Title IX does not compound these dilemmas—rather, the fairness in educational systems that Title IX demands reinforces the attention that must be paid to the educational and entrepreneurial interests of higher educational institutions in today's era of college athletics reforms.

Women's sports have been blamed for financial woes in college athletics and idealized for their seeming alignment with amateurism (Hoffman, Iverson, Allan, & Ropers-Huilman, 2010). While these discourses distract us from understanding the real promise of Title IX, they provide a useful framework to investigate Title IX in the context of college athlete rights. Rather than predict the outcomes of how the law should apply in the current landscape of college athletics of reforms, this chapter explores the ways in which Title IX tethers women's and men's sports despite the gender-separate administration of intercollegiate athletics.

TITLE IX CONTEXT

Title IX, passed in 1972, was not originally conceived as an athletics policy. It was developed as a way to ameliorate discrimination against women in access to educational opportunities in educational institutions. The law states, "No person in the United States shall, on the basis of sex, be excluded from participation in, be denied the benefits of, or be subjected to discrimination under any education program or activity receiving federal financial assistance." It covers 10 areas in education—access to higher education, career education, employment, math and science, standardized testing, athletics, pregnant and parenting students, the learning environment, sexual harassment, and technology (US Department of Education, 2015). Within athletics, Title IX requires equal treatment in 12 aspects of intercollegiate athletics (US Department of Education, n.d.). They are grouped into: (1) accommodation of interests and abilities, (2) scholarships, and (3) 10 areas of benefits and services (National Women's Law Center, n.d., NWLC, education, & Title IX, athletics).

Areas of Intercollegiate Athletics Regulated by Title IX

1. Effective accommodation of interests and abilities of members of both sexes in sports and competition levels
2. Scholarships—athletics financial aid
3. Equipment and supplies
4. Scheduling of games and practice time
5. Travel and per diem allowances
6. Availability of coaches and their compensation
7. Locker rooms, practice and competitive facilities
8. Medical and training facilities and services
9. Publicity
10. Recruitment
11. Availability of tutors and their compensation
12. Housing and dining facilities and services

Complying with Title IX

Compliance with accommodation of interests and abilities is determined by a three-part test that focuses on equity in participation. Under the three-part test, the university must demonstrate one of three measures to satisfy that accommodation of interests and abilities has been met. These are: (1) show a history of increasing women's opportunity, (2) demonstrate that the interests of women have been fully accommodated, or (3) see to it that the proportion of women athletes is equal to the proportion of undergraduate women students at the college or university. The last measure, also known as the safe harbor, is often the most straightforward option for compliance, but it is also the most controversial. The "safe harbor" designation after the 1996 *Cohen v. Brown University* case has been criticized and cast as a quota system that harms men's opportunities in sports other than football. However, rather than maintaining a consistent and deliberate increase in more opportunities for women athletes, institutions quickly eliminated men's programs and blamed Title IX requirements. Furthermore, universal compliance has still not been achieved. Among all NCAA institutions, women's participation in 2013–14 was 43.4 percent, compared to 56.6 percent for men (NCAA, 2014a). Division I has 46.4 percent women athletes, Division II has 41.5 percent, and Division III has 41.7 percent participating in NCAA championship sports (NCAA, 2014a).

The second factor, equity in scholarships or grants-in-aid, means that the athletic financial aid distributed to men's and women's athletes must be distributed in proportion to participation rates. According to the 2013 revenues and expenses reports by the NCAA, women receive 43 percent of all scholarship dollars in Division I programs, and Division II departments distribute 45 percent of their scholarship dollars to women (NCAA 2014b). Division III does not offer scholarships or grants-in-aid for participating in athletics, to men or women. This area of equity receives far less attention, especially when participation rates are compared with the overall number of women undergraduates (Heckman, 1997). The last of the 12 areas, equity in benefits and services, stipulates that there must be equal access in the quality and quantity in resources, such as equipment and supplies, travel support, and use of facilities. There must be fairness in scheduling games and practices and in assigning and paying quality coaches.

Why has it been so difficult for institutions to comply with participation and scholarship equity? One of the structural barriers to compliance with Title IX in scholarships and participation opportunity is that football has no gender partner sport. Unlike almost any other sport that institutions offer, women's and men's teams are separate, but there is a team for both genders. There is no gender partner sport for football and few sports that can match the number of participants or financial distribution of scholarships. Combine these structural challenges with the financial reality that many football programs recruit heavily out of state; that further tips the distribution of recruiting and scholarship resources heavily to men's programs, and many institutions are not in compliance with an equitable distribution of resources or participation rates.

Complying without Football

These structural and legal realities have been tested in Congress and in the courts. The Tower Amendment was introduced to Congress in 1974. The Tower Amendment sought to exclude revenue-producing sports from inclusion in Title IX. Eventually defeated, the amendment would have eliminated any sport that produced revenue, including donations, from any financial or participation calculation under Title IX (Acosta & Carpenter, 2005; Hogshead-Makar & Zimbalist, 2007). In 1979 a state gender equity case was making its way through the Washington state-level court system, in which the Washington State Superior Court ruled that, given these structural realities, football should be left out of any discussion of gender equity for women athletes (Hoffman, Hoffman, & Kotila, 2008). In short, football operates "under business principles" and is largely a "self-sustaining sport," therefore, these distinct features should exclude it from measures of gender equity. The lower court ruled that football should be defined as a business endeavor, not an educational endeavor. In *Blair v. Washington State University*, the lower court attempted to differentiate football as a business model, citing the fact that football is operated for profit under business principles.

However, in 1987 the State Supreme court ruled differently and reversed the lower court decision. This ruling explicitly defined football as an educational endeavor, noting that football is a large and essential part of intercollegiate athletics at the university. By describing football as an educational endeavor rather than a business enterprise, *Blair* also reinforced the structure of college athletics that women's sports would accommodate. The lower court focus on football as a business and the state policy's exclusive focus on proportionality represent deeply held assumptions that drive the policy and discourse on equity in college athletics.

DISCOURSES OF TITLE IX

Title IX law emerged from the social climate and context of the Civil Rights era, which formulated liberal feminist thought. Liberal feminist thought rests on several foundational elements. Namely, it relies on mandate (e.g., government intervention) to promote social change. The emphasis is on gender similarity, and inequality is addressed through legal, political, and institutional struggles for the rights of individuals. It promotes advocacy to give women equal access to the same opportunities men have. In college athletics football provides a powerful baseline by which to judge gender similarity and giving equal access to athletic opportunity, scholarships, and athletic department benefits and services. Title IX and its provisions for measuring equity in participation and resources lack the tools to measure equity without men's sports as the baseline. In sport, women as a subordinated group strategically align with the dominant group to avoid or mitigate discrimination (Brake, 2013). Sport becomes further linked to masculinity and men's interests, and sport evades any challenge as a masculinist construct (Brake, 2013).

As a result, Title IX has ensured the development of an infrastructure for women's athletic opportunities in higher education. However, because the standard for equity is largely based on men's opportunities in college football, it has had the unintended effect of further reinforcing a masculinist approach to women's athletic opportunity. The result has been discursive practices that connect Title IX policy and women's athletics to men's sports, namely, college football.

Equal Access to Scholarships

Title IX's implications for equal treatment have emerged as key features of the college sports landscape. The law was passed at a time when women athletes were also advocating for more resources and opportunity in athletics. Women's athletics was governed under the newly formed Association for Intercollegiate Athletics for Women (AIAW)—also in 1972—with a model that emphasized more engagement and opportunity for women athletes to participate in the leadership and decision making of the AIAW. As part of a student-oriented athletics model, athletic scholarships were banned.

However, the restriction ended in 1973, following a lawsuit by women players and coaches from two colleges in Florida (Festle, 1996). This advocacy by athletes for scholarships is important for two reasons. First, it is a rare example of college athletes fighting for college athlete rights. Secondly, it reveals the gendered discourse that positioned the "women's educational" model of the AIAW with no scholarships in contrast to the NCAA "men's commercial model." In short, this gendering of women's athletics under the AIAW, and the subsequent passing of Title IX, positions the discourse on women in sport as educational and amateur. This discourse is situated in deliberate contrast to the men's NCAA model as commercial and professional, even after the demise of the AIAW and the highly commercialized experience of women's sports today.

Amateurism

These amateur, educational discourses of Title IX have been leveraged by some in college athletics to position the amateur model as focused on the self-development of the participant with little acknowledgment of the financial realities of participating at a high level in intercollegiate athletics. These discourses have been used as a cover for the highly commercial examples of college football and basketball. College sports are gender-separate and often contrasted in policy discourses. Athletics policy reform discourse often suggests that administrators should use the gendered "women's" educational model to achieve a closer approximation of amateurism or that Title IX is somehow a barrier to structural or legislative changes that would benefit all athletes.

Furthermore, these discourses are gendered. That is, women's sports are constructed as educational, and men's sports are designated as commercial. These gendered approaches further reinforce long-standing discourses of the role of women in sports, and in college sports in particular. Today, women's athletics continue to be cast as educational and amateur, despite the highly visible examples of commercialized women's athletic events. Such events are not limited to women's basketball, with its ability to draw national TV audiences to several games a year and early in the national championship tournament. Conference and institutional television networks dedicated to college sports increasingly carry programming covering women's contests and competition. For example, the University of Utah has developed a fast-paced, television-friendly meet format, complete with big video screen entertainment, music, cheerleaders, and contests to attract fans in person and on television. Utah's attendance at gymnastics meets is consistently greater than every other women's NCAA sport, including the University of Connecticut and the University of Tennessee women's basketball programs. It even draws more than most Women's National Basketball Association teams (Branch, 2015).

Youth sport tournaments and special events support a $7 billion travel industry for elite "select" or "travel" teams. In addition, the precollege family investment for early specialization includes fees, equipment, and private coaching estimated at $300 to $1,000 per year per athlete. The childhood youth sports industry, for many boys and girls in pursuit of a college athletics scholarship, is not congruent with a definition of "amateur" based on the self-development of the individual at the college level.

To say that women's sports are simply educational and not commercial is just not true anymore. From the sophisticated youth sports system and travel industry that has grown around select tournaments, getting a college scholarship is big business for women as well as men. Keeping gendered discourses in check is important as we talk about college athletics reform.

Discourses in Opportunity

When institutions are unwilling or unable to fully support intercollegiate athletics, Title IX is also used as a tool to cut some men's sports as a way to invest more in other areas of the department. When men's sports are cut, athletic departments can claim, "Title IX made me do it," pointing to the ambitions and opportunities of women athletes as problematic in a system that does not provide institutional support. Athletics budgets of the 1970s were strained long before Title IX was implemented; that led to cutting men's sports in support of more resources for football (Thelin, 2000). Because institutions are unwilling or unable to financially support athletics and they rely heavily on external funding, the budget issues are not new. Title IX simply provides a more convenient excuse.

Because we are blaming women's interests rather than exploring the institutional responsibility of funding athletics, more pressure is put on a largely Black, male labor force. When adding a racialized lens to the gendered discourse at the Division I "Power Five" level, it should come as no surprise that this exerts more pressure on a Black, male labor force to support a largely white, women's sport system of participants (Hawkins, 2010).

RECOMMENDATIONS

Title IX's application in sports offers an opportunity to evaluate how themes of equity in education might serve all college athletes. As reforms are proposed and new policy models take shape, it is essential to ask not only what Title IX requires but also to recognize that this policy should not be used to reform college sports or resist reforms. Neither of these approaches is an appropriate use of the law.

Revenue Generation and College Athlete Benefits

Under Title IX, the law has been consistent that the amount of revenue generated by an individual athlete or team on behalf of the institution is not the determining factor for equity. Institutions and athletics governing associations will need to keep the interests of all athletes at the forefront in today's era of reform. Under Title IX all athletes need to be treated in similar ways in regard to additional financial benefits or opportunity to profit from their athletics participation.

We should not be tempted to use Title IX or any other policy to retract from changes to provide fair treatment to all college athletes. If reforms such as four-year scholarships or unionization benefit some athletes, then Title IX not only asks, but requires, that women's athletic interests are considered equally.

Support for Women's Sports

If as, in the past, athletic departments are expected to fund themselves, athletic departments cannot continue to rely just on the labor force of men's sports. Investment in the promotion of women's sports is essential to give women's athletics the opportunity to be self-sustaining. Given the mandate to operate sports at a high level, with little institutional support and the persistent pathway to more commercialization, institutions should investigate digital platforms and media opportunities to promote women's sports more. The mantra "If you build it they will come" has not been fully realized in today's media landscape. With ESPN and other cable outlets seeing a shift in cable subscribers, new models that fully represent the interests of women's sports are crucial to the success of women's athletic interests.

CONCLUSION

In the emergence of reforms focused on college athlete rights, two dominant discourses have emerged that invoke Title IX or women's sports as an obstacle to college athlete rights reform or as a device to stall efforts to create opportunities that benefit all athletes. How do these discourses reveal themselves in the current reform era? The first is, "We can't reform because Title IX won't allow it." The public discourse focuses on not being able to afford the financial costs to treat everyone the same. This discourse is a tired economic argument that has been used over Title IX's 40-year history. At the very least, the affordability argument leverages Title IX as a convenient excuse for previous budget challenges. When viewed with a gendered and racialized lens, the use of Title IX to position rights of one group over the rights of another reveals deeply held assumptions about the treatment of college athletes. Under these discursive practices, Title IX is used to justify the exploitation of Black men to preserve the athletic benefits for (mostly) white women athletes.

Alternative, but less prominent, is the return to the discursive practices of using Title IX as a tool to leverage reform. Because Title IX is explicitly educational, there could be attempts to use this policy to further tether the commercialized model to educational interests. Given the defeat of the Tower Amendment and the case of *Blair v. Washington State University,* where the court ruled that, if athletic departments are to retain their educational status, then everyone must be treated the same, including football programs. Football, despite its commercial interests, must remain educational under the law. Given that Title IX's theoretical foundation promotes equity based on a male-gendered standard—that women are entitled to whatever the men have—in most athletic departments that standard is what the men's football team has.

These deeply held sociocultural assumptions and legal limitations are not held in isolation. There are other sociohistorical considerations that accentuate today's financial realities and help explain why balancing interests in the gender-separate context remains a challenge in college athletics reform.

According to Smith (2001), for colleges and universities, whether they are "mercantile or educational," their first instinct is survival, then prosperity. US higher education institutions prosper because of their ability to sell themselves to the public. College sports are no different and have always been sold to the public. Reliance on commercial practices in college sports is compounded, because higher education institutions have insisted that sports must be conducted as amateur but financed "along lines that are clearly professional and commercial" (Smith, 2001, p. 3). This dilemma of reconciling amateur and commercial ideals has been deeply entrenched from the beginning. This dilemma, coupled with limited federal intervention, has led to struggles for competitive equity in educational sport settings that are not easily reconciled, if reconciled at all.

From the first crew race between Harvard and Yale in 1852, college athletics quickly grew into something where athletic departments were expected to develop highly competitive athletic programs with little to no institutional support (Smith, 2001). As such, institutions are unwilling or unable to pay for sports out of the educational budget, and many institutions fund athletics through external, commercial sources.

Title IX in its initial implementation appeared to compound the financial pressures in intercollegiate athletics, but this assumption is unfounded and misplaced. The pressure Title IX places on budgets provides a useful distraction. However, it has also been used as a tether to draw revenue sports back to the educational mission. Interpretation of gender equity law in the separate context of sport clearly states that the amount of revenue generated cannot trump the principles of equal opportunity.

The gender-separate nature of college sports is further intensified by a gendered cultural view of athletic participation. The long-standing commercial approach to college athletics that has positioned men's college football as a $6 billion industry today has called many of the practices in the treatment of college athletes within higher education into question. Title IX requires that we provide opportunity, financial aid, and benefits in a gender-separate system. Yet it is more complex than that when providing equal opportunity in an inherently lopsided financial system.

The intense demands on college football players and basketball players within this system to fund the entire athletic department are generating a new reform discourse on these issues. Rather than use Title IX to suggest that reforms cannot be done because the costs associated with providing better opportunities for one group would be too costly for all groups, we need to pay much closer attention to the benefit of a college scholarship for all athletes.

QUESTIONS FOR DISCUSSION

1. Sports are offered as gender-separate athletic opportunities under the law but are not required. Does the gender-separate approach remain the best way to offer equitable opportunities for all athletes in the context of today's reforms?

2. What should be the definition of amateurism that acknowledges women's and men's athletics today?

3. To fund women's sports independently from men's football, should institutions commercialize women's sports more or invest additional institutional dollars to the entire athletic department?

References

Acosta, R. V., & Carpenter, L. J. (2005). *Title IX*. Champaign, IL: Human Kinetics.

Bok, D. (2003). *Universities in the marketplace: The commercialization of higher education*. Princeton, NJ: Princeton University Press.

Brake, D. L. (2013). Discrimination inward and upward: Lessons on law and social inequality from the troubling case of women coaches. *Indiana Journal of Law and Social Equality, 2*(1), Article 1.

Branch, J. (2015, February 25). At their meets, the audience flips, too. *New York Times*. Retrieved from http://www.nytimes.com/2015/02/26/sports/at-packed-utah-womens -gymnastics-meets-marketing-earns-high-scores-too.html

Festle, M. J. (1996). *Playing nice: Politics and apologies in women's sports*. New York: Columbia University Press.

Hawkins, B. (2010). *The new plantation: Black athletes, college sports, and predominantly white NCAA institutions*. New York: Palgrave Macmillan.

Heckman, D. (1997). The Women's Sports Foundation report on Title IX, athletics and the Office for Civil Rights. Women's Sports Foundation.

Hoffman, J. L., Hoffman, H. L., & Kotila, A. (2008). Athletics gender equity in the State of Washington: The 20th anniversary of Blair v. Washington State University. *Journal for the Study of Sports and Athletes in Education, 3*(1), 273–294.

Hoffman, J. L., Iverson, S., Allan, E. J., & Ropers-Huilman, R. (2009). Title IX policy and intercollegiate athletics: A feminist poststructural critique. In E. J. Allan, S. Iverson, & R. Ropers-Huilman, eds., *Reconstructing Policy in Higher Education: Feminist Poststructural Perspectives* (pp. 129–146). New York: Routledge.

Hogshead-Makar, N., & Zimbalist, A. S. (Eds.). (2007). *Equal play: Title IX and social change*. Philadelphia, PA: Temple University Press.

National Women's Law Center. (n.d.). Check it out: Is the playing field level for women and girls at your school? Retrieved from http://www.nwlc.org/resource/check-it-out -playing-field-level-women-and-girls-your-school

National Women's Law Center. (n.d.). NWLC, education, & Title IX, athletics. Retrieved from http://nwlc.org/issue/athletics/.

NCAA. (2014a). Student-Athlete Participation: 1981–82—2013–14 Sports Sponsorship and Participation Rates Report. Indianapolis, IN.

NCAA. (2014b). Archives of NCAA revenue and expenses report by division. Retrieved from http://www.ncaa.org

Smith, R. (2001). *Play-by-play: Radio, television, and big-time college sport*. Baltimore, MD: Johns Hopkins University Press.

Staurowsky, E. J. (2014, March 28). Title IX should not confuse the issue of college sports unions. *New York Times*. Retrieved from http://www.nytimes.com/roomfordebate /2014/03/27/scholars-players-and-union-members/title-ix-should-not-confuse-the -issue-of-college-sports-unions

Thelin, J. (2000). Good sports?: Historical perspective on the political economy of intercollegiate athletics in the era of Title IX, 1972–1997. *Journal of Higher Education, 71*(4), 391–410.

US Department of Education Office of Civil Rights. (n.d.). Equal opportunity in intercollegiate athletics: Requirements under Title IX of the education amendments of 1972. Retrieved from http://www2.ed.gov/about/offices/list/ocr/docs/interath.html

US Department of Education Office of Civil Rights. (2015, October 15). Title IX and sex discrimination. Retrieved from http://www2.ed.gov/about/offices/list/ocr/docs/tix_dis.html

The State of Concussion Protocols

Paperwork or Policies?

Whitney Griffin

The human brain contains over 80 billion neurons, or brain cells. Diagnosing, assessing, and managing sport-related concussions are contingent upon our current understanding of billions of neurons and their functions, locations, and

KEY TERMS

▶ Sport concussion

▶ Compliance

▶ Return to play

▶ Return to learn

▶ Management

connectivity. As information is synthesized about concussion definitions, diagnoses and management warrant refinement. A concussion is a traumatically induced transient disturbance of brain function and involves a complex physiological process (Harmon et al., 2013). It is the complex nature of this process that has prevented a universal agreement on the definition of concussion (Hunt & Asplund, 2010). Research has revealed that concussions are induced by biomechanical forces, result in functional and metabolic changes rather than structural changes, and correlate with symptom severity (Harmon et al., 2013; Henry, Tremblay, Boulanger, Ellemberg, & Lassonde, 2010; McCrory et al., 2013). According to the American Medical Society for Sports Medicine position statement, concussions are a subset of mild traumatic brain injuries (mTBI) and at the less severe end of the brain injury spectrum (Harmon et al., 2013). It is estimated that about 3.8 million sport-related concussions occur in the United States per year; however, as many as 50 percent may go unreported (Langlois, Rutland-Brown, & Wald, 2006). By those estimates, there may be over 7.6 million sport-related concussions that affect otherwise healthy individuals each year.

As sport concussions have become a rising public health concern in the last decade, commissioned research has increased accordingly. However, with more answers have come more questions, and we know less than we know more. The National College Athletic Association (NCAA) governs 1,066 member institutions and more than 450,000 college athletes annually (Baugh et al., 2015). The NCAA Concussion Policy is derived from the consensus statement in the 4th International Conference on Concussion in Sport; it states that "the authors acknowledge that the science of concussion is evolving, and therefore management and return to play (RTP) decisions remain in the realm of clinical judgment on an individual basis" (McCrory et al., 2013, p. 1).

Despite exigent progress and advancement, concussion research is not exempt from critical inquiry and scientific merit. Several methodological issues have been examined in over 300 published research reports on mTBI. Some of the most common methodological flaws include not clearly stating the research question, suboptimal or inappropriate research design to test the research question, substandard or inappropriate analysis strategies, and use of small samples leading to inadequate statistical power (Carroll, Cassidy, Holm, Kraus, & Coronado, 2004). Because the quality of individual studies varies so greatly, the applicability of the findings are limited and published recommendations are based on consensus, usual practice, or opinion (Kay, Weber, & McLeod, 2014). The purpose of this chapter is to examine the evidence that supports recommendations related to concussion definition, assessment, management, and return to physical and cognitive activity. First, current knowledge gaps are outlined in four major elements of concussion management plans: neuropsychological assessment, sequelae/follow-up, return to play (RTP), and return to learn (RTL). Second, perspectives from the NCAA commissioners are presented. Finally, recommendations for future study are made based on the state of current concussion education and policy compliance.

TESTING AND ASSESSMENT

While there is an abundance of neuropsychological test batteries and sideline assessment tools, no single test has demonstrated enough sensitivity to warrant comprehensive results. It is recommended that neuropsychological tests be utilized as only one part of a multidisciplinary approach (Kay, Weber, & McLeod, 2014). The model of using preseason baseline testing followed by repeat testing within one to two days of injury is now being used at several levels of sport competition. The rationale for comparing an athlete's preconcussion and postconcussion functioning in preseason baseline neurocognitive testing is to compare to increase the accuracy of RTP decisions and determine when the athlete has fully recovered (Schatz, Moser, Solomon, Ott, & Karpf, 2012). Yet, the reliability, validity, and feasibility of baseline testing remain uncertain (Stewart et al., 2012). There has been a "lack of requisite statistical information to aid in interpreting neuropsychological test scores in athletes at all levels" (Barr, 2003, p. 92). Athletes may be motivated to purposefully create a low threshold for comparison by performing below their highest potential during preseason baseline testing (Bailey, Echemendia, & Arnett, 2006). Test batteries may not be feasible because they are time consuming, expensive, and require a trained neuropsychologist to interpret results and to be attentive to the possibility of invalid test performance (Schatz et al., 2012). Among 20 self-report concussion scales and checklists identified,

McLeod and Leach (2012) found that 7 had published psychometric properties and only one was empirically driven.

Clinical and nonclinical factors must be considered in concussion evaluation and diagnosis. So far, researchers have identified modifying biopsychosocial factors that affect test interpretation, including age, gender, test setting, fitness level, sport setting, psychiatric conditions, learning disability, and medical history (Dessy, Rasouli, Gometz, & Choudhri, 2014; Stewart et al., 2012). "However, the sensitivity, specificity, validity and reliability of these standardized tests remain largely undefined, particularly among different age groups, cultural groups and settings" (Dessy et al., 2014, p. 60). No single instrument should be used in isolation to diagnose a concussion or evaluate recovery (Stewart et al., 2012). Additionally, clinicians must be aware of the advantages and limitations of whichever method is implemented in the concussion evaluation and management plan (Dessy et al., 2014; McLeod & Leach, 2012).

SEQUELAE AND FOLLOW-UP

The suspected diagnosis of concussion may include one or more of the five clinical domains: (1) somatic (e.g., headache) and/or emotional symptoms (e.g., lability), (2) physical signs (e.g., loss of consciousness or amnesia), (3) behavioral changes (e.g., irritability), (4) cognitive impairment (e.g., slow to answer questions or follow instructions and/or slowed reaction time), and/or (5) sleep disturbance (e.g., drowsiness) (Stewart et al., 2012, p. 435).

Though symptoms may appear mild, they can significantly and negatively impair an athlete's ability to function physically, cognitively, and psychosocially. Onset of symptoms may be delayed for several hours, and athletes may attempt to mask their symptoms (Stewart et al., 2012). Other risk factors/modifiers of concussion management that have been documented so far are sport position and style of play, age, gender, duration of loss of consciousness, mental health issues, previous concussion, genetics, mood disorders, migraines, and learning disabilities and attention disorders (Harmon et al., 2013; McCrory et al., 2013).

There is no single biological marker of concussion (McCrea et al., 2003). Current neuroimaging tools lack adequate sensitivity to detect subtle damage and understand the severity of changes in brain function, making an initial concussion diagnosis difficult (Borich et al., 2013; Guskiewicz, 2013). As neuroimaging techniques are becoming more sensitive and sophisticated in contributing to the diagnosis and prognosis of concussion, results suggest that "recovery may be more prolonged than previously thought" (Borich et al., 2013, p. 134). Consequently, athletes may be cleared to return to play well before full recovery has occurred. Inappropriate concussion management can leave players increasingly vulnerable to repeated trauma and susceptible to a higher risk of a subsequent concussion seven to ten days after the initial concussion, since players who sustain one concussion in a season are three times more likely to sustain a second in the same season (Borich et al., 2013; Guskiewicz, Weaver, Padua, & Garrett, 2000; Littleton & Guskiewicz, 2013).

RETURN TO PLAY

One of the most controversial and litigious elements of concussion management is when an athlete should be allowed to *safely* return to play (RTP). Concussions differ from other athletic injuries because of the heavy reliance on observable symptoms and on an athlete's subjective reporting of symptoms (Borich et al., 2013; Guskiewicz, 2013). It is well documented that athletes do not volunteer symptoms in high school and college sports (Delaney, Lamfookon, Bloom, Al-Kashmiri, & Correa, 2015; McCrea, Hammeke, Olsen, Leo, & Guskiewicz, 2004; Torres et al., 2013). Some reasons for underreporting and knowingly hiding symptoms are: lack of appropriate knowledge of symptoms and consequences, athlete knowledge and attitude toward concussion, and coach approachability (Chrisman, Quitiquit, & Rivara, 2013; Cournoyer & Tripp, 2014; Register-Mihalik et al., 2013).

RTP should be individualized, gradual, and progressive (Harmon et al., 2013). Yet, a significant barrier in standardizing RTP protocols is the variable rate of individual recovery. Literature on concussion symptom resolution varies from 15 minutes, 5 to 7 days, 7 to 10 days, 2 weeks, and 3 months to 1 year (Carroll, Cassidy, Peloso, Borg, von Holst, Holm, et al., 2004; McCrea et al., 2003; McCrory et al., 2013). Current NCAA RTP protocol states that athletes diagnosed with a sport concussion must be removed from play, must not return to sport-related activity for at least one calendar day, and are to be evaluated by a health care provider with expertise in sport-related concussion (NCAA, 2013). The graduated RTP protocol is a stepwise progression in six stages. Athletes should continue to proceed to the next level if asymptomatic at the current level after 24 hours: (1) no activity, (2) light aerobic exercise, (3) sport-specific exercise, (4) noncontact training drills, (5) full-contact practice, (6) return to play (McCrory et al., 2013). Generally, the full rehabilitation protocol would take approximately one week if an athlete remains asymptomatic both at rest and with provocative exercise. It is essential to note that all RTP guidelines are consensus-based, not evidence-based (Borich et al., 2013; Giza et al., 2013).

RETURN TO LEARN

Cognitive difficulties that are compromised postconcussion such as attention, new learning retention, processing speed, and flexibility are also the most essential for academic performance. If a concussed athlete has a learning disability prior to injury, the return to full cognitive activities could be convoluted and extremely challenging (Littleton & Guskiewicz, 2013). Premature RTP and re-turn to learn (RTL) can exacerbate symptoms, yet it has been documented that athletes are returned to sport and school too soon, from elementary to college levels (Carson et al., 2014). There are no standardized guidelines for returning athletes to school, and even if written forms of restrictions and adjustments ex-isted there is no guarantee that a school can or will comply (Halstead et al., 2013; Harmon et al., 2013). Furthermore, current data is insufficient to show that any postconcussion intervention or neurocognitive rehabilitation enhances recovery or diminishes long-term consequences (Giza et al., 2013; Hunt & Asplund, 2010). The term "cognitive rest" is ambiguously defined, and there is insufficient clar-ity about how or when a period of reduced stimulation should be implemented (Carson et al., 2014). In sum, "most guidelines for management of concussion in sport use vague, graded exercise approaches, with a focus upon return to play, often neglecting guidelines that support return to cognitive and psychosocial activities" (Stewart et al., 2012, p. 441).

WHAT THE COMMISSIONERS ARE SAYING

In April 2010 the NCAA Executive Committee adopted concussion policy and leg-islation that requires each member institution to have a concussion management plan on file. Each plan should meet the minimum requirements of:

> (a) An annual process that ensures student-athletes are educated about the signs and symptoms of concussions. Student-athletes must acknowledge that they have received information about the signs and symptoms of concussions and that they have a responsibility to report concussion-related injuries and illnesses to a medical staff member; (b) A process that ensures a student-athlete who exhibits signs, symptoms or behaviors consistent with a concussion shall be removed from athletics activities . . . and evaluated by a medical staff mem-ber . . . ; (c) A policy that precludes a student-athlete diagnosed with a concus-sion from returning to athletic activity . . . for at least the remainder of that calendar day; and (d) A policy that requires medical clearance for a student-athlete diagnosed with a concussion to return to athletics activity . . . as deter-mined by a physician . . . or the physician's designee. (NCAA, 2013, p. 64)

Deciding on and enforcing punitive measures for concussion protocol noncom-pliance is a root issue in college athlete safety and well-being. In January 2015, the Power Five conferences (Atlantic Coast Conference, Big 12, Big Ten, South-eastern Conference, and Pac-12) in Division I created the Concussion Safety Pro-tocol Committee to annually review and approve schools' written procedures for handling concussions. In February 2015, the Big 12 Conference announced a new concussion policy in addition to existing NCAA concussion protocols to give full autonomy to medical staff in deciding when an athlete can return to play. Big 12 members will be required to follow the NCAA's 2014 Inter-Association Consensus Guidelines for Concussion Diagnosis and Management, which state that institutions should have on file a team physician–directed concussion management plan and the specific protocol for evaluation and management of a concussion. It is not clear if there are consequences if a Big 12 school is found to be noncompliant.

While this moves the ball forward, the committee does not have enough support to attach penalties to RTP concussion guidelines. The commissioners in charge of making policy have several paramount factors to consider. Big 12 commissioner Bob Bowlsby supports penalties, and he commented on the dangers of coach totalitarianism: "They want to have local control and their coaches saying, 'I don't want to be told what to do on the sideline' . . . The fact is there are places where coaches are making return-to-play decisions and that's not right. It's not right for young people. It's not right from a competitive standpoint. It's the wrong approach to it. Those decisions ought to be vested in the hands of medical personnel singularly" (Solomon, 2015, p. 2). Creating punitive policies is not without bureaucratic deterrents. Metro Atlantic Athletic Conference (MAAC) commissioner Rich Ensor expressed that he doesn't see the need for penalties: "There's a tendency to think that a penalty will solve the problem. I've come to believe we have way too many compliance problems and end up with a lot of paperwork instead of implementing policies in a coherent manner. Invariably, for every rule there are 10 exceptions. If we find out in a year or two there are still gaps, we can always return to rules and enforcement" (Solomon, 2015, p. 3). Indeed, excessive compliance problems and paperwork do stand in the way of college athlete well-being.

Who is responsible for concussion management and college athlete safety? Conference USA commissioner Britton Banowsky stated his wait-and-see approach until medical professionals agree on how to best treat concussions: "I believe we should let some time and analysis happen before we figure out what kind of rule structure should be attached to that" (Solomon, 2015, p. 3). How much data will be collected and analyzed before policies are enacted to protect college athletes? The Atlantic 10 commissioner, Bernadette McGlade, said: "I think everyone is trying to make sure whatever goes into place is enforceable and can be done if there's a penalty structure in place. On the one hand, I understand that taking some time. But I don't think you can take forever" (Solomon, 2015, p. 2).

RECOMMENDATIONS

The NCAA and the US Department of Defense launched a $30 million initiative in 2014 to enhance the safety of college athletes and service members. The joint initiative will include research on concussion and head impact exposure. This concussion study has the potential to address the following research recommendations, which are derived from current knowledge gaps.

Concussion education is perhaps the most blatant recommendation. However, the NCAA currently mandates that institutions provide concussion education without specifying content or delivery. A pilot study of the NCAA Concussion Policy evaluation and implementation of concussion education found that there were no significant improvements in knowledge and only a very small decrease in intention to continue playing while experiencing symptoms of a concussion (Kroshus, Daneshvar, Baugh, Nowinski, & Cantu, 2013). The first study to examine compliance in a large sample of NCAA member schools across all divisions of competition yielded dismal results: 30 respondents at 27 schools reported their school did not have a concussion management plan, 175 respondents from 140 schools were unsure whether their school had a concussion management plan, and 135 schools had conflicting responses about whether the school had a concussion management plan (Baugh et al., 2015). More research is needed to understand the extent to which schools are adopting and implementing the required components of concussion management plans, since it is becoming increasingly clear that knowledge is not sufficient for change. Those institutions without a concussion management plan are responsible for the rights and well-being for thousands of collegiate athletes each year. "At minimum, improved distribution of, and communication about, concussion management plans between stakeholders at NCAA member schools is advised" (Baugh et al., 2015, p. 7).

The NCAA recommends but does not require that member institutions provide coaches with concussion education. Thus, coaches who seek concussion education must do so voluntarily. Mandating concussion education to coaches is as imperative as educating college athletes, since coach approachability is a significant predictor in symptom reporting (Chrisman, Quitiquit, & Rivara, 2013). Another stakeholder in the RTP decision is the athletic trainer. Yet, it is unknown how athletic trainers are clinically applying current research and recommendations. According to one study, athletic trainers have greatly decreased their use of clinical examinations and symptom evaluations when assessing and managing concussions (Lynall, Laudner, Mihalik, & Stanek, 2013). Specifically, even though more athletic trainers appear to be using all three components of the concussion assessment battery than in the past, the overall percentage who use all three domains remains low. One factor that affects athletic trainers' compliance is their attitude toward recommended guidelines. Athletic trainers who do not believe they have the power or resources to implement concussion management recommendations are less likely to do so (Rigby, Vela, & Housman, 2013). Future interventions should take into account athletic trainers' attitudes and to surround them with a support group of team physicians and other qualified health care providers (Rigby, Vela, & Housman, 2013).

Finally, the language of the NCAA Concussion Policy is addressed. The verbiage of the policy includes a bureaucratic escape route, since schools that have not implemented full plans or portions of their plans are not technically violating NCAA policy: "As written, the NCAA Concussion Policy only requires the presence of a plan and not that the plan is actually implemented . . . Perhaps the most important next step is for the NCAA to revise the language of its concussion policy to reflect the necessity of plan implementation" (Baugh et al., 2015, pp. 8–9). In revising the language of current policies, it is recommended that the NCAA not fall victim to ineptitude. Dr. Brian Hainline, chief medical officer of the NCAA, described ineptitude at the National Summit on Sports Concussions as knowledge without application (personal communication, June 5, 2015). As a billion-dollar industry, the NCAA must expend its benefits, resources, and energies on the athletes they deem to protect. For example, it would behoove the organization to develop and implement policies that they can monitor and enforce, such as limiting contact during football practice and reducing the number of regular season football games.

CONCLUSION

Amidst policy administration, litigation, and increasing fatal injury counts, it is easy to forget that President Theodore Roosevelt helped to establish the NCAA in 1906 specifically for player safety reasons. Concussions can be compared to snowflakes in that no two are alike: "No checkbox system can be applied to every concussion, and because concussions are diverse and unique injuries that affect each athlete differently, we must learn how to treat them individually" (Guskiewicz, 2013, p. 441). As a result, no two treatment programs can be identical (Borich et al., 2013). What we do know is that concussions are invisible, hard to detect, and symptoms can be easily lied about. Currently, standardization of neuropsychological assessment, follow-up procedures, and RTP and RTL protocols are recommended but nonexistent. At the 2015 NCAA convention, Atlantic Coast commissioner John Swofford remarked about the legislative autonomy for the Big Five conferences: "I've never attended a convention where the primary focus of most of what was being discussed was about the student-athlete and the student-athlete's experiences" (Hill, 2015, p. 1). Better late than never.

QUESTIONS FOR DISCUSSION

1. How might the NCAA enforce stringent concussion protocols the way it tracks amateurism violations?

2. What can coaches, parents, trainers, and players do / not do to create a safe concussion-reporting environment?

3. What is the most effective concussion education medium for coaches, clinicians, athletic trainers, learning specialists, and athletes?

References

Bailey, C., Echemendia, R., & Arnett, P. (2006). The impact of motivation on neuropsychological performance in sports-related mild traumatic brain injury. *Journal of the International Neuropsychological Society, 12,* 475–484. doi: 10.1017/S1355617706060619

Barr, W. (2003). Neuropsychological testing of high school athletes: Preliminary norms and test-retest indices. *Archives of Clinical Neuropsychology, 18,* 91–101.

Baugh, C., Kroshus, E., Daneshvar, D., Filali, N., Hiscox, M., & Glantz, L. (2015). Concussion management in US college sports: Compliance with national collegiate athletic association concussion policy and areas for improvement. *American Journal of Sports Medicine, 43*(1), 47–56. doi: 10.1177/0363546514553090

Borich, M., Cheung, K., Jones, P., Khramova, V., Gavrailoff, L., Boyd, L., & Virji-Babul, N. (2013). Concussion: Current concepts in diagnosis and management. *Journal of Neurologic Physical Therapy, 37*(3), 133–139. doi: 10.1097/NPT.0b013e31829f7460

Carroll, L., Cassidy, D., Holm, L., Kraus, J., & Coronado, V. (2004). Methodological issues and research recommendations for mild traumatic brain injury: The WHO collaborating centre task force on mild traumatic brain injury. *Journal of Rehabilitation Medicine, 43,* 113–125.

Carroll, L., Cassidy, J., Peloso, P., Borg, J., von Holst, H., Holm, L., . . . Pepin, M. (2004). Prognosis for mild traumatic brain injury: Results of the WHO collaborating centre task force on mild traumatic brain injury. *Journal of Rehabilitation Medicine, 43,* 84–105.

Carson, J., Lawrence, D., Kraft, S., Garel, A., Snow, C., Chatterjee, A., . . . Fremont, P. (2014). Premature return to play and return to learn after a sport-related concussion. *Canadian Family Physician, 60,* 310–315.

Chrisman, S. P., Quitiquit, C., & Rivara, F. P. (2013). Qualitative study of barriers to concussive symptom reporting in high school athletics. *Journal of Adolescent Health, 52*(3), 1–6. doi:10.1016/j.jadohealth.2012.10.271

Cournoyer, J., & Tripp, B. (2014). Concussion knowledge in high school football players. *Journal of Athletic Training, 49*(5), 654–658. doi: 10.4085/1062-6050-49.3.34

Delaney, J., Lamfookon, C., Bloom, G., Al-Kashmiri, A., & Correa, J. (2015). Why university athletes choose not to reveal their concussion symptoms during a practice or game. *Clinical Journal of Sports Medicine, 25*(2), 113–125.

Dessy, A., Rasouli, J., Gometz, A., & Choudhri, T. (2014). A review of modifying factors affecting usage of diagnostic rating scales in concussion management. *Clinical Neurology and Neurosurgery, 122,* 59–63.

Giza, C., Kutcher, J., Ashwal, S., Barth, J., Getchius, T., Gioia, G. A., . . . Zafonte, R. (2013). Summary of evidence-based guideline update: Evaluation and management of concussion sports. *Neurology, 80*(24), 2250–2257. doi: 10.1212/WNL.0b013e31828d57dd

Guskiewicz, K. (2013). When treating sport concussion, check the boxes, but also go the extra mile. *Journal of Athletic Training, 48*(4), 441.

Guskiewicz, K., Weaver, N., Padua, D., & Garrett, W. (2000). Epidemiology of concussion in collegiate and high school football players. *American Journal of Sports Medicine, 28*(5), 643–650.

Halstead, M., McAvoy, K., Devore, C., Carl, R., Lee, M., & Logan, K. (2013). Returning to learning following a concussion. *Pediatrics, 132*(5), 948–957.

Harmon, K., Drezner, J., Gammons, M., Guskiewicz, K., Halstead, M., Herring, S., . . . Roberts, W. (2013). American medical society for sports medicine position statement: Concussion in sport. *British Journal of Sports Medicine, 47*(1), 15–26. doi:10.1136/bjsports-2012-091941

Henry, L., Tremblay, S., Boulanger, Y., Ellemberg, D., & Lassonde, M. (2010). Neurometabolic changes in the acute phase after sports concussions correlate with symptom severity. *Journal of Neurotrauma, 27,* 65–76. doi: 10.1089/neu.2009.0962

Hill, O. (2015, January 17). NCAA Big 5 passes athletic scholarship value increases, concussion protocol. Retrieved June 15, 2015, from http://www.foxsports.com/college-football/story/ncaa-big-ten-big-12-acc-pac-12-sec-concussion-athletic-scholarship-011715

Hunt, T., & Asplund, C. (2010). Concussion assessment and management. *Clinical Sports Medicine, 29*(1), 5–17. doi: 10.1016/j.csm.2009.09.002

Kay, M., Weber, M., & McLeod, T. (2014). Assessment, management and knowledge of sport-related concussion. *Clinical Bottom Line,* June, 36–38.

Kroshus, E., Daneshvar, D., Baugh, C., Nowinski, C., & Cantu, R. (2013). NCAA concussion education in ice hockey: An ineffective mandate. *British Journal of Sports Medicine, 48*(2), 135–140.

Langlois, J., Rutland-Brown, W., & Wald, M. (2006). The epidemiology and impact of traumatic brain injury: A brief overview. *Journal of Head Trauma Rehabilitation, 21*(5), 375–378.

Littleton, A., & Guskiewicz, K. (2013). Current concepts in sport concussion management: A multifaceted approach. *Journal of Sport and Health Science, 2*(4), 227–235. doi: 10.1016/j.jshs.2013.04.003

Lynall, R., Laudner, K., Mihalik, J., & Stanek, J. (2013). Concussion-assessment and management techniques used by athletic trainers. *Journal of Athletic Training, 48*(6), 844–850.

McCrea, M., Guskiewicz, K., Marshall, S., Barr, W., Randolph, C., Cantu, R., . . . Kelly, J. (2003). Acute effects and recovery time following concussion in collegiate football players: The NCAA concussion study. *Journal of the American Medical Association, 290*(19), 2556–2563.

McCrea, M., Hammeke, T., Olsen, G., Leo, P., & Guskiewicz, K. (2004). Unreported concussion in high school football players: Implications for prevention. *Clinical Journal of Sport Medicine, 14*(1), 13–17.

McCrory, P., Meeuwisse, W., Aubry, M., Cantu, R., Dvorak, J., Echemendia, R., . . . Turner, M. (2013). Consensus statement on concussion in sport: The 4th international conference on concussion in sport held in Zurich, November 2012. *British Journal of Sports Medicine, 47,* 250–258.

McLeod, T., & Leach, C. (2012). Psychometric properties of self-report concussion scales and checklists. *Journal of Athletic Training, 47*(2), 221–223.

NCAA. (2013). Guideline 2i: sports related concussion. In *2013–2014 NCAA Sports Medicine Handbook.* Indianapolis, IN: NCAA.

Register-Mihalik, J., Guskiewicz, K., McLeod, T., Linnan, L., Mueller, F., & Marshall, S. (2013). Knowledge, attitude, and concussion-reporting behaviors among high school athletes: A preliminary study. *Journal of Athletic Training, 48*(5), 645–653. doi: 10.4085/1062-6050-48.3.20

Rigby, J., Vela, L., & Housman, J. (2013). Understanding athletic trainers' beliefs toward a multifaceted sport-related concussion approach: Application of the theory of planned behavior. *Journal of Athletic Training, 48*(5), 636–644.

Schatz, P., Moser, R., Solomon, G., Ott, S., & Karpf, R. (2012). Prevalence of invalid computerized baseline neurocognitive test results in high school and collegiate athletes. *Journal of Athletic Training, 47*(3), 289–296. doi: 10.4085/1062-6050-47.3.14

Solomon, J. (2015, February). Why the NCAA won't adopt concussion penalties— at least not yet. CBS Sports. Retrieved June 15, 2015, from http://www.cbssports.com

/collegefootball/writer/jon-solomon/25073014/why-the-ncaa-wont-adopt-concussion
-penalties——at-least-not-yet.

Stewart, G., McQueen-Borden, E., Bell, R., Barr, T., & Juengling, J. (2012). Comprehensive assessment and management of athletes with sport concussion. *International Journal of Sports Physical Therapy, 7*(4), 433–447.

Torres, D. M., Galetta, K. M., Phillips, H. W., Dziemianowicz, E. M. S., Wilson, J. A., Dorman, E. S., . . . Balcer, L. J. (2013). Sports-related concussion: Anonymous survey of a collegiate cohort. *Neurology Clinical practice, 3*(4), 279–287. doi:10.1212 /CPJ.0b013e3182a1ba22

4–4 Transfer Restrictions on College Football and Athlete Freedom

Gerald Gurney

Each year, prospective college students are faced with the challenge of selecting the best university to gain an education, experience developmental growth, and prepare themselves for successful futures. Many academic and nonacademic considerations are taken into account when making this decision, such as issues of affordability, proximity to home, academic reputation, prestige of program of study, peer choices, and even amenities in residence halls (Moldoff, n.d.). Students who are academically gifted or have other special talents must also take into account the level of academic challenge or opportunity for skill development that the university offers.

> **KEY TERMS**
>
> ▶ National Letter of Intent
>
> ▶ 4–4 Transfer
>
> ▶ NCAA
>
> ▶ Residence Requirement
>
> ▶ Revenue sports

Though the college selection process may be made very carefully, an unfamiliar living environment, unexpected academic challenges, and important life events lead many students to feel that it is in their best interest to transfer to another university. A 2011 US Department of Education report by the National Center of Educational Statistics found that 25.7 percent of first-time four-year college students in the 2003–04 class transferred to another four-year institution during their six-year enrollment. This common event allows students of all majors to reconsider the selection process and attend a different institution with no restrictions. Just like before, college selection decisions are compounded when the student is academically gifted or has a special talent or skill that is incorporated into the college experience. Students who connect with faculty mentors or engage in an artistic apprenticeship might feel compelled to follow a professor who has taken residence at another college. For example, students majoring in or participating in music, dance, or debate may elect to leave the institution at any time to advance their education or hone their talents elsewhere. Academically gifted students with prized scholarship awards may decide to transfer to another institution without returning their financial aid. The wide variety of reasons that lead to a student's decision to transfer to another university makes any restriction of a student's ability to transfer seem difficult to defend.

As with any other college students, transferring is a common reality among college athletes. Just as what happens with other students with special talents or skills who attend universities, another set of factors is taken into account in the college selection process. Because athletes attending institutions that are part of the National Collegiate Athletic Association (NCAA) are subject to the rules of that association, this introduces another set of considerations that may increase the likelihood of deciding to transfer and should be taken into account when evaluating whether to transfer to another institution. In 2012, Mark Emmert, the president of the NCAA, expressed concern that 40 percent of athletes in men's basketball in Division I left their original universities by the end of their sophomore year (Halley & Wieberg, 2012). An athlete's ability to transfer and the circumstances surrounding the move are among the areas of focused attention in NCAA legislation. The requirements and restrictions of the NCAA on an athlete's ability to transfer include a standard one-year in-residence requirement and, in some cases, a financial aid restriction. When agreeing to participate in NCAA-sanctioned athletic programs, students have no choice but to abide by rules that limit their abilities to attend another university, even if it is in their best personal, educational, or professional interests.

This chapter aims to provide a foundation for understanding NCAA rules specific to college athletes who have attended one four-year institution and wish to transfer to another four-year institution, referred to as 4–4 transfers. Information included in this chapter is designed to explain and promote discussion regarding the following:

1. Transfer restrictions for NCAA athletes and the rationale for such restrictions

2. Penalties and restrictive 4–4 transfer provisions for NCAA athletes specific to the sports of football and men's basketball

3. Exceptions to the NCAA 4–4 transfer rules and the rationale for such exceptions

4. Legal implications for NCAA 4–4 transfer restrictions

5. Ethical implications for NCAA 4–4 transfer restrictions

THE NCAA: A BILLION-DOLLAR INDUSTRY ON COLLEGE CAMPUSES

In order to understand the rationale of the NCAA's creation of restrictions on transferring college athletes, it is important to understand the financial magnitude of the NCAA as an organization. College sports, particularly NCAA Division I football and men's basketball, are annually an $8 billion industry, roughly the size of the National Football League, and have become part of the fabric of modern American society. On a crisp fall afternoon, stadiums seating in excess of 100,000 paying fans are packed with supporters of college football (Mayyasi, 2013). In 2010, the NCAA signed a 14-year, $10 billion contract with CBS and Turner Sports to televise the NCAA Division I Men's Basketball Championship, referred to as "March Madness." In 2014–15, the new College Football Playoff will pay $50 million to each of the five Power Five conferences (ACC, Big Ten, Big 12, SEC, and Pac-12) (Dosh, 2014).

To compete at the highest levels in the NCAA Division I Football Bowl Subdivision (FBS), participating universities feel compelled to invest in a skyrocketing coaching marketplace. In 2015, the highest-paid head college football coach's salary exceeded $8 million. The average salary of head coaches in 2014 reached a reported $1.75 million, up 75 percent from 2007. Successful college coaches with long-term contracts at their universities are often lured by more lucrative offers from other schools that are willing to purchase buyout clauses in their contracts. Such was the case when the University of Florida settled a $7.5 million buyout with Colorado State University in December 2014 for the services of head coach Jim McElwain (Holden, 2014).

Other job markets in college sports, such as athletic directors, assistant coaches, athletic administrative personnel, and athletic support personnel specialists, have also outpaced salary levels at our nation's universities at alarming rates. Presently, the escalation of salaries and the heavy investments universities are making in athletics seems endless. The aspiration of athletic dominance and perceived prestige associated in major college sports is costly, frequently at the expense of taxpayers and the student body through fees (Baumbach, 2014).

The Players

To maintain the highest levels of athletic competitiveness, universities must attract and retain elite athletes from high schools and community colleges who are also capable of meeting university curricular requirements and NCAA eligibility rules. Prospective athletes hoping to compete in the highest levels of football and men's basketball often have professional sport aspirations and must use NCAA member institutions to display their skills for their professional future. In exchange for their athletic talent and a 40- to 50-hour year-round training schedule, college athletes, through a renewable agreement of financial aid, are offered scholarships that may total the value of the cost of attendance for that university. In this agreement, college athletes are promised an opportunity for a world-class education at an American university and the opportunity to hone their athletic skills for advancement to the ranks of professional athletics. While this exchange may seem like an equitable arrangement, these agreements, termed National Letter of Intent (NLI), come with several stipulations.

The college athlete recruited in football and men's basketball is unique in that, arguably, he is the only student on campus there to provide entertainment for the masses while attempting to fulfill the promise of the revenue stream in Division I. His value is tied to the coach's style of play, and his contributions to the scoreboard. Frequently, college athletes in these sports meet minimum NCAA eligibility standards and have an academic profile and level of college preparedness that falls well below the published admissions standards for the institution. These students are commonly admitted through a backdoor policy known as *special admissions*. The NCAA legislated academic eligibility standards in response to charges of the disparate impact on certain student groups on standardized exam requirements, and it instituted a sliding scale for grade point averages (GPA) and standardized test scores. This scale removed the previously established minimum requirement of a composite 17 on the ACT or 820 on the SAT, and instead it allows any score on a standardized test as long as it is coupled with a corresponding high school GPA. The emphasis on high school GPA has highlighted the variation of academic rigor found in school systems around the country and multiple methods of increasing a GPA without a corresponding increase in knowledge. This has resulted in academically underskilled athletes graduating from high school but still meeting the GPA requirement to gain admission to selective institutions. With these athletes far behind the rest of the student body in these institutions, this preparedness gap has contributed to the academic mismatch apparent at many of the major universities participating in Division I football and men's basketball (Gurney, 2011).

The Decision to Transfer

While college athletes have many of the same experiences as other students, including those that lead to transferring to another institution, some factors specific to athletic participation contribute to a desire to transfer from the university. Although the college athlete has signed the NLI, the promise of an education and a successful college experience at that institution are dependent on multiple factors. College coaches may overestimate the skills of a high school player, and he is deemed a recruiting mistake. The player's physical development may fall short of what was anticipated, resulting in underperformance and a mismatch for the level of competition. A head coach may be fired or leave for a more lucrative coaching opportunity. The player's relationship with the head coach or an assistant coach is sometimes strained and may prompt a transfer. Athletic injury is often an intervening factor that could alter athletic participation and affect the decision to transfer. The academic challenge, or requirements for necessary academic remediation, that the athlete faces may lead to athletic ineligibility or dissatisfaction with the curricular opportunities available to the athlete (Winters & Gurney, 2012).

Whether the college athlete's decision to transfer is due to the athletic reasons stated above or factors from other parts of the college experience, he must contend with a number of obstacles or penalties if he wishes to receive an athletic scholarship and continue his college athletic career.

Rules of the Game

The National Letter of Intent

The first obstacle that an athlete encounters unwittingly is a provision found in the National Letter of Intent, a binding agreement that a prospective athlete signs to end the recruitment process and designate the institution that he wishes to attend. The NLI program is managed by the NCAA and governed by the Collegiate Commissioners Association. For the high school athlete, the NLI Signing Day marks the end of the intense recruitment process. In exchange for an offer of athletic-related aid for at least one year, the 635 universities participating in the NLI program agree to cease all recruitment and honor the athlete's commitment to attend a designated school. For the sport of football, National Signing Day, the first Wednesday in February, is celebrated with great fanfare, and students are thrust into the regional or national spotlight. The television network ESPN covers the signing of the nation's top recruit each year. High schools have press conferences to record the signing of their star athletes. College coaches host press conferences to introduce the next class of incoming stars.

The rationale that the Collegiate Commissioners Association uses for this contract is that, by signing the agreement and ceasing recruiting activity, the prospective athlete may then focus on educational objectives without distraction. What may not be clear to the student is that accompanying this revelry and excitement is a transfer penalty in which, if the athlete does not complete one full academic year at the designated university, then a one-year residency requirement and the loss of one year of athletic eligibility will be imposed. For an athlete who realizes that his choice of institution was a mistake prior to the end of the first academic year, one of his four opportunities to participate in his sport will be forfeited. To be released from this basic penalty, the athlete must request a formal release from the institution. Depending on the circumstances and the thought of losing the athlete to a competing team, the university has the choice to deny the release. This release, which must be signed by the school's athletic director and approved by the coach, allows the student or his parents to communicate with another school's coach. As noted on the NLI website (http://www.nationalletter .org), if the institution denies the release, the athlete may submit a written appeal to the NLI Review Committee within 30 days after the denial.

What prospective college athletes and their parents rarely understand is the imbalance of the NLI. The letter acts as a contract and is heavily weighted in favor of the university. The contract binds the student to the institution for which he signed for at least one year. The NLI simply serves as a means to restrict the athlete from being raided by other schools prior to enrollment. The confusion for the student and parents is the accompanying institutional offer of financial aid. An athlete must sign the offer when submitting the NLI. By signing the offer of financial aid, the university is committed to the athletic scholarship if the athlete enrolls at that school. This offer is binding for the university with or without having a signed NLI. Other than ending the recruitment process, one could argue that there is no purpose for the student to sign the document. A highly recruited athlete, for example, could get as many as a dozen financial aid offers prior to Signing Day. In theory, he could simply sign one or all of the financial aid offers and leave the universities in suspense until classes or practice begins. By doing so, the athlete is not bound to the basic transfer penalty clause should he change his mind.

Transfer Residence Requirement

Another obstacle confronting the athlete wishing to transfer from one four-year institution to another is the residence requirement rule. No other student classification is bound by this rule except for the college athlete, and no other classification of athlete is more restricted than those participating in high-profile, revenue-generating sports. NCAA Bylaw 14.5.1 defines the basic penalty applied to student-athletes wishing to transfer from a four-year institution to another four-year institution. Unless the athlete qualifies for a recognized exemption, he or she must complete one full academic year in residence (not able to compete in the sport or travel with the team).

In its *Transfer 101* guide, the NCAA describes the legislation surrounding transfer restrictions as essential to ensure a successful transition to the next school (NCAA, 2014). This rationale has sparked much debate, as the NCAA has permitted freshman college football and basketball players to be eligible for immediate competition since 1972. Critics point out that the NCAA suggests that a transfer student who is academically eligible to participate needs to sit out for an entire year to focus on his studies or to adjust to the new university. If the NCAA deems freshmen who have no adjustment period to university life as eligible to participate immediately, then an academically eligible sophomore or junior college athlete, arguably better adept at navigating college life, should also be immediately eligible to keep the rationale consistent. Critics maintain that immediate freshman eligibility and subsequent transfer ineligibility are conflicting ideas that the NCAA claims are rooted in academic concern (Students first, athletes second, 1999).

One-time Transfer Exception

In response to the criticism, the NCAA has developed a one-time transfer exception to the basic transfer requirement, which outlines four conditions that must be met to avoid serving the one-year residency requirement. For complete details, refer to NCAA Bylaw 14.5.5.2.10 in the *Division I Manual*. These conditions are (1) the student is not a participant in FBS football, men's ice hockey, basketball, or baseball; (2) the student has not transferred previously from a four-year institution; (3) the student would have been academically eligible to compete had they stayed at the institution; and (4) the institution the student is departing will provide a written statement of approval (a "release") that the student not be subject to the residency rules. If *all four* conditions are not met, then the student cannot take advantage of the NCAA's one-time transfer exception. While this grants relief to many athletes, students in high-profile, revenue-generating sports are not eligible for this exception. Football, basketball, men's ice hockey, and, more recently, baseball are all capable revenue streams of the athletics department and are featured sports in which fans typically purchase tickets for admission. The NCAA seeks to create a competitive balance between its member institutions at each of its three divisions. Establishing a transfer penalty, particularly for football and men's basketball at FBS schools, clearly limits the movement of elite athletes. By doing so, the rule impedes an athlete's ability to change institutions for the sake of competitive balance (Yasser & Fees, 2005).

Permission to Contact

As outlined in NCAA Bylaw 13.1.1.3 in the *Division I Manual,* any representative of a four-year institution is prohibited from contacting a student-athlete without the receipt of a signed release from the present university. Any communication, if brought to light, would constitute an NCAA violation for the recruiting institution. If no release is granted to that athlete and the student still decides to transfer, then the athlete will not be eligible for athletic aid for an entire academic year. The student's head coach may deny permission to contact or limit the places to transfer. Some athletic conferences, such as the Big 12, presently have rules preventing the transfer from one member institution to another within the conference. Coaches do not relish the prospect of losing a game because a former team member used his talents against his old team. Failure to receive permission to contact does not prohibit the athlete from transferring but denies him the opportunity to receive athletic aid during the residence requirement, which makes the cost of attending college unaffordable for many students. Although athletes may appeal a denial to contact, the athlete is largely at the mercy of his head coach, who determines where he may go and whether he may receive athletic-related financial aid.

Waivers

Apart from the restriction on free movement for athletes in revenue-generating sports, the NCAA considers a number of conditions as waivers to the basic residence requirement. Some reasons for a waiver of transfer regulation requests include mandatory military service, documented academic misinformation, waivers involving medical injury, being run off by a team, and demonstration of financial hardship (NCAA Division I Legislative Council Subcommittee for Legislative Relief, 2013).

RECOMMENDATIONS

College athletes are subject to harsh penalties if they wish to transfer to another four-year institution. No single group of athletes is more penalized than those participating in the revenue-generating sports of football, basketball, men's ice hockey, and baseball. The consequences set in place by the NCAA and the NLI frequently make the transfer infeasible for the athlete. Because of this, these penalties carry ethical and legal implications.

Legal Implications

Ray Yasser compared the NCAA transfer restrictions to common law covenants on employees who leave companies to start their own businesses or work for competitors (Yasser & Fees, 2005). While courts have historically been hesitant to classify college athletes as employees, recent legal cases reflect a change in thought. The finding of the National Labor Relations Board (NLRB) in Region 13 in favor of Northwestern University football players to be employed by the university, allowing them to form a worker's union, marked the first decision of its kind (Northwestern University, 2014). If college athletes are employees, then they are entitled to employee rights and can engage in collective bargaining through their union. The initial decision of the Region 13 board was appealed to the NLRB. In August 2015, the NLRB declined to assert its jurisdiction in the case, citing that a ruling in favor of a single team's petition would not promote labor stability, due to the nature of FBS football, and dismissed the petition (NLRB, 2015).

Another indication of a change in thought came with the initial decision in *O'Bannon v. NCAA* (2014) in favor of the plaintiffs, who filed to ensure compensation for athletes for the use of their likenesses for commercial purposes. A September 2015 opinion before the Ninth Circuit Court of Appeals panel agreed in part with the initial ruling that NCAA rules are not exempt from antitrust scrutiny and the district court's remedy of expanding scholarships up to the full cost of attendance. However, it struck down the district court's remedy to provide football and basketball players $5,000 per year in trust, citing lack of sufficient evidence. The plaintiffs have since filed petition for an *en banc* hearing (O'Bannon v. NCAA, 2015). More recently, an NCAA transfer rule antitrust case has been filed in federal court. Devin Pugh, a former college football player at Weber State, seeks to allow college football and basketball athletes freedom of transfer and to abolish the current cap on scholarships at 85. After a Weber State coaching change, Mr. Pugh's scholarship was not renewed. According to the plaintiff, scholarship offers at other Division I institutions were rescinded when the NCAA denied him a waiver. Mr. Pugh subsequently enrolled in a lower competitive division, where his scholarship was reduced and his cost of education required additional student debt (Strauss, 2015).

Because the NCAA makes a transfer waiver distinction between athletes participating in revenue-generating sports and those participating in Olympic sports, some critics feel this is an unfair ruling that serves to target a specific demographic of student. The NCAA is no stranger to lawsuits related to cultural bias or having racial or ethnic implications. The restriction on the free movement of athletes in revenue-generating sports, most of whom are African American, is a potential legal and ethical issue for the NCAA. Taylor Branch termed this phenomenon a vestige of "the plantation mentality" and exploitation of the Black athlete (Branch, 2011).

Ethical Implications

The one-time transfer exception prohibition on football and men's basketball denotes the supposition of athlete ownership that is more restrictive than professional team agreements with their athletes. Once a professional athlete meets the terms of his contract, he may take his services to another team with no penalty. For college athletes, the requirement of the permission to contact form demonstrates a subservient relationship put in place by the NCAA in which student-athletes are forced to engage.

College athletes from non-revenue-generating sports may use the NCAA's one-time transfer exception to compete immediately at another institution, but those from revenue-generating sports such as football and men's basketball cannot compete for one year after transferring. This is particularly unfair, because these sports represent the highest-paid group of coaches, who are free to move to the highest-bidding institution. The only reason for the residency penalty is to protect the institutions' and coaches' investments in their athletic talent. College athletes should share in the same freedom to explore other institutional and academic options that their coaches do (Dennie & Gurney, 2012).

As with most issues in national organizations with large sums of money at stake, solutions are complex. The intended and unintended consequences of each decision must be considered. Every decision should be made with the best interest of the college athlete at the core of the plan. Protecting the rights and well-being of athletes is of paramount importance. With this in mind, the following recommendations are presented.

The NLI program ought to end its athlete penalty clauses. While the document serves the purpose of ending the nuisance of recruitment for the student, athletes should not be penalized with a loss of eligibility if they desire to transfer.

The National College Players Association (NCPA), headed by former UCLA football player Ramogi Huma, has been an influential national advocacy group for college athletes. Its mission and goals statement includes a guarantee that all athletes who wish to transfer be granted a release so that they are not restricted from receiving financial aid. The NCPA correctly cites the release process as a contradiction of the NCAA's educational mission. In addition, the NCPA seeks an end to the sport restrictions on the one-time transfer rule. As stated on the NCPA website (http://www.ncpanow.org), it advocates an end to restrictions on athletes to pursue their personal and academic goals.

In 2012, Dennie and Gurney offered a number of suggested reforms for intercollegiate athletics. Among the recommendations aimed at maintaining amateurism in collegiate athletics is an elimination of the transfer penalty.

CONCLUSION

In the NCAA's Principle of Sound Academic Standards, it is stated that student-athletes "shall be an integral part of the student body" (NCAA, 2015, p. 4). It should follow that the same freedom to transfer to another university enjoyed by the student body should be afforded to college football and basketball players.

It is abundantly clear that transfer restrictions are rooted in the proprietary relationships that the university and the NCAA assume with athletes in revenue-generating sports. The NCAA insists that athletes are students first and foremost, not employees. If this is the case, then NCAA legislation should reflect the standards of every other student on campus, the freedom to stay or transfer to other schools.

QUESTIONS FOR DISCUSSION

1. Suppose you are the athletic director at a large Division I university. You are personally opposed to the NCAA's 4–4 transfer restrictions but would never violate NCAA rules professionally. What are some ways in which you could instruct your administrators, coaches, and staff to minimize the impact of the legislation on college athletes?

2. Consider the listed recommendations found in this chapter. What might be some unintended consequences of these recommendations? Develop strategies or suggestions for how you might be able to address them.

3. Many are of the opinion that students elect to participate in college sports and choose to subject themselves to the rules and regulations of the NCAA. Apply this rationale to the legal and ethical considerations presented in this chapter. How does this line of thinking enable college athletes? How does this line of thinking limit them?

References

Baumbach, J. (2014, October 4). Special report: College football coaches' salaries and perks are soaring. *Newsday*. Retrieved from http://www.newsday.com

Branch, T. (2011, September 7). The shame of college sports. *The Atlantic*. Retrieved from http://www.theatlantic.com

Dennie, C. S., & Gurney, G. S. (2012, January 8). It's time for the NCAA to get it right. *Chronicle of Higher Education*. Retrieved from http://chronicle.com

Dosh, K. (2014, December 1). College football playoff payouts / revenue distribution for 2014–15. Business of College Sports. Retrieved from http://businessofcollegesports.com

Gurney, G. S. (2011, April 10). Stop lowering the bar for college athletes. *Chronicle of Higher Education*. Retrieved from http://chronicle.com

Halley, J., & Wieberg, S. (2012, June 24). Athlete movement in Division I basketball raising "alarm." *USA Today*. Retrieved from http://www.usatoday.com

Holden, W. C. (2014, December 4). CSU buyout settled, Jim McElwain will be new Florida football coach. KDVR. Retrieved from http://kdvr.com

Mayyasi, A. (2013, May 17). The pseudo-business of the NCAA. Priceonomics. Retrieved from http://priceonomics.com

Moldoff, D. K. (n.d.). Top 10 reasons why students transfer. College Transfer. Retrieved from http://www.collegetransfer.net

NCAA. (2014). Transfer 101: Basic information you need to know about transferring to an NCAA college. Retrieved from http://www.ncaa.org

NCAA. (2015). *2014–2015 NCAA Division I manual* (January version). Retrieved from http://www.ncaapublications.com

NCAA Division I Legislative Council Subcommittee for Legislative Relief. (2013, June 18). Information standards, guidelines and directives. NCAA. Retrieved from https://www.ncaa.org/sites/default/files/DI%2BSLR%2BGuidelines.pdf

NLRB. (2015). Board Unanimously Decides to Decline Jurisdiction in Northwestern Case. Retrieved from https://www.nlrb.gov/news-outreach/news-story/board-unanimously -decides-decline-jurisdiction-northwestern-case

Northwestern University, Case 13-RC-121359 (NLRB, 2014) (unpublished board decision).

O'Bannon v. National Collegiate Athletic Association, 7 F. Supp. 3d 955 (N.D. Cal. 2014).

O'Bannon v. National Collegiate Athletic Association, 9 F. Supp. 9d (Cal. 2015).

Strauss, B. (2015, November 5). Ex-Player suit challenges NCAA's transfer rules. *New York Times*. Retrieved from http://www.nytimes.com

Students first, athletes second. (1999, June 11). *New York Times*. Retrieved from http://www.nytimes.com

US Department of Education. (2011). Six-year attainment, persistence, transfer, retention, and withdrawal rates of students who began postsecondary education in 2003–04 (NCES 2011–152). Retrieved from http://nces.ed.gov/pubs2011/2011152.pdf

Winters, C. A., & Gurney, G. S. (2012). Academic preparation of specially-admitted student-athletes: A question of basic skills. *College & University Journal, 88*(2), 2–9. Retrieved from http://www.aacrao.org/

Yasser, R., & Fees, C. (2005). Attacking the NCAA's anti-transfer rules as covenants not to compete. *Seton Hall Journal of Sports and Entertainment Law,* 15(2). Retrieved from TU Law Digital Commons website: http://digitalcommons.law.utulsa.edu/

Due Process in College Sports

Steven J. Silver

The US Constitution provides basic rights to citizens accused of wrongdoing. Americans enjoy the rights to counsel, to receive notice of the charges against them, to confront accusers at a trial in front of a jury of their peers or at an administrative hearing, and to present exculpatory evidence. Whether the police are levying criminal charges or a government agency is seeking to dismiss an employee, everyone possesses inalienable rights to a fundamentally fair process before losing their freedom or property at the hands of a local, state, or federal government action.

KEY TERMS

▶ Procedural due process

▶ Substantive due process

▶ State actor

▶ Restitution Rule

▶ Injunction

Those rights diminish, however, as soon as an athlete decides to compete in the National Collegiate Athletic Association (NCAA). Take, for example, former University of Kentucky pitcher James Paxton. In 2009, the Toronto Blue Jays drafted Paxton in the first round of the Major League Baseball Draft (Sandler, 2011). Paxton turned down a $1 million offer from the Blue Jays so he could return to college. Shortly after the new school year began, a university official told Paxton that he had to interview with an NCAA investigator. If he refused, he would face expulsion. Yet, even if he cooperated, he could still lose his scholarship. The school also advised Paxton not to tell anyone, even his parents, about the NCAA's request for an interview (Sandler, 2011). Meanwhile, the entire time, Paxton had no idea what he allegedly had done wrong. Later, the NCAA revealed that Paxton had impermissibly retained a sports agent when determining whether to accept the Blue Jays' million-dollar offer or return to college.[1]

Faced with a lose-lose situation, Paxton declined the ominous interview and hired an attorney to sue the NCAA. Paxton's lawsuit focused on whether he had a right to written notice, an evidentiary hearing, and similar protections afforded to all other students by the University of Kentucky's Code of Student Conduct and the Kentucky Constitution (Johnson, 2010). Both the trial and appellate courts held that he had no due process rights whatsoever. See *Paxton v. Univ. of Ky.*, No. 09-CI-6404 (Ky. Cir. Ct., Jan. 19, 2010) (denying motion to dismiss and motion for temporary injunction). As a result, Paxton missed his senior season and fell to the fourth round of the next MLB Draft.

Although Paxton is now enjoying a professional baseball career with the Seattle Mariners, his plight illustrates how the NCAA and its member institutions do not provide written notice or evidentiary hearings to college athletes before taking adverse eligibility actions against them. They are guilty until proven innocent. In other words, the NCAA openly denies college athletes due process, because, as this chapter will examine, the Constitution effectively does not apply to the NCAA, which is a private, unincorporated nonprofit association (Hunter & Mayo, 1999).

THE PILLARS OF DUE PROCESS

Section One of the Fourteenth Amendment of the US Constitution provides that "no state shall make or enforce any law which shall abridge the privileges or immunities of citizens of the United States; nor shall any state deprive any person of life, liberty, or property, without due process of law."[2] This is known as the "due process clause." At its core, due process is "the principle that the government must respect all of the legal rights owed to a person" (Gill, 2015).

Throughout the early twentieth century, the US Supreme Court issued major decisions "incorporating" the Bill of Rights to the states through the Fourteenth Amendment (Chemerinsky, 2006, pp. 503–505). In effect, this meant that most of the protections provided to citizens through the Bill of Rights, such as the First Amendment's freedom of speech or the Sixth Amendment's right to counsel, would apply equally to federal, state, and local governments. As former Supreme Court Justice Felix Frankfurter explained, the concept of due process prevents actions that "offend those canons of decency and fairness which express the notions of justice of English-speaking peoples." See *Adamson v. Cal.,* 332 U.S. 46, 47 (1947).

Broadly, the due process clause provides both procedural and substantive due process. Procedural due process "refers to the procedures that the government must follow before it deprives a person of life, liberty, or property. Classic procedural due process issues concern what kind of notice and what form of hearing the government must provide when it takes a particular action" (Chemerinsky, 2006, p. 545). Procedural due process comprises two fundamental elements—notice and a hearing. There is no specific form of notice, as it varies per each case (Chemerinsky, 2006, pp. 581–83). At a minimum the person potentially losing property or liberty must be informed of the specific charges or issue to allow an opportunity for a defense. A hearing is defined at its basic level as "a proceeding wherein an issue of law or fact is adjudicated and evidence is presented to help determine the facts at issue" (Hunter, Shannon, & McCarthy, 2013, p. 66).

The other type of process—substantive due process—asks whether "the government has an adequate reason for taking away a person's life, liberty, or property. In other words, substantive due process looks to whether there is a sufficient justification for the government's action" (Chemerinsky, 2006, p. 546). Even when proper notice and hearing procedures are followed, a government's actions are still challengeable if there is no justification for the action. Although substantive due process issues do sometimes arise in the intercollegiate athletics context, most challenges to the NCAA's authority stem from the lack of procedural due process. From a legal standpoint, this leads to three basic questions:

1. Is participating in college sports a right?

2. Is a suspension from a given sport a deprivation of that right?

3. Was there adequate notice and a hearing before the action was taken?

The last question is fairly simple. Either there was notice and a hearing or not. The first two questions, though, are more difficult legal inquiries that require case-by-case factual analyses. Unlike when the government seeks to take a person's land for a highway construction project and thereby deprives him or her of physical property, the property rights of a college athlete are less tangible. Scholarships, national television exposure, and competing in front of professional league scouts are all benefits of competing in the NCAA that could amount to legitimate property interests.

However, the Supreme Court has explained that to have a property interest in a benefit, "a person clearly must have more than an abstract need or desire for it. He must have more than a unilateral expectation of it. He must, instead, have a legitimate claim of entitlement to it." See *Bd. of Regents of State Colls. v. Roth*, 408 U.S. 564, 577 (1972). Additionally, the Fourteenth Amendment is designed to protect a person's reputation. As one federal district court explained, "Where a person's good name, reputation, honor, or integrity is at stake because of what the government is doing to him, notice and an opportunity to be heard are essential." See *Stanley v. Big Eight Conference*, 463 F. Supp. 920, 934 (W.D. Mo. 1978).

Who can deprive a person's property rights without affording due process became clear soon after the ratification of the Fourteenth Amendment when the Supreme Court declared that "the provisions of the Fourteenth Amendment . . . all have reference to State action exclusively, and not to any action of private individuals." See *Virginia v. Rives*, 100 U.S. 313, 318 (1879). This is now known as the "state action doctrine." For the Constitution's protections of individual liberties such as due process to apply, there must be an action by a state entity or individual acting under color of state law. See 42 U.S.C. § 1983. The Constitution provides no protection against abuses by private actors. According to the Supreme Court, the state action doctrine "preserves an area of individual freedom by limiting the reach of federal law and federal judicial power." See *Lugar v. Edmondson Oil Co.*, 457 U.S. 922, 936 (1982).

This leads to the key question that has plagued athletes, coaches, administrators, and the judicial system for decades—is the NCAA a state actor? If it is, then it must provide due process rights to athletes based on the plain language of the Fourteenth Amendment.

NCAA DODGES DUE PROCESS

Early in the debate over the status of the NCAA, courts regularly ruled that it was a state actor and had to provide due process. See, for example, *Regents of the Univ. of Minn. v. NCAA,* 560 F.2d 352 (8th Cir. 1977, *cert denied,* 434 U.S. 978 (1977); *Howard University v. NCAA,* 510 F.2d 213 (D.C. Cir. 1975); *Associated Students, Inc. v. NCAA* (493 F.2d 1251 (9th Cir. 1974)). For instance, in *Buckton v. NCAA,* a Massachusetts district court found that the NCAA was a state actor in a case involving the suspension of two Boston University hockey players because the NCAA was in a "symbiotic relationship" with its member institutions. See 366 F. Supp. 1152 (D. Mass. 1973). Then, in *Parrish v. NCAA,* the Fifth Circuit determined that the NCAA was a state actor when suspending basketball players due to low GPAs, because "the NCAA by taking upon itself the role of coordinator and overseer of college athletics—in the interest both of the individual student and of the institution he attends—is performing a traditional governmental function." See 506 F.2d 1028, 1032–33 (5th Cir. 1975).

After a string of decisions throughout the 1970s holding that it was a state actor, the NCAA needed a solution to avoid constant litigation and repeated courtroom losses. The obvious solution, which was the one proposed by its own general counsel, was to reform its disciplinary proceedings to provide full due process rights to athletes. Remarkably, on July 10, 1973, outside general counsel George H. Gangwere authored a memorandum to NCAA executive director Walter Byers advocating for due process rights for athletes. Attorney Gangwere advised:

> This memo will show you: (1) that even though there may be no constitutional right to participate in intercollegiate athletics there may be a sufficient interest in such participation to require the observance of due process before one can be deprived of it and (2) that the courts have not been consistent in deciding whether or not participation in intercollege athletics is such a substantial interest that it requires due process protection. Certainly where the eligibility of potential professional athletes or "super stars," or the continuation of a grant in aid are involved it would not be difficult for a court to find such a substantial interest . . . *It is our recommendation, therefore, that the member institutions be urged to give notice and an opportunity for a hearing to student athletes in any infractions action wherein it is proposed to suspend eligibility or aid.* (Johnson, 2010, p. 471) (emphasis added)

The following year, Stephen Horn, the president of Cal State, Long Beach University proposed adopting Gangwere's recommendation at the NCAA's 1975 Annual

Convention (Johnson, 2010). However, rather than provide due process to its athletes, the NCAA rejected the advice of its own general counsel and the proposals of Mr. Horn. Instead, it adopted two rules at that monumental 1975 convention that continue to shape how the NCAA operates today.

First, instead of reforming itself so that athletes would not have reasons for taking the organization to court, the NCAA created a rule that penalized any person or entity that sued it. This unique rule is now known as the Restitution Rule. Currently codified as NCAA Bylaw 19.7, the Restitution Rule provides that if an athlete initially deemed ineligible by the NCAA gains a court order to stop the NCAA's penalty, but later loses his or her lawsuit on appeal or has an injunction revoked, then the NCAA can vacate victories, enact postseason bans on the entire team, force the member institution to forfeit television revenue for games in which the targeted athlete participated, or levy any other monetary fine it deems appropriate. This unprecedented rule had one goal in mind—to prevent athletes from exercising their rights in court. In fact, at that 1975 NCAA Convention's General Round Table, Edgar Sherman of Muskingum College bragged that the Restitution Rule "would help to discourage legal actions against the NCAA in several ways" (Johnson, 2010, p. 476). Furthermore, the Restitution Rule all but guarantees that the university will side with the NCAA and not its own students, for fear of facing monetary sanctions or the loss of television revenue. Following the NCAA's lead, nearly all of the nation's individual state interscholastic athletic organizations have now adopted identical bylaws to incorporate the perverse incentives of the Restitution Rule at the high school level (Porto, 2015).

Penalizing anyone who dared sue the NCAA was not enough, though. At the same 1975 convention, Wake Forest University professor and future NCAA executive, Jack Sawyer, made the proposal to adopt a penalty structure whereby the NCAA could insulate itself from future due process litigation by not actually punishing athletes directly (Johnson, 2010). Instead, the NCAA would recommend penalties that schools levied themselves. If the school refused to do so, or challenged the NCAA's recommendation, it risked harsher penalties. This all but mandated schools to impose whatever punishments the NCAA would recommend. The NCAA approved the proposal, and it went into effect immediately. As James Paxton's attorney summarized, "By the stroke of a pen, the NCAA enacted the charade that, since it does not directly punish college athletes, it does not have to afford them any due process whatsoever" (Johnson, 2010, p. 487).

THE CASE THAT FOREVER CHANGED COLLEGE ATHLETICS

Despite its own belief that it had insulated itself from having to provide athletes with due process, the NCAA had still never received a final resolution as to whether it was a state actor or not. Courts throughout the country had come down on both sides of the question since that 1975 convention. However, with the Restitution Rule in effect, fewer athletes were likely to challenge the NCAA's power. It was not until a coach challenged his own alleged deprivation of due process that the NCAA gained a free pass to ignore the Fourteenth Amendment.

That coach was legendary University of Nevada, Las Vegas (UNLV) basketball coach Jerry Tarkanian. When he arrived at UNLV in 1973, Tarkanian inherited a mediocre 14–14 team. Four years later, he had the Runnin' Rebels in the Final Four. In his 19 seasons with UNLV, Tarkanian amassed a 509–105 record with three Final Four appearances and one NCAA title. When he died in 2015, Las Vegas dimmed all the lights along the Strip—something previously done only for the likes of Frank Sinatra, Elvis, and John F. Kennedy (Pierce, 2015). Although a giant in Las Vegas, Tarkanian was a thorn in the NCAA's side. His meteoric success brought intense scrutiny from the NCAA.

In 1977, UNLV informed Tarkanian that it was going to suspend him for two years after the NCAA issued a "show cause" order on UNLV to prove why harsher penalties should not be imposed. See *Nat'l Collegiate Ath. Ass'n v. Tarkanian,* 488 U.S. 179, 181 (1988). The NCAA had conducted a two-and-a-half-year investigation into UNLV's basketball program and found 10 violations by Tarkanian. Of course, Tarkanian refuted the allegations and submitted affidavits and sworn statements directly contradicting testimony of the NCAA enforcement staff. See *Tarkanian v. NCAA,* 741 P.2d 1345 (Nev. 1987). Ultimately, the NCAA told UNLV—a public university—that it had three options:

1. Reject the sanction requiring it to disassociate Tarkanian from the athletic program and risk heavier sanctions;

2. Accept the NCAA's proposed two-year suspension; or

3. Leave the NCAA completely.

UNLV decided to suspend Tarkanian rather than risk worse sanctions or commit athletic suicide by leaving the NCAA. The day before his suspension went into effect, Tarkanian filed an action in Nevada state court for declaratory and injunctive relief because he had been deprived of due process. Note that, since the NCAA is an unincorporated entity, it can be sued in any state.

Ultimately, Tarkanian obtained injunctive relief and an award of attorney's fees against both UNLV and the NCAA. The Nevada Supreme Court had concluded that the NCAA was a state actor and that it had deprived Tarkanian of his due process rights because his contract with UNLV established "a property interest in continued employment" (*id.* at 1349.) The Nevada Court explained further that "the right to discipline public employees is traditionally the exclusive prerogative of the state. UNLV cannot escape responsibility for disciplinary action against employees by delegating that duty to a private entity . . . By delegating authority to the NCAA over athletic personnel decisions and by imposing the NCAA sanctions against Tarkanian, UNLV acted jointly with the NCAA" (*id.* at 1348).

The NCAA appealed to the US Supreme Court, where it eked out a narrow 5–4 victory with the typically liberal Justice John Paul Stevens joining Justices Rehnquist, Blackmun, Scalia, and Kennedy in writing the majority opinion. Justice Stevens prefaced his opinion with a stark reminder of the limitations of the Constitution. He wrote, "Embedded in our Fourteenth Amendment jurisprudence is a dichotomy between state action, which is subject to scrutiny under the Amendment's Due Process Clause, and private conduct, against which the Amendment affords no shield, no matter how unfair that conduct may be." See 488 U.S. at 191. The court went on to detail that the NCAA "cannot be regarded as an agent of UNLV" and thus was not a state actor (*id*. at 196). It explained, "Just as a state compensated public defender acts in a private capacity when he or she represents a private client in a conflict against the State, the NCAA is properly viewed as a private actor at odds with the State when it represents the interests of its entire membership in an investigation of one public university" (*id*. at 196). In addition, Justice Stevens found that "it would be more appropriate to conclude that UNLV has conducted its athletic program under color of the policies adopted by the NCAA, rather than that those policies were developed and enforced under color of Nevada law" (*id*. at 200).

Lastly, the court remarked that if UNLV did not want to abide by NCAA rules, then it was free to withdraw its membership from the NCAA. Justice Stevens explained, "Tarkanian argues that the power of the NCAA is so great that the UNLV had no practical alternative to compliance with its demands. We are not at all sure this is true, but even if we assume that a private monopolist can impose its will on a state agency by a threatened refusal to deal with it, it does not follow that such a private party is therefore acting under color of state law" (*id*. at 197). In a footnote, the court went even further to support its contention that UNLV had a legitimate choice to leave the NCAA, as it concluded that "the university's desire to remain a powerhouse among the Nation's college basketball teams is understandable, and nonmembership in the NCAA obviously would thwart that goal. But that UNLV's options were unpalatable does not mean that they were nonexistent" (*id*. at n. 19).

Justice Bryon White, writing the dissent, simply summed up his opinion that "it was the NCAA's findings that Tarkanian had violated NCAA rules, made at NCAA conducted hearings, all of which were agreed to by UNLV in its membership agreement with the NCAA, that resulted in Tarkanian's suspension by UNLV. On these facts, the NCAA was 'jointly engaged with [UNLV] officials in the challenged action,' and therefore was a state actor" (*id*. at 202).

FREE REIGN TO AVOID DUE PROCESS

That slim 5–4 margin was all the NCAA needed to cement its status as a private entity immune from the obligations of the Fourteenth Amendment. In the nearly 30 years since the *Tarkanian* decision, neither the Supreme Court nor any circuit court of appeals has classified the NCAA as a state actor that owed its athletes and coaches due process rights.

The plight of former University of Connecticut (UConn) basketball player Ryan Boatright offers a prime example of how the *Tarkanian* decision has allowed the NCAA to ignore basic due process rights. Although college sports fans had long known of the NCAA's surreptitious investigations and harsh penalties for myriad violations, from accepting free meals (Norwood, 2003) to autographing the wrong memorabilia (Schroeder, 2013), columnist Joe Nocera brought the organization's utter disregard for due process to a mass audience on the pages of the *New York Times* in 2012. Nocera's opened the first of two columns about Boatright with a chilling reminder of just how little had changed since the Supreme Court granted the NCAA a free pass from the Constitution in *Tarkanian:*

> In America, a person is presumed innocent until proved guilty. Unless that is, he plays college sports. When the NCAA investigates an athlete for breaking its rules, not only is he presumed guilty but his punishment begins before he knows what he's accused of. He is not told who his accuser is. The NCAA will delve into the personal relationships of his relatives and demand their bank statements and other private records. And it will hand down its verdict without so much as a hearing. Reputations have been ruined on accusations so flimsy that they would be laughed out of any court in the land. Then again, the NCAA isn't a court of law. It's more powerful. (Nocera, 2012, January 23, para. 1)

So what did Boatright do that resulted in UConn suspending him six games without a hearing and ordering him to pay a $4,100 fine? Nothing. Boatright did not break any NCAA rules. Rather, based on a tip from a convicted felon and ex-boyfriend of Boatright's mother, Tanesha Boatright, the NCAA learned that Tanesha had borrowed money from an old friend (Reggie Rose, brother of NBA player Derrick Rose) to pay for her flights to attend campus visits with her son since the universities recruiting Boatright could only pay for his airfare.

Suspending Boatright was not enough, though. The NCAA began calling his mother multiple times per day threatening her with further punishment for her son if she did not cooperate. This led to NCAA investigators interrogating Mrs. Boatright in the middle of the night for more than eight hours without an attorney by her side (Nocera & Strauss, 2016). They demanded to see her bank statements and credit card bills, they questioned the salesman who sold her a car, and they even interviewed her co-workers. Ultimately, Boatright missed nine games and had his and his family's reputation tarnished. The NCAA was able to do this without a hearing, without allowing Boatright to confront his accuser, and without the aid of legal counsel.

Boatright and Paxton are not alone. For instance, in 2010, a total of 16 University of North Carolina (UNC) football players, including future NFL players Marvin Austin, Greg Little, and Mike McAdoo, were suspended for varying lengths because of alleged improper contact with sports agents and the receipt of impermissible benefits. As professor Dr. Emmett Gill Jr. detailed, the lack of due process was apparent in every step of the UNC saga:

> When NCAA officials initially questioned the UNC student-athletes, none had an attorney present. Some of the student-athletes did not have access to all of the documents the UNC athletic department exchanged with the NCAA during the hypothetical bylaw interpretation and reinstatement processes. When UNC submitted paperwork to the NCAA pertaining to student-athletes' alleged academic fraud, the university did not share the content with one accused student-athlete. Moreover, the UNC football student-athletes did not have the opportunity to refute conflicting evidence prior to being declared ineligible and withheld from NCAA competition. At least one student-athlete involved in the investigation did not secure representation until nine months into the saga. Lastly, per NCAA appeal requirements, prior to being afforded the opportunity to appeal ineligibility and reinstatement denial decisions, a student-athlete has to admit to violating the bylaws. (Gill, 2015, para. 4)

Unfortunately, what the UNC athletes experienced is the new norm in the post-*Tarkanian* NCAA. Suspensions are handed down before the athlete has an opportunity to mount a defense. There is no right to an attorney, and if an athlete wants to appeal a decision, he or she must admit wrongdoing. The NCAA shoots first and asks questions later. It enjoys this freedom because challenging the NCAA in court is most often a losing proposition since *Tarkanian*.[3] Moreover, unless a particular athlete can afford legal representation, his or her school is not going to provide assistance because of the severe retaliatory ramifications embedded within the Restitution Rule. When it comes to due process issues, the NCAA is essentially above the law.

RECOMMENDATIONS

The most basic reform needed in intercollegiate athletics is a guarantee of due process. In modern college athletics, where the NCAA serves as the NFL's minor league and basketball's March Madness tournament generates billion-dollar television deals, there is simply too much at stake to jeopardize an athlete's career and reputation without due process. What the NCAA should do to shield itself from future litigation and protect the rights of its athletes is to enact the recommendations of its own lawyer from back in the 1970s. This means providing notice and a hearing in any infractions or eligibility action.

First, the NCAA needs to adopt an innocent-until-proven-guilty framework. Rather than suspend an athlete immediately, the NCAA should notify the athlete in writing of the accusations against him or her. This notice should contain the specific infringing conduct, the bylaws allegedly violated, and the potential penalties. After receiving notice, the NCAA should allow a grace period for the athlete to continue to compete while gathering exculpatory evidence, locating witnesses, and potentially hiring an attorney. This amnesty window could range from 10 to 60 days depending upon the circumstances and whether the athlete was in season or not. Currently, once a school learns of an NCAA investigation, the school often immediately suspends the athlete for fear of having to later forfeit any games in which the affected athlete participates. By providing proper notice and an amnesty period, the schools would not have to risk unnecessarily punishing the athlete.

Once an athlete receives notice of an alleged infraction, he or she should have an opportunity to retain an attorney. If the athlete cannot afford one, the member institution should provide private, outside counsel. Certainly, there are costs involved in providing legal counsel. However, each conference could retain an attorney for all of its members and split the costs. In a sense it would be akin to an athletic public defender.

The NCAA should then hold a fair and public hearing. At the hearing, the athlete should have the ability to testify, introduce evidence, and cross-examine witnesses. The hearing should follow a set of preordained rules akin to the Federal Rule of Civil Procedure or the American Arbitration Association rules to ensure that both the NCAA and the athlete have equal access to all potential evidence before the hearing. Otherwise, the hearing is a trial by ambush without proper due process.

More importantly, the public hearing should occur before an arbitrator or tribunal that is neutral and independent. The Court of Arbitration of Sport (CAS) could provide a model as to how the NCAA could implement a neutral arbitration process to adjudicate infractions and eligibility disputes. Based in Switzerland, CAS uses about 300 arbitrators from numerous countries who hear and decide almost all disputes involving the Olympics and Union of European Football Associations (UEFA).

Lastly, the NCAA should abolish the Restitution Rule before a court finds it unconstitutional. Penalizing an athlete's teammates and university for simply exercising his or her civil rights in a court of law is unnecessarily punitive. If the NCAA stands behind its bylaws and its enforcement process, then it should have no problem affording its athletes notice and a fair hearing before a public tribunal.

CONCLUSION

Even though the plight of college athletes in acquiring basic due process rights seems hopeless at times, it is crucial to remember that violating an NCAA rule is not a crime. The NCAA does not make laws. It is a collection of voluntary members who have agreed to a set of arbitrary rules. With public opinion skewing almost exclusively negative toward the NCAA and an increasingly liberal Supreme Court, the right challenge to the NCAA's due process avoidance at the right time could undo the *Tarkanian* decision. The Restitution Rule on its own is ripe for a constitutional challenge. See *Bloom v. NCAA,* 93 P.3d 621, 628 (Colo. App. 2004) (cautioning the NCAA that the Restitution Rule renders an athlete's right to seek judicial remedies "meaningless").

In addition to future legal challenges to overturn the *Tarkanian* precedent, Congress could always decide to act on behalf of college athletes. Congress can regulate the NCAA through its interstate commerce power as it can condition funds provided to higher education institutions, and remove nonprofit tax exemptions (Potuto, 2012). Congress has held hearings to investigate concerns about the NCAA's procedures in the past, so there is no reason why it could not do so again (Despain, 2015; Gill, 2015). Although motivating Congress to act on anything seems far-fetched in the current political climate, it is not a total fantasy. Between the creation of the autonomous Power Five conference, looming antitrust lawsuits, and skyrocketing revenues, change is coming. In terms of due process rights, it is not a matter of if but when. Athletes must not only increase their awareness of their rights but commit to exercising them whenever necessary.

QUESTIONS FOR DISCUSSION

1. If the Supreme Court were to reverse itself and declare the NCAA a state actor, what other athletes' rights would become subject to constitutional challenges?

2. In *Tarkanian,* the Supreme Court split 5–4. Did the majority reach the correct decision? Why or why not?

3. Does playing college athletics constitute a legitimate constitutional right? Why or why not?

Notes

1. Since Paxton's confrontation with the NCAA, the Power Five conferences revoked the prohibition against agents for baseball players drafted out of high school. However, current NCAA players are still not allowed to hire agents if drafted prior to graduation (Siegrist & Silver, 2016).

2. The Fifth Amendment also mandates that "no person shall be . . . deprived of life, liberty, or property, without due process of law."

3. High school athletes fare much better in court, as the US Supreme Court ruled that state high school athletic governing bodies are state actors in the seminal case of *Brentwood Acad. v. Tenn. Secondary Sch. Ath. Ass'n,* 531 U.S. 288 (2001).

References

Chemerinsky, E. (2006). *Constitutional law: Principles and policies*. New York: Aspen.

Despain, J. J. (2015). From off the bench: The potential role of the US Department of Education in reforming due process in the National Collegiate Athletic Association. *Iowa Law Review, 100*(3), 1285–1326. doi:10.2139/ssrn.2490113

Gill, E. (2015). The UNC football investigation and student-athlete due process: The legal, public policy, and social justice implications. *Entertainment and Sports Lawyer, 32*(2). Retrieved from http://www.americanbar.org/publications/entertainment-sports-lawyer/2015/firstedition/the-unc-football-investigation-and-student-athlete-due-process.html

Hunter, R. J., Jr., & Mayo, A. M. (1999). Issues in antitrust, the NCAA, and sports management. *Marquette Sports Law Journal, 10*(69): 69–85. Retrieved from http://scholarship.law.marquette.edu/sportslaw/v0110/iss1/5

Hunter, R. J., Shannon, J. H., & McCarthy, L. (2013). Fairness, due process and the NCAA: Time to dismiss the fiction of the NCAA as a "private actor." *Journal of Politics and Law, 6*, 63. doi:10.5539/jpl.v6n4p63

Johnson, R. G. (2010). Submarining due process: How the NCAA uses its Restitution Rule to deprive college athletes of their right of access to the courts . . . Until Oliver v. NCAA. *Florida Coastal Law Review, 9*(459).

NCAA Division I Manual. (2016). Indianapolis, IN: NCAA.

Nocera, J. (2012, January 20). Guilty until proved innocent. *New York Times*. Retrieved from http://www.nytimes.com/2012/01/21/opinion/nocera-guilty-until-proved-innocent.html

Nocera, J. (2012, January 23). Living in fear of the NCAA. *New York Times*. Retrieved from http://www.nytimes.com/2012/01/24/opinion/nocera-living-in-fear-of-the-ncaa.html

Nocera, J., & Strauss, B. (2016). *Indentured: The inside story of the rebellion against the NCAA*. New York: Penguin Random House.

Norwood, R. (2003, July 31). Utah is penalized for rules violations. *LA Times*. Retrieved from http://articles.latimes.com/2003/jul/31/sports/sp-utah31

Pierce, C. P. (2015, March 2). Jerry Tarkanian: Coach, terror of the NCAA, and one of the last honest men in Las Vegas. Grantland. Retrieved from http://grantland.com/the-triangle/jerry-tarkanian-ncaa-las-vegas-unlv-rebels/

Porto, B. L. (2015). The NCAA's Restitution Rule: Bulwark against cheating or barrier to appropriate legal remedies? *Roger Williams University Law Review, 20*(2), 335–373.

Potuto, J. R. (2012). The NCAA state actor controversy: Much ado about nothing. *Marquette Sports Law Review, 23*(1): 1–67. doi:10.2139/ssrn.2006562

Sandler, J. (2011, February 5). The Blue Jays that got away. *National Post*. Retrieved from http://news.nationalpost.com/sports/mlb/the-blue-jays-that-got-away

Schroeder, G. (2013, August 16). Analysis: The Johnny Manziel autograph case. *USA Today*. Retrieved from http://www.usatoday.com/story/sports/ncaaf/sec/2013/08/15/johnny-manziel-texas-am-ncaa-investigation-autographs-for-money/2662257/

Siegrist, A., & Silver, S. (2016, March). NCAA begins to change culture in wake of Oliver Case. *Journal of NCAA Compliance*, 3–9.

College Athletes and Collective Bargaining Laws

Neal H. Hutchens and Kaitlin A. Quigley

Should college athletes be permitted to engage in collective bargaining activities and join unions? Yes, according to a March 2014 decision by a regional director of the National Labor Relations Board (NLRB) involving football players at Northwestern University. Under the decision, scholarship football players at the university qualified as employees for purposes of the National Labor Relations Act (NLRA), entitling them to vote on forming a collective bargaining unit (i.e., to be represented by a union). On review, however, the NLRB reversed the regional director's decision and declined to exercise jurisdiction in the case. The decision not to exercise jurisdiction meant the board offered a narrow ruling, one that did not weigh in on the issue of whether scholarship athletes should qualify as employees under the NLRA. Accordingly, the issue of collective bargaining rights for college athletes continues as an undecided legal question under federal labor law.

Especially given the limited scope of the Northwestern decision by the NLRB, debate over the collective bargaining rights of college athletes continues. The effort at Northwestern University to unionize scholarship football players provides an opportunity to review legal aspects related to collective bargaining initiatives by college athletes. This chapter, in addition to examining the Northwestern case, explores more generally the legal standards applicable to collective bargaining activities by college athletes. Additionally, the authors consider several of the key implications stemming from legal recognition or denial of unionization rights for college athletes.

KEY TERMS

▶ National Labor Relations Board

▶ National Labor Relations Act

▶ Collective bargaining

▶ Right to work laws

▶ Labor law

COLLECTIVE BARGAINING RIGHTS IN HIGHER EDUCATION

A broader statutory and legal framework encompasses the issue of collective bargaining (i.e., unionization) efforts by college athletes, with important facets at both the federal and state levels. A key legal distinction involves the bifurcated system of legal authority over public- and private-sector collective bargaining. Private colleges and universities (such as Northwestern University) are subject to the NLRA and fall under the jurisdiction of the NLRB. State law controls the collective bargaining rights available to individuals in public higher education. State legal standards can also impact collective bargaining in both public and private contexts through the existence of what are known as right to work laws, which are described further below. The following sections provide an overview of the legal standards governing collective bargaining rights in private and public higher education.

COLLECTIVE BARGAINING RIGHTS AT PRIVATE COLLEGES AND UNIVERSITIES

The National Labor Relations Act

Until the 1930s, legal protections for collective bargaining activities by employees existed only for railroad workers (Saltzman, 1998). After overcoming initial rejection from the US Supreme Court to a broader collective bargaining law, Congress approved the NLRA in 1935 as part of the package of New Deal initiatives enacted in the wake of the Great Depression. The legislation authorized the creation of the NLRB to administer the act and to oversee union elections. The NLRA, as amended in 1947 by the Taft-Hartley Act, continues to provide the legal framework and standards that govern collective bargaining in the private sector.

The NLRB serves as the federal agency designated under the law to implement the requirements and provisions of the NLRA. Five members, appointed by the president and approved by the Senate, compose the board, which operates with independent legal authority. The appointment process for members means that the board's interpretation of particular legal provisions of the NLRA can shift back and forth, depending on the prevailing political winds and the resulting influence on the board's composition.

The board hears administrative cases involving allegations of unfair labor practices made pursuant to the NLRA, and, as with the Northwestern case, reviews decisions from the NLRB's 26 regional offices dealing with union elections and representation issues. Following a board ruling, a party may opt to appeal the decision to an appropriate US court of appeals. From there, a party may ask the US Supreme Court to review the case, a request that could be accepted or declined, as happens with the overwhelming majority of review petitions submitted to the Supreme Court.

The Northwestern case, discussed more extensively later in the chapter, centers on a petition submitted to the NLRB for scholarship football players at the university to be able to vote on whether to form a collective bargaining unit (i.e., a union). For the NLRB to authorize such a representation election, the football players must qualify as employees for purposes of the NLRA, a point disputed by the university. It is important to note that the legal right of a group of employees to vote on the formation of a collective bargaining unit does not mean they will decide to do so.

While the NLRB, pursuant to the NLRA, oversees collective bargaining in the private sector, state labor laws can also impact collective bargaining activities for private entities. Most notably, 25 states have enacted right to work laws that permit employees to opt out of joining a union and paying dues, even if these individuals receive wages and benefits negotiated by the collective bargaining unit (National Conference of State Legislatures, n.d.).

Private Higher Education and the NLRA

The Northwestern case arises in a context in which the NLRB has previously addressed matters related to collective bargaining in private higher education. Initially, in a 1951 decision, the board declined to interpret the NLRA as covering employees at private colleges and universities (Saltzman, 1998). Reversing course in 1970, the board determined that the law encompassed private higher education employees. The extension of the provisions of the NLRA to private higher education has not translated into collective bargaining eligibility for all employees or for all campus constituencies seeking designation as an employee for purposes of the NLRA. Instead, at various points, the board has engaged in a process of determining whether certain groups qualify or not as employees under the law (e.g., graduate student workers) and which employees are eligible to participate in collective bargaining activities protected by the NLRA (e.g., faculty members).

The twists and turns of collective bargaining rights for full-time faculty in private higher education illustrate how the interpretation of the NLRA can evolve and change, including one based on the US Supreme Court's interpretation of the law. After the board's decision in 1970 that interpreted private colleges and universities as subject to the provisions of the NLRA, it then determined that full-time faculty at private, nonprofit institutions qualified under the law to engage in collective bargaining activities. But, in *Yeshiva University* (1980), the Supreme Court reversed the board, holding that full-time faculty members constituted managerial employees under the NLRA and, as such, were ineligible to engage in collective bargaining activities protected by the law.

Prior to the Northwestern case, the board had previously addressed the issue of when a particular position qualifies as an "employee" or "student" for purposes of the NLRA. In a 1999 decision, the board held that medical residents (commonly referred to as house staff) constituted employees under the NLRA (Boston Medical Center Corporation, 1999), a position reaffirmed in a 2014 case decided by an NLRB regional director (Ichan School of Medicine at Mt. Sinai, 2014). Medical centers in these cases argued that the residents performed functions and roles that made them more akin to students than to employees.

The NLRB has also considered whether to classify graduate students serving as teaching or research assistants as employees under the NLRA. The board has flip-flopped on this question. In a 1972 decision, the board determined that graduate student teaching and research assistants were ineligible to engage in collective bargaining for purposes of the NLRA (Adelphi University, 1972). Then, it overturned this stance in a 2000 decision, deciding that such graduate assistants constituted employees under the law (New York University, 2000). But, and reflective of how political forces help shape the board's composition and stance toward interpreting the NLRA, the board reversed course again in 2004, declaring that graduate student teaching and research assistants did not qualify as employees under the law (Brown University, 2004). The board appeared potentially ready to address the issue of graduate student teaching and research assistants again in 2013, but the parties in the case reached a resolution where New York University voluntarily permitted graduate students to organize (Jaschik, 2013).[1] The Northwestern case arises in a context punctuated by previous (and ongoing) debates regarding the "student" or "employee" question under the NLRA.

COLLECTIVE BARGAINING AT PUBLIC COLLEGES AND UNIVERSITIES

The availability (or not) of collective bargaining rights for public sector employees represents a matter of state law, not the NLRA; this includes public colleges and universities. Some states have labor laws that permit collective bargaining by various groups of eligible public employees. In terms of higher education faculty, for example, California, New York, New Jersey, Illinois, and Michigan contain almost three-fourths of faculty members who belong to collective bargaining units. These faculty are overwhelmingly employed in public institutions because of the curtailment of unionization by private higher education faculty which resulted from the *Yeshiva* (1980) decision (Berry & Savarese, 2012). Some states permit graduate students (or even undergraduate students in some instances) to form collective bargaining units, though many states refuse to classify such student workers as employees for purposes of state labor law. The Coalition of Graduate Employee Unions (CGEU) reports 31 recognized student employee unions in the United States, with all but one of these at public institutions (CGEU, n.d.).[2]

For college athletes at public colleges and universities, their collective bargaining rights (like other constituencies in public higher education) depend on state law. Accordingly, the matter of collective bargaining rights for college athletes at public institutions represents an issue for determination on a state-by-state basis. Likely instructive in relation to college athletes, even in states that otherwise permit collective bargaining by at least some public higher education employees, many of these states do not classify student workers (e.g., graduate student teaching or research assistants) as employees under the state's collective bargaining law (Berry & Savarese, 2012). Perhaps even more telling, in response to the initial Northwestern decision and resulting consideration of potential unionization efforts by college athletes at public institutions, Ohio and Michigan both enacted provisions that exclude college athletes at public colleges and universities as employees for purposes of the states' collective bargaining laws (New, 2014; Thompson, 2014).

THE NORTHWESTERN UNIVERSITY DECISION

The Regional Director's Opinion

As a private institution, Northwestern University falls under the NLRB's jurisdiction. An NLRB regional director, Peter Sung Ohr, determined that scholarship football players at the university qualified as employees under the NLRA and also represented an appropriate collective bargaining unit. As such, the regional director ordered that an election should proceed for the scholarship football players to vote on whether to form a collective bargaining unit.

A key issue addressed in the regional director's decision centered on the classification of the scholarship football players as students or employees under the NLRA. The test applied by the regional director defined an employee as "a person who performs services for another under contract of hire, subject to the other's control or right of control, and in return for payment" (Northwestern University, 2014, p. 13). Looking to this definition, the regional director determined that the football players and the university engaged in a contractual relationship in which the players performed "football-related services" in exchange for the compensation (i.e., tuition and room and board) provided via their scholarships (Northwestern University, 2014, p. 14).

In reaching the determination that scholarship football players qualified as employees under the NLRA, the regional director deemed several factors dispositive. Ohr discussed that the scholarship football players performed services that resulted in a substantial economic benefit to Northwestern, noting in the opinion that the football program generated revenues in the range of $235 million from 2003 to 2012. The regional director also discussed that the university likely derived an economic benefit from increased enrollment and alumni giving because of success on the football field.

While the football players did not collect salaries, Ohr concluded that the scholarship football players "nevertheless receive[d] a substantial economic benefit for playing football" (Northwestern University, 2014, p. 14). This compensation, according to the regional director, included the cost of tuition and fees, room and board, and books during a player's four or five years as a scholarship student-athlete. According to Ohr, "the monetary value of these scholarships totals as much as $76,000 per calendar year and results in each player receiving total compensation in excess of one quarter of a million dollars" during an individual's football career at Northwestern (Northwestern University, 2014, p. 14).

The regional director also deemed it central to his analysis that the scholarship football players signed a "tender" agreement that provides the players with "detailed information concerning the duration and conditions under which the compensation [from the university] will be provided to them" (Northwestern University, 2014, p. 14). Ohr stated that the fact that players could lose their scholarships for failure to remain on the team or to abide by team rules indicated the contractual nature of the relationship between the scholarship football players and the university.

In deciding that an employer-employee relationship existed, the regional director described the "strict and exacting control" exercised by coaches over the scholarship football players' yearly and daily schedules. From the regional director's perspective, the substantial hours devoted by the college athletes to football, for which they earned no academic credit, undercut arguments to characterize them primarily as students rather than employees for purposes of the NLRA. Along with the substantial time commitment made by players, Ohr also discussed how the rules and conditions imposed on scholarship football players far exceeded those placed on the general student population and also extended to the regulation of private matters not directly related to football duties. Among the rules imposed, football players had to gain permission to hold outside employment, receive consent to drive a personal vehicle, obtain approval for their living arrangements, refrain from using swear words in public, and adhere to various standards related to academic performance.

The football players agreed as well, noted the regional director, to abide by multiple social media rules. These included restrictions on content the college athletes could post on social media. Football players also had to "friend" designated coaches on their social media pages as part of the monitoring of players' social media activities. Additionally, football players pledged not to profit off their image or reputation during their playing career at Northwestern, while at the same time permitting the institution and the Big Ten Conference to use and profit from the use of their name, likeness, or image for any purpose. While acknowledging that the university placed many of the requirements on players discussed in the opinion to ensure compliance with NCAA standards, the regional director concluded that this state of affairs did not alter the fact that the university exerted substantial control over the players' daily lives, both in terms of the numerous rules imposed and the time commitment exacted from scholarship football players.

Based on these foregoing factors, Ohr decided that scholarship football players at Northwestern qualified as employees under the NLRA. The regional director stated that reaching this determination did not conflict with the board's decision in *Brown* (2004), where it declared that graduate student teaching and research assistants are not employees under the NLRA. He pointed out the additional oversight of football players compared to graduate student assistants. The regional director also emphasized the players did not engage in their duties primarily for academic reasons, as they did not accrue academic credit for participation in football.

The regional director also concluded that the proposed bargaining unit appropriately excluded walk-on football players, since they did not receive the same kinds of compensation (i.e., scholarship aid) as scholarship football players. Determining all conditions satisfied per the requirements of the NLRA, he ordered an election to determine whether the scholarship football players wished to form a collective bargaining unit.

NLRB Review of the Regional Director's Decision

As noted, the NLRB overturned the regional director's decision on narrow jurisdictional grounds. Thus, the board did not engage in substantive discussion of many of the issues raised in the case or the regional director's opinion. Instead, the NLRB declined to address these issues, stating in its decision that "whether we might assert jurisdiction in another case involving grant-in-aid scholarship football players (or other types of scholarship athletes) is a question we need not and do not address at this time" (Northwestern University, 2015, p. 1).

In its decision, the board determined that even if scholarship football players otherwise qualified as employees under the NLRA, it would not assert jurisdiction in the case based on the following rationale: "Our decision is primarily premised on a finding that, because of the nature of sports leagues (namely the control exercised by the leagues over the individual teams) and the composition and structure of FBS [Football Bowl Subdivision] football (in which the overwhelming majority of competitors are public colleges and universities over which the Board cannot assert jurisdiction), it would not promote stability in labor relations to assert jurisdiction in this case" (Northwestern University, 2015, p. 3). The NLRB described the case as raising novel questions, pointing out no previous petition for recognition of collective bargaining rights under the NLRA by a single college team or group of college teams. It stated in its opinion that "scholarship players do not fit into any analytical framework that the Board has used in cases involving other types of students or athletes" (Northwestern University, 2015, p. 3). According to the board, the fact that players participated in a co-curricular activity to receive a scholarship differentiated them from cases involving student graduate assistants and student custodians and cafeteria workers. Likewise, according to the NLRB, the status of the players as students made the circumstances distinct from cases involving professional athletes.

While not engaging substantive legal questions regarding college athletes and collective bargaining, the NLRB stated that institutions, particularly those in the FBS, operate in ways not unlike professional sports enterprises and "are engaged in the business of staging football contests from which they receive substantial revenues" (Northwestern University, 2015, p. 4). As with professional sports leagues, the board discussed the existence of a "symbiotic relationship among the various teams, the conferences, and the NCAA" (Northwestern University, 2015, p. 4).

This interconnectedness, stated the board, meant that any determination related to Northwestern scholarship football players affected the NCAA and its member institutions and the Big Ten Conference to which Northwestern belonged. As such, asserting jurisdiction over a single team—which differed from previous cases that dealt with leagues—failed to "promote stability in labor relations" (Northwestern University, 2015, p. 5). The board discussed that only 17 of some 125 FBS teams were private and, therefore, under the jurisdiction of the NLRB, as public institutions are subject to state law. The lack of authority over most FBS teams contended the NLRB would disrupt labor stability if it were to assert jurisdiction over Northwestern. The board also discussed changes to the status of scholarship players, such as the NCAA decision to permit the awarding of guaranteed four-year scholarships as well as ongoing calls for reform, as a reason to withhold jurisdiction in the case.

While the board declined to assert jurisdiction in the Northwestern case, it has demonstrated continuing interest in the collective bargaining rights of students. The NLRB has once again taken up the issue of the status of graduate assistants under the NLRA (Jaschik, 2015). Future developments related to collective bargaining and graduate students could indicate a future willingness on the part of the board to consider again the issue of college athletes and collective bargaining. And, as noted by the board in its Northwestern decision, "subsequent changes in the treatment of scholarship players could outweigh the considerations that motivate our decision today" (Northwestern University, 2015, p. 6). Especially given the narrow scope of the NLRB decision, the topic of college athletes and collective bargaining will be subject to future litigation, activism, and debate.

RECOMMENDATIONS

While the NLRB declined to assert jurisdiction and uphold the regional director's decision, the Northwestern case highlighted issues that could arise if the board were to assert jurisdiction in a future case. A key consideration relates to the reach of the NLRA and the board's authority. Though the NCAA membership consists of both public and private institutions, as pointed out earlier, NLRB authority extends only to private colleges and universities. If the NLRB were to uphold collective bargaining rights for college athletes at private institutions, the organization would face an environment in which some college athletes could engage in collective bargaining activities while others could not. The legislation enacted in Michigan and Ohio excluding college athletes at public institutions from joining unions in reaction to the Northwestern case reveals how a checkered landscape could exist for intercollegiate athletics in relation to unionization. As the NLRB, courts, and lawmakers weigh in on issues related to college athletes and collective bargaining, they should proceed thoughtfully in weighing arguments for and against permitting college athletes to join unions.

Beyond the immediate issue of collective bargaining rights for college athletes, the Northwestern case highlights broader tensions existing in intercollegiate athletics. Facets of the enterprise increasingly function more like a professional undertaking, including the treatment of college athletes, resulting in what has been termed the creation of the "student-athlete-employee" (Snyder, Hutchens, Jones, & Sun, 2015). At the same time, other aspects of intercollegiate athletics still enhance and emphasize the amateur and educational aspects of the college athlete experience. The Northwestern case serves as a valuable reminder of the challenges facing the NCAA and colleges and universities to ensure that rhetoric matches sufficiently with reality. The task will not be easy.

Whether college athletes constitute employees for purposes of labor law also has relevance beyond collective bargaining contexts. An especially notable example involves state worker's compensation laws, which cover employees injured or disabled while performing job-related duties. Classification of college athletes for purposes of labor law could influence ongoing discussion and debate over whether college athletes should qualify for coverage under these laws. Likewise, courts have scrutinized amateurism arguments in litigation, contending that the NCAA should compensate college athletes for the use of their likeness in NCAA marketing efforts (O'Bannon v. NCAA, 2015).

Despite the outcome—or the lack of one, in important respects—in the Northwestern case, the perceived imbalance over the treatment of college athletes versus the money that is now a part of, and at stake in, particular sports and divisions of play (e.g., the Football Bowl Subdivision), sports has created a difficult path for institutions and the NCAA to navigate. Rather than respond to the kinds of issues raised in the Northwestern case with only platitudes, the NCAA and colleges and universities need to respond to these challenges and critiques in a meaningful way.

CONCLUSION

The Northwestern case raised important questions for intercollegiate athletics and higher education more generally. Future litigation could force the NCAA to revise its policies and procedures to accommodate an intercollegiate athletics environment in which collective bargaining takes place at some institutions. While the effort to achieve collective bargaining rights for scholarship football players at Northwestern failed in this instance, the board can and does reverse its positions, meaning that unionization efforts could take place again. Beyond the purview of collective bargaining, the Northwestern case highlights challenges confronting the NCAA and institutions regarding the treatment of college athletes and the extent to which the logics of business compete with notions of amateurism and the educational mission.

QUESTIONS FOR DISCUSSION

1. Do you believe that scholarship college athletes should qualify as employees for purposes of the National Labor Relations Act? Why or why not?

2. What would be some of the key impacts on intercollegiate athletics if scholarship college athletes at private colleges and universities were allowed to join unions?

3. What kinds of implications might collective bargaining rights for college athletes have in relation to Title IX considerations?

Notes

1. An important point from this successful organizing effort on behalf of graduate students at New York University relates to the fact that a private college or university may voluntarily choose to recognize a collective bargaining unit.

2. The private institution represented is New York University, which was discussed previously.

References

Adelphi University, 195 NLRB 639 (1972).

Berry, J., & Savarese, M. (2012). *Directory of US faculty contracts and bargaining agents in institutions of higher education.* New York: National Center for the Study of Collective Bargaining in Higher Education and the Professions.

Boston Medical Center Corporation, 330 NLRB 152 (1999).

Brown University, 342 NLRB 483 (2004).

CGEW. (n.d.). [Listing of Recognized US Student Employee Unions.] Retrieved from http://www.thecgeu.org/wiki/United_States.

Ichan School of Medicine at Mt. Sinai, No. 29-RC-112517, 2014 WL 2002992 (NLRB) (February 25, 2014). Retrieved from WestlawNext.com

Jaschik, S. (2013, November 27). Union election, not NLRB vote. InsideHigherEd. Retrieved from http://www.insidehighered.com/news/2013/11/27/nyu-and-uaw-agree -terms-election-teaching-assistant-union#sthash.FJDgjjbO.dpbs

Jaschik, S. (2015, October 23). NLRB returns to grad student unions. InsideHigherEd. Retrieved from https://www.insidehighered.com/news/2015/10/23/nlrb-returns-issue -graduate-student-unions-private-institutions

National Conference of State Legislators. (n.d.). Right-to-work states. Retrieved from http://www.ncsl.org/research/labor-and-employment/right-to-work-laws-and-bills .aspx#chart

New, J. (2014, December 30). New Michigan law bars college athletes from unionizing. InsideHigherEd. Retrieved from https://www.insidehighered.com/quicktakes/2014/12/30/new-michigan-law-bars-college-athletes-unionizing

New York University, 332 NLRB 1205 (2000).

NLRB v. Yeshiva University, 444 U.S. 672 (1980).

Northwestern University, No. 13-RC-121359 (March 26, 2014). Retrieved from http://www.nlrb.gov/news-outreach/news-story/nlrb-director-region-13-issues-decision-northwestern-university-athletes

Northwestern University, No. 13-RC-121359 (August 17, 2015) [NLRB decision]. Retrieved from https://www.nlrb.gov/news-outreach/news-story/board-unanimously-decides-decline-jurisdiction-northwestern-case

O'Bannon v. National Collegiate Athletic Association, 802 F.3d 1049 (2015).

Saltzman, G. M. (1998). Legal recognition of collective bargaining in higher education. In National Education Association, ed. *The NEA 1998 almanac of higher education* (pp. 45–58). Washington, DC: National Education Association.

Snyder, E. M., Hutchens, N. H., Jones, W. A., & Sun, J. C. (2015). Social media policies in intercollegiate athletics: The speech and privacy rights of student-athletes. *Journal for the Study of Sports and Athletes in Education, 9*(1), 50–74. doi: http://dx.doi.org/10.1179/1935739715Z.00000000035

Thompson, C. (2014, June 16). Kasich signs tax credit for low-income workers. Cincinnati.com. Retrieved from http://www.cincinnati.com/story/news/politics/2014/06/16/kasich-signs-tax-credit-low-income-workers/10652421/

PART THREE

The Commercial Enterprise of College Sports

The popularity of big-time college sports continues to increase, and the funds that flow into athletics programs have created major commercial entertainment with considerable revenue-generating capabilities. Concerns have been raised about the business practices and increasing commercialism in college sports, as well as issues of fairness for college athletes. Part three sheds light on these concerns. First, in chapter 9, Angela Lumpkin explores the adverse impact of commercialism on athletes in revenue- and non-revenue-generating sports, with particular attention to special admissions, eligibility maintenance, and coaches. Conference realignment—a critically important topic that is often underresearched and overlooked in college sports—is the focus of chapter 10. Here, Earl Smith and Angela J. Hattery explore its role in exorbitant spending by athletic departments and the threat to the mission and fundamental values of colleges and universities. And in chapter 11, Andy Schwarz and Daniel A. Rascher discuss competitive balance and financial solvency arguments, as well as concerns about the compensation of college athletes. ■

Commercialism in College Sports Undermines Athletes' Educational Opportunities and Rights

Angela Lumpkin

The revenue-producing college sports of football and men's basketball are highly commercialized, with the exception that the athletes who directly bring in the revenues are classified as amateurs. The National Collegiate Athletic Association (NCAA) has argued vehemently that athletes are students participating in an avocation and not employees. Specifically, the NCAA's principle of amateurism affirms, "Student-athletes shall be amateurs . . . and their participation should be motivated primarily by education and by the physical, mental and social benefits to be derived . . . Student-athletes should be protected from exploitation by professional and commercial enterprises" (NCAA, 2014–15, article 2.9).

> **KEY TERMS**
>
> ▶ Revenue-producing athletes
>
> ▶ Commercialism
>
> ▶ Academic exploitation
>
> ▶ Restrictive NCAA rules
>
> ▶ Coach control over athletes

Not so!, claim critics. For example, in exposing the shame of college sports, Branch (2011) has argued, "The real scandal is not that students are getting illegally paid or recruited, it's that two of the noble principles on which the NCAA justifies its existence—'amateurism' and the 'student-athlete'—are cynical hoaxes, legalistic confections propagated by the universities so they can exploit the skills and fame of young athletes" (para. 12). R. A. Smith (2011) affirmed that athletes playing on revenue-producing football and men's basketball teams often are not amateurs nor serious about getting an education.

The educational myths of college sport are based on principles espoused in the NCAA's constitution, such as defining amateurism as whatever the NCAA says it is, limiting financial aid to the cost of attendance, and stating that student-athletes are admitted and governed by the same academic standards as other students. It should be noted that other organizations, such as the International Olympic Committee and Amateur Athletic Union, historically also adopted and enforced amateurism upon its competitors, a practice ended decades ago. This chapter exposes these hypocrisies and demonstrates how commercialism in football and men's basketball in the Atlantic Coast Conference (ACC), Big Ten Conference, Big 12 Conference, Pacific 12 Conference (Pac-12), and Southeastern Conference (SEC) (known as the Power Five conferences) undermine the educational opportunities and financial well-being of athletes. Specifically, this chapter will describe how many of the factors protecting athletes' educational well-being are elusive, including granting special admissions and majoring in eligibility, and coaches and commercialized college sports are dominating the lives of athletes to the athletes' detriment. Recommendations for substantive change are provided.

THE MYTH OF A FREE EDUCATION

Sitting in the living rooms of high school seniors, college coaches promise educational opportunities if these highly skilled athletes will choose to attend their institutions in exchange for playing the sports they love. Coaches' sales pitches are persuasive, especially for adolescents whose parents' socioeconomic circumstances preclude their having this opportunity without sports. The opportunity to earn a college education that could open careers otherwise inaccessible to these athletes, and maybe even become professional athletes, is a huge enticement for signing a National Letter of Intent to attend and play for a specific college.

Once a 17-year-old and his or her parent or guardian sign a legally binding National Letter of Intent, however, reality sets in. This free education is accompanied by several limitations, including the academic underpreparation of many athletes for the rigors of college; reliance on tutors to complete course assignments; an emphasis on maintaining eligibility instead of academic achievement; dissuasion from taking certain courses and declaring certain majors; challenges of missing a large number of classes for practices, travel, and competitions; and failure to graduate. A free education is hardly free. In reality, athletes receive grants-in-aid as payment for relinquishing control over their lives, educationally and athletically. When athletes are paid to play through grants-in-aid, it could be argued, their status changes from student to employee, thus entitling them to benefits such as workers' compensation when injured while practicing and competing.

Academic Underpreparation and Special Admissions

High schools differ widely in the educational preparation of students; therefore, educational opportunities linked to the socioeconomic statuses of adolescents vary dramatically. These two factors significantly affect the future academic performances of football and men's basketball players. In an attempt to quiet critics about the underpreparation of prospective student-athletes, the NCAA membership passed several rule changes over the past few decades to stiffen the initial eligibility requirements (Clotfelter, 2011; Crowley, 2006). For example, the NCAA requires minimum grade point averages (GPAs) in high school courses, minimum standardized test scores, a minimum on a sliding scale combining GPAs and test scores, and completion of a specified number and type (core) of high school courses to emphasize that prospective student-athletes must be better prepared to succeed in college.

Simultaneously, coaches of football and men's basketball teams competing in the Power Five conferences convinced college administrators to admit highly talented athletes who fail to meet institutional admission requirements applied to other students, even if these athletes meet the NCAA's minimal eligibility requirements. Football and basketball players admitted preferentially inevitably enroll in classes with students much better prepared to succeed in college than they are, and these athletes face a continuous struggle to achieve academically and maintain eligibility.

Reliance on Tutors and Advisors to Maintain Eligibility

Athletes understand the education promised to them is contingent on their being eligible to play, which is vitally important, because many football and men's basketball players attend college to play, often with unrealistic aspirations of becoming professional athletes (Beamon & Bell, 2002; Estimated Probability of Competing, 2015). If these athletes are underprepared academically, then it will not be surprising that they welcome help writing papers and passing tests to maintain their eligibility. Football and men's basketball players are required to attend classes, and hundreds of thousands of dollars are spent paying class checkers to ensure attendance. However, academic progress also requires them to complete their homework, including their reading and writing assignments.

Coaches and athletic directors have argued that athletes deserve to have tutors provided by the athletic department because of their special admission status and the time demands placed on them. A few athletic department employees, however, have succumbed to pressures from coaches and athletes to do athletes' academic work to keep them eligible and influence instructors to give athletes unearned grades or preferential treatment. When athletes allow others to do their work or they fail to expend sufficient time and effort learning, they are cheating themselves and violating institutional and NCAA rules.

Limitations on Courses to Take and Majors to Declare

Once coaches have academically underprepared, revenue-producing athletes admitted, the onus falls on athletic department advisors "to steer them into the least demanding majors and courses that will ensure their eligibility to compete" (Gurney et al., 2015, p. 2). Because athletes on most campuses are privileged to enroll before most other students, they get their preferred sections and times, including those taught by the athlete-friendly faculty members recommended by advisors. Sometimes, athletes are enrolled in independent studies and sections of courses where they are promised grades of A or B with little or no work, as happened in the "paper classes" at the University of North Carolina at Chapel Hill (Wainstein, Jay, & Kukowski, 2014).

Advisors sometimes discourage athletes from choosing majors requiring afternoon classes and labs. On many campuses, upon advisor recommendations, athletes choose less rigorous curricula, which leads to the clustering of athletes in one or two majors. Such a choice of major may have nothing to do with the interests and career aspirations of football and men's basketball players, which are thereby discounted. Such actions prioritizing eligibility to play over obtaining an education result in defrauding athletes of their educational opportunities.

Failure to Make Progress toward a Degree and Graduate

In an attempt to keep athletes and academic support personnel in athletics from focusing on eligibility, NCAA rules require athletes to declare majors prior to the beginning of their third year of enrollment and annually make satisfactory progress toward their degrees. In 2003 with the enactment of the Academic Progress Rate (APR), the NCAA required teams based on each athlete's academic eligibility and retention to achieve a minimal score or face restrictions on the team (Academic Progress Rate Explained, 2015). In 2004, the NCAA introduced the Graduation Success Rate (GSR), used to report annually what percentage of athletes graduated, which often reveals that football and men's basketball players are less likely to graduate than other athletes and the overall student body. The APR and GSR have been attacked as flawed because they can be manipulated by athletic department personnel (Gurney & Southall, 2012). The NCAA's academic rules dealing with academic progress and graduation may help athletes better prepare for life after sports, because they hold athletes accountable for making progress toward earning degrees with the assistance provided by institutions. However, the APR and GSR may have the unintended consequence of academic support personnel being pressed by coaches and other athletic department administrators to keep athletes eligible by clustering athletes in certain majors and violating institutional and NCAA rules governing the academic performances of athletes.

Athletes, especially those preferentially admitted, frequently exhaust their eligibility to play after four years, yet are woefully short of graduating (Beamon & Bell, 2002; Eckard, 2010). The subsequent disappearance of their grants-in-aid leaves many athletes financially unable to earn their degrees. Another factor is, many athletes chase an elusive dream of playing professional football or basketball, and even among those who make it (only 1–2 percent), their dreams are shattered (Beamon & Bell, 2002; Estimated Probability of Competing, 2015). The absence of a college degree leaves many adrift with a bleak future.

Creative efforts in keeping athletes eligible motivated the Knight Commission on Intercollegiate Athletics to advocate for changes in commercialized college sports. It called for academic integrity (1991), academic reform (2001), and rewarding practices to prioritize academic values (2010). NCAA rules, Knight Commission reports, and the exposure of academic fraud have minimally deterred the educational exploitation of athletes.

Missing Classes for Practices, Travel, and Competitions

College athletes miss numerous classes for practices, travel, and competitions. The commercialization of football and men's basketball programs in the power conferences is dictated by television. Between 2010 and 2014, for example, CBS, TBS, TNT, and truTV are paying the NCAA $10.8 billion (NCAA, 2010) to broadcast the men's Division I basketball tournament. ESPN is paying $7.3 billion to broadcast the college football playoffs over 12 years (Boudway, 2015). Athletic conferences sign contracts to have games televised on days of the week and times dictated by the media. The realignment of conferences based on broadcasting media footprints and generation of revenue instead of geography has resulted in longer travel times and additional missed classes. The number of games has increased, and games commanding lucrative payouts to conferences and athletic departments are emphasized.

With the increased emphasis on winning, coaches often demand that athletes miss classes for practices on game days as well as the day before for away games. No class time seems too sacred to be taken over by teams' practices, travel, or competitions. The extraordinary time demands that coaches require interfere with athletes meeting their academic responsibilities (Gurney et al., 2015), which will be discussed in the following section.

NCAA RULES GOVERNING AND COACHES' CONTROL OVER ATHLETES

The NCAA stipulates the amount of financial aid each athlete can receive and for how many years, whether an athlete who transfers can compete in football and men's basketball, and encroachments on due process rights. Coaches exert immense control over the lives of athletes. For example, coaches' excessive time demands on athletes make their commitment equivalent to a full-time job.

Financial Aid Limitations

In an effort to eliminate widespread violations of its amateur code by football coaches and boosters, in 1957 NCAA-member institutions first allowed awarding grants-in-aid to athletes, even though this directly violated its espousal of amateurism (Smith, 2011). While the allowable grant-in-aid of tuition, fees, room, board, and books has remained largely unchanged for decades, Huma and Staurowsky (2012) exposed the price of poverty associated with football and men's basketball in the Power Five conferences, as many of the football and men's basketball athletes on these teams live below the federal poverty line. Many athletes, such as Shabazz Napier after his University of Connecticut basketball team won the national championship, have claimed to have gone hungry and lacked basic necessities or received benefits disallowed by NCAA rules to survive. Since a "full ride" fails to pay the full cost of attendance, the allowable amount of a grant-in-aid remains a controversial issue today. Athletes in revenue-producing sports who bear the burden of financing the highly commercialized college sport enterprise (Huma & Staurowsky, 2012) reap only the financial benefits the member institutions of the NCAA permit. Based on the NCAA's one-sided rules, Lopiano et al. (2015) concluded that there is a "huge conflict of interest when million-dollar-a-year coaches and administrators are rewarded for college athlete exploitation" (p. 7). These authors stated that athletes should receive the full cost of education. The NCAA's cartel-like rules not only limit the amount of financial aid each athlete can receive but also stipulate how many football and men's basketball grants-in-aid can be awarded. The number of grants-in-aid in these sports and other sports is also linked with the equal opportunity required by Title IX of the 1972 Education Amendments.

Between 1973 and 2011, the NCAA limited these grants-in-aid to one-year, renewable grants solely at the coach's discretion, which "renders athletes silent or substantially voiceless when it comes to their own welfare by exerting pressure on them to remain compliant if they wish to achieve their goals of either remaining in college or developing their athletic talent in pursuit of professional careers" (Huma & Staurowsky, 2012, p. 7). Because coaches and institutions wish to control expenditures for grants-in-aid and maintain control over athletes, few four-year grants have been awarded, even though these are now permitted (Solomon, 2014). Because coaches, not the faculty or other institutional personnel, decide on grant-in-aid renewals, it could be argued that, instead of these grants-in-aid being educational or academic in focus, they provide further evidence of a promised education for play.

Transfer Restrictions

NCAA rules and coaches exert immense control over athletes who wish to transfer institutions for academic or athletic reasons. When a Division I football and men's basketball athlete signs a National Letter of Intent, he cannot contact another Division I college to inquire about transferring without the written permission of his current athletic director. The NCAA also stipulates that athletes who transfer to a Power Five conference in football or men's basketball must complete a full academic year of residence before being eligible to compete, even if the coach who recruited him leaves. The Division I institution to which a football or men's basketball player transfers is precluded by NCAA rules from awarding this athlete a grant-in-aid, which means that without the financial means to pay for his own education he seldom transfers. In order to protect economically valuable athletic assets, these NCAA rules and actions of coaches and athletic directors discourage revenue-producing athletes from transferring (McCormick & McCormick, 2010b).

Despite these restrictive rules disfavoring athletes, coaches' pressure on and controls over athletes may tempt athletes to transfer or quit prior to exhausting their eligibility. When an athlete fails to meet performance expectations or falls into disfavor, the coach may decide not to renew his grant-in-aid so it can be awarded to a new or better player. The decision to renew a one-year grant-in-aid can be made solely by the coach.

Stated Time Limitations Fail to Represent Reality

Coaches not only dictate how much time athletes spend in highly regimented physical training, sport practices, film study, and team meetings, but they also indirectly expect athletes to dedicate twice as many hours as the allowable 20 hours per week in-season to skill development. In a study conducted for the NCAA, Brown (2011) found the average number of self-reported hours spent per week in-season involved in athletic activities in 2010 in Division I was 43.3 in the Football Bowl Subdivision and 39.2 in men's basketball. As these numbers demonstrate, athletes choose to dedicate many hours to honing their skills to impress coaches to gain more playing time or ensure that their grants-in-aid are renewed.

Given the pressures on coaches to win to keep their jobs, the commercialized collegiate sport model precludes an off-season with demands for skill development and conditioning that never cease. Even though college sports are touted as extracurricular, character-building, amateur pastimes for regular college students, being a commercialized football or men's basketball player playing in a Power Five conference is a full-time job that precludes opportunities to engage fully in other college experiences.

Lack of Due Process Rights

Under the guise of amateurism and promoting competitive equity, NCAA rules prohibit athletes from financially capitalizing on the commercial use of their names, images, and likenesses. Branch (2011) has argued that athletes are denied fundamental due process when they are required to transfer their promotional rights forever. The paternalistic domination of the NCAA and coaches over thousands of college athletes who annually enter into servitude obscures the reality of their exploitation (McCormick & McCormick, 2006). "The denial of fundamental due process for college athletes has stood unchallenged in public discourse. Like other NCAA rules, it emanates naturally from the premise that college athletes own no interest in sports beyond exercise, character-building, and good fun" (Branch, 2011). Some athletes, however, may choose to give up some of their rights in exchange for the promise of an education.

Another egregious exploitation of revenue-producing athletes is the NCAA's continual claim that they are students first and athletes second. McCormick and McCormick (2006) denied this self-serving categorization: "Grant-in-aid athletes in revenue-generating sports at NCAA Division I institutions are employees under the common law. They perform services for the benefit of their universities under an agreement setting forth their responsibilities and compensation, are economically dependent upon their universities, and are subject virtually every day of the year to pervasive control by the athletic department and coaches. Put somewhat differently, employee-athletes perform services for their universities under a contract of hire which subjects them to the universities' control and in return for payment" (p. 97). They argued that the services performed by gifted football and men's basketball athletes facilitate institutions' and the NCAA's commercial interests and are unrelated to their education. Moreover, Byers (1995) claimed he developed and mandated use of the term *student-athlete*. McCormick and McCormick (2006) suggested that the term *student-athlete* was used "to camouflage their true function as employees in the commercial college sports entertainment industry" (p. 135).

The following is an example of the lack of due process, if persistence of an apartheid system in college sports in the Power Five conferences represents absence of equal protection under the law as guaranteed by the Fourteenth Amendment to the US Constitution. "This system, made up of numerous NCAA rules, effectively sanctions the exploitation of mostly African-American young men for the enormous pecuniary gain of mostly European Americans associated with major universities, athletic organizations, and corporations, as well as for the great entertainment of millions of mostly European Americans" (McCormick & McCormick, 2010a, p. 14). That is, if mostly African American athletes generate huge revenues enjoyed by coaches, athletic administrators, and athletes in non-revenue-producing sports, when they have no voice in making the rules permitting this, where is their equal protection? Mostly African American football and men's basketball players generate millions of dollars while the rules preclude them from profiting from their athletic talents in the marketplace (McCormick & McCormick, 2010b).

Commercialism in college sports undermines athletes' educational opportunities and rights, yet many positives exist. Rather than eliminating college sports, substantive changes could help ameliorate many of the problems and concerns. Several recommendations are offered.

RECOMMENDATIONS FOR CHANGE

Huma and Staurowsky (2012) have recommended four substantive changes to prevent athletes in revenue-producing sports from living below the federal poverty line: (1) fully fund athletes' cost of attendance, (2) allow athletes, if they choose, to take advantage of their commercial opportunities, (3) allow revenue-producing athletes to place a portion of the revenues they help earn in an educational lockbox for their postgraduation years, and (4) award multiyear grants-in-aid. After serving 36 years as its executive director, Walter Byers urged the NCAA to free athletes from the straitjacket of its monopolist rules by making five substantive changes: (1) eliminate restrictions on and control over athletes' income, (2) allow athletes to hold jobs by significantly reducing time demands of their sports, (3) allow football and men's basketball athletes to transfer institutions without restrictions, (4) permit athletes to consult with sports agents to aid in making informed decisions about their futures, and (5) guarantee workers' compensation for athletes to demonstrate a genuine concern for their health and safety (Byers, 1995). N. Smith (2015) has suggested revising or eliminating the National Letter of Intent, revising unfair transfer rules, guaranteeing grants-in-aid for four years, getting rid of the no-agent rule, following the National Basketball Association's rules for underclassmen declaring for the draft (i.e., let the marketplace decide), improving due process for athletes accused of wrongdoing by the NCAA, and allowing some version of pay for play.

In support, and as an extension of these suggestions, the following changes could help restore academic integrity, ensure the financial well-being of football and men's basketball players, and eliminate the hypocrisy and untenable controls that NCAA rules and coaches exert on the lives of athletes.

1. Treat athletes like all other students relative to meeting college admission requirements.

2. Make first-year students who meet college admission requirements athletically ineligible so they can acclimate to college academically.

3. Once admitted to a college, base athletic eligibility on college grades, not on high school grades and standardized test scores.

4. Ensure that athletes have nonrestrictive choices of courses and majors.

5. Eliminate athletic advisors and tutors and provide athletes with the same academic support services as the general student population.

6. Free football and men's basketball players to transfer institutions for academic and athletic reasons.

7. Limit the number of competitions and missed classes for practices, travel, and competitions.

8. Enforce the 20-hour in-season and 8-hour off-season rules for all athletic-related activities.

9. Provide football and men's basketball athletes funding for the years needed to earn a degree.

10. Guarantee to each athlete commercial publicity rights for his name, likeness, and image while playing in college and after his collegiate playing days are completed.

11. End the financial exploitation of athletes competing in revenue-producing sports.

12. Guarantee due process whenever conflicts with coaches occur.

13. Educate athletes about the unrealistic possibility of a professional sport career.

14. End the practice of all students subsidizing the athletic department and its sport teams.

CONCLUSION

The academic rights of students who happen to be athletes should be protected so they receive their promised education, rather than being routinely admitted academically underprepared, awarded grades to maintain their eligibility even though course work did not merit these grades, and enrolled in independent studies or less demanding courses with athlete-friendly instructors (Gurney et al., 2015). Limiting grants-in-aid to less than the cost of attendance; onerous transfer restrictions; excessive time demands of practicing, traveling, and competing year-round; and the absence of due process rights indicate a serious disregard for the well-being of football and men's basketball players. Some athletes have filed lawsuits against the NCAA because of its hypocritical and restrictive rules and denial of athletes' financial and personal rights. As these actions suggest, the status quo is unlikely to continue without major changes.

QUESTIONS FOR DISCUSSION

1. Given the highly commercialized college sport enterprise in football and men's basketball, how can these athletes take full advantage of the educational opportunities made possible through their athletic talents?

2. How can constitutional and legal guarantees of individual rights be employed to prevent NCAA rules and coaches from exerting excessive control over the lives of football and men's basketball players?

3. Based on the recommendations offered, what actions should be taken to justify the continued sponsorship by institutions of higher education of football and men's basketball teams?

References

Academic progress rate explained. (2015). NCAA. Retrieved from http://www.ncaa.org/about/resources/research/academic-progress-rate-explained

Beamon, K., & Bell, P. A. (2002). "Going pro": The deferential effects of high aspirations for a professional sports career on African-American student athletes and White student athletes. *Race & Society, 5,* 179–191.

Boudway, I. (2015). ESPN's college football playoff money machine is just getting started. Bloomberg. Retrieved from http://www.bloomberg.com/news/articles/2015-01-13/espns-college-football-playoff-money-machine-is-just-getting-started

Branch, T. (2011, October). The shame of college sports. *The Atlantic.* Retrieved from http://www.theatlantic.com/magazine/archive/2011/10/the-shame-of-college-sports/308643/

Brown, G. (2011, January 13). Second GOALS study emphasizes coach influence. NCAA.org. Retrieved from http://ncaa.org/

Byers, W., with Hammer, C. (1995). *Unsportsmanlike conduct: Exploiting college athletes.* Ann Arbor: University of Michigan Press.

Clotfelter, C. T. (2011). *Big-time sports in American universities.* New York, NY: Cambridge University Press.

Crowley, J. N. (2006). *In the arena: The NCAA's first century.* Indianapolis, IN: NCAA. Retrieved from http://www.ncaapublications.com/productdownloads/AB06.pdf

Eckard, E. W. (2010). NCAA athlete graduation rates: Less than meets the eye. *Journal of Sport Management, 24,* 45–59.

Estimated probability of competing in athletics beyond the high school interscholastic level. (2015). NCAA. Retrieved from http://www.ncaa.org/about/resources/research /estimated-probability-competing-college-athletics

Gurney, G., Lopiano, D., Porto, B., Ridpath, D. B., Sack, A., Willingham, M., & Zimbalist, A. (2015). *The Drake Group calls upon the NCAA, its member institutions and higher education regional accreditation agencies to fulfill athlete academic protection responsibilities.* [Position statement]. The Drake Group. Retrieved from http:// thedrakegroup.org/2015/04/16/fulfill-athlete-academic-protection-responsibilities/

Gurney, G. S., & Southall, R. M. (2012, August 9). College sports' bait and switch. ESPN. Retrieved from http://espn.go.com/college-sports/story/_/id/8248046/college-sports -programs-find-multitude-ways-game-ncaa-apr

Huma, R., & Staurowsky, E. J. (2012). *The price of poverty in big time college sport.* National College Players Association. Retrieved from http://www.ncpanow.org/research/body /The-Price-of-Poverty-in-Big-Time-College-Sport.pdf

Knight Commission on Intercollegiate Athletics. (1991). *Keeping faith with the student athlete.* Retrieved from http://www.knightcommission.org/images/pdfs/1991-93 _kcia_report.pdfKnight Commission on Intercollegiate Athletics. (2001). *A call to action: Reconnecting college sports and higher education.* Retrieved from http:// www.knightcommission.org/images/pdfs/2001_knight_report.pdf

Knight Commission on Intercollegiate Athletics. (2010). *Restoring the balance: Dollars, values, and the future of college sports.* Retrieved from http://knightcommission.org /images/restoringbalance/KCIA_Report_F.pdf

Lopiano, D., Porto, B., Gurney, G., Ridpath, D. B., Sack, A., Willingham, M., & Zimbalist, A. (2015). *The Drake Group position statement: Compensation of college athletes including revenues from commercial use of their names, likenesses, and images.* The Drake Group. Retrieved from http://thedrakegroup.org/2015/03/26/position -statement-032615/

McCormick, R. A., & McCormick, A. C. (2006). The myth of the student-athlete: The college athlete as employee. *Washington Law Review, 81,* 71–157. Retrieved from http:// digitalcommons.law.msu.edu/

McCormick, R. A., & McCormick, A. C. (2010a). Major college sports: A modern apartheid. *Texas Review of Entertainment & Sports Law, 12,* 13–51. Retrieved from http:// digitalcommons.law.msu.edu/

McCormick, R. A., & McCormick, A. C. (2010b). A trail of tears: The exploitation of the college athlete. *Florida Coastal Law Review, 11,* 639–665. Retrieved from https:// www.fcsl.edu/law-review

NCAA. (2010). CBS Sports, Turner Broadcasting, NCAA reach 14-year agreement. Retrieved from http://www.ncaa.com/news/basketball-men/2010-04-21/cbs-sports -turner-broadcasting-ncaa-reach-14-year-agreement

NCAA. (2015). *2015–2016 Division I manual.* Retrieved from http://www.ncaapublications .com.

Smith, N. (2015, April 6). College basketball is great, but it could be better for its players. *The Cauldron*. Retrieved from https://the-cauldron.com/college-basketball-is-great -but-it-could-be-better-for-its-players-bd5c8c59fcdc

Smith, R. A. (2011). *Pay for play: A history of big-time college athletic reform*. Urbana: University of Illinois Press.

Solomon, J. (2014). Schools can give out 4-year athletic scholarships, but many don't. CBS Sports. Retrieved from http://www.cbssports.com/collegefootball/writer/jon -solomon/24711067/schools-can-give-out-4-year-scholarships-to-athletes-but-many -dont

Wainstein, K. J., Jay, A. J., III, & Kukowski, C. D. (2014). Investigation of irregular classes in the Department of African and Afro-American Studies at the University of North Carolina at Chapel Hill. Retrieved from http://carolinacommitment.unc.edu/reports _resources/investigation-of-irregular-classes-in-the-department-of-african-and-afro -american-studies-at-the-university-of-north-carolina-at-chapel-hill-2/

Conference Realignment and the Evolution of New Organizational Forms

Earl Smith and Angela J. Hattery

For unto every one that hath shall be given, and he shall have abundance: but from him that hath not shall be taken away even that which he hath.

Robert K. Merton (1968)

Conference realignment is a relatively new social movement in college sports. Yet, it is one that is destined to change forever intercollegiate sports as we know it (Smith & Hattery, 2015). As well, conference realignment is one of the most important issues facing intercollegiate sport since the movements toward integration for African American athletes and the process of implementing Title IX. Though colleges and universities have moved between athletic conferences in the past, most of this movement has been about conference expansion and conference concentration. What is unique about the movement that began in and around 2012 are both the *cause* and the *volume* of movement. On July 1, 2013, 49 (15 percent) institutions in Football Bowl Subdivision (FBS) and Football Championship Subdivision (formerly Division I and Division I-A) moved conferences (table 10.1). Not only did teams move, but the realignment involved the dismantling of a major conference and the emergence of a new entity, a grouping of conferences that refer to themselves and are referred to by others as the Power Five conferences (table 10.2).

It is well understood that the Power Five conferences represent the athletic programs/institutions with what are widely believed to be the best football teams in the country. Second, the causes of this movement are the potentially huge sums of money that institutions believe they will have access to, the scramble to be positioned so that an institution's football team is eligible to compete for the national championship, and attempts to consolidate power away from the National Collegiate Athletic Association (NCAA). It is only incidental that several basketball programs are also in the Power Five, but many of the best basketball

> **KEY TERMS**
>
> ▶ Intercollegiate athletics
>
> ▶ Conference realignment
>
> ▶ Student fees
>
> ▶ Athletic subsidies
>
> ▶ Arms race

TABLE 10.1.	
National Collegiate Athletic Association (NCAA) Conferences	
Division I Conferences	
Football Bowl Subdivision	11
Football Championship Subdivision	14
Nonfootball, multisport conferences	13
Division II Conferences	25
Division III Conferences	46
Total Conferences =	**109**

Source: NCAA (2013b).

TABLE 10.2.	
Power Five Conferences (approximately 65 institutions)	
Atlantic Coast Conference (ACC)	
Big Ten Conference	
Big 12 Conference	
Pacific 12 Conference (Pac-12)	
Southeastern Conference (SEC)	

Source: NCAA, http://www.ncaa.com.

teams are not represented. What is left out of the discussions of conference realignment is the impact on institutions of higher learning, the colleges and universities that continue to house and, in the vast majority of cases, financially subsidize intercollegiate athletics.

This chapter will examine the ways in which conference realignment has the potential to leave colleges and universities literally bankrupt while chasing the increasingly elusive dream of winning national championships and cashing in on the associated windfall of revenues.

THEORETICAL FRAMEWORK

To best capture the conference realignment social movement, we employ the sociological concept of social movement theory adequately defined and used by Professor Aldon Morris (2000). The theory holds that when organizations attempt broad-based change, initially you observe unorganized behavior. Morris (2000) put it thus: "These theories argued that social movements were a form of collective behavior that emerged when significant social and cultural breakdowns occurred. As a form of collective behavior, social movements were considered spontaneous, unorganized, and unstructured phenomena that were discontinuous with institutional and organizational behavior . . . Thus, social movements and movement participants were viewed as non-rational, given the unpredictability and heavy emotional content of movements" (p. 445). Conceptualizing the Power Five conference realignment as a social movement for the betterment of the 65 institutions involved allows us to focus more on the impact on the colleges and universities, both inside and outside of the Power Five and on the athletes—mostly male football players—and how the unintended consequences may impact all three stakeholders: institutions (colleges and universities), the NCAA, and college athletes.

CONFERENCE REALIGNMENT DEFINED

For this chapter, conference realignment is to mean the systematic movement of institutions from one athletic conference to another in order to better access financial resources. Add to this, schools are looking to place themselves in a better position to access one of the three College Football Playoff (CFP) bowl games. Athletic directors and college football coaches have made this intention clear in statements related to both television contracts and the opportunity to play for the national championship. These remarks are typically made by those coaches and athletic directors who are bemoaning the fact that because of their conference affiliation they are consistently left out of the opportunity to compete for the national championship and/or play in major bowl games, such as what is referred to in 2016 as the New Year's Six. For example, after the 2007 Tostitos Bowl upset by Boise State University—a team that resides in a mid-major conference—there was much conversation about developing strategies that would allow Boise State and other nonmajor conference football teams to have access to bowl games. As no strategy emerged, Boise State initiated the first move, which ultimately failed, of what became the conference shake-up of the early twenty-first century.

THE POWER FIVE CONFERENCE REALIGNMENT MOVEMENT

The 65 teams making up the Power Five conference realignment movement also seek to concentrate power and resources among themselves. This movement creates a multitiered system of haves and have-nots. And, as conference movement has been around forever, the defining situation took place in 2014, wherein the Atlantic Coast Conference (ACC), Big Ten Conference, Big 12 Conference, Pacific 12 Conference (Pac-12), and Southeastern Conference (SEC) broke away from the rest of the NCAA Division 1 FBS and set in place exceptions to NCAA rules that apply *only to the institutions in the Power Five conferences*. In brief, the new rules or exemptions allow for policies such as paying cost-of-attendance stipends (between $2,000 and $5,000 per athlete); insurance benefits for players, money for players to travel home, expansions of staff, fewer restrictions on recruiting, and so on (Bennett, 2014).

For further clarity we add that the Power Five conference realignment movement is akin, in many ways, to the myth of meritocracy (see Guinier, 2015), and it runs parallel to the "Rare Event Rule in Inferential Statistics," wherein something like winning the national championship in football or the Final Four in basketball will never happen no matter what. That is to suggest that, even among the 65 schools in the Power Five conference model, no more than a handful of these teams have ever won or come close to winning a national championship. Since 2000, only 15 teams have contended for the national championships, all but one from what were the conferences that became the Power Five. Of these 15 teams, half competed more than once for the national championship and four (i.e., University of Southern California, Ohio State University, University of Florida, and the University of Alabama) have won more than one title. This concentration is even narrower when looking at head football coaches: the University of Alabama's Nick Saban is responsible for four titles (three at Alabama and one at Louisiana State University), and Ohio State's Urban Myer is responsible for three titles (two at the University of Florida, and one at Ohio State University)—all within the time period from 2000 to 2015. Put differently, 50 of the 65 power teams never have and likely never will win or even compete for a national a title. And, yet, the simple idea that they might propels universities and athletic departments to spend unprecedented amounts of money (table 10.3).

How can we explain the fact that otherwise reasonable adults make what appear to be such unreasonable decisions that have lasting financial implications on the institutions where they are employed and which they lead? Because of dominant ideology (Therborn, 1980) and the meritocratic belief system that is fundamental to the ideology of the American Dream (Smith, 2014), these decisions bleed into athletic departments. College and university presidents, athletic directors, coaches, players, parents and fans year in and year out fail to pay attention to what sociologist Émile Durkheim (1982) calls social facts. For Durkheim social facts "consist of representations and actions" (p. 59). He goes on to define the term: "A social fact is any way of acting, whether fixed or not, capable of exerting over the individual an external constraint; or: which is general over the whole of a given society whilst having an existence of its own, independent of its individual manifestations" (p.59).

The discourse here is that conference realignment has negative consequences. Most, if not all, of these are hidden from sight so as not to obscure or complicate the seemingly irrational decision making of powerful, mostly white, men who control not only the majority of athletic departments but also colleges and universities. And, these negative consequences will be experienced not only by the 50 of the 65 institutions in Power Five conferences who will likely never compete for a national championship, but more so by the hundreds of colleges and universities that feel compelled to dump millions of dollars into athletic programs—

TABLE 10.3.

National Champions—Football

Miami (2)	Florida St.
Oklahoma (2)	Missouri
Oklahoma State	Utah
Ohio State (3)	Alabama (4)
USC (4)	Auburn
LSU (3)	TCU
Texas	Notre Dame
Florida (2)	

Source: NCAA, http://www.ncaa.com/history/football/fbs.

a phenomenon we often call "keeping up with the Joneses" (Smith, 2015). This approach is based on the myth that doing so will allow these programs to remain competitive both on the playing field and in the stiff competition for revenues, all at the expense of their primary mission: educating young men and women.

This chapter then, not only defines conference realignment but goes on to analyze the conference realignment social movement from the perspective of the myth of meritocracy (Guinier, 2015), which holds that working hard, investing, saving, and deferring gratification will ensure one access to the just rewards. Unfortunately, winning championships does not come from a belief in the ideology; the power to compete for national championships—the power to recruit the best players, hire the best coaches, and so forth is concentrated in the Power Five and even more narrowly among a very elite set of institutions. And, no matter the money that an institution pays, it will likely never crack that elite group (table 10.4).

CONFERENCE REALIGNMENT: AN OVERVIEW

Intercollegiate athletic conferences were originally established to organize schools by both size and geography. Conference realignment has been going on for decades but has exploded beginning around 2011. In short, conference commissioners—who are all white men—are scrambling to assemble and reconfigure conferences in ways that give them the most potential to make money. And, though most, if not all, of the institutions engaged in realignment argue that they will profit from such moves, there is very little in these discussions about the ways in which money would be distributed to each individual school and/ or how the movement will or may impact the NCAA or athletes. Rather, as we suggest, this movement is about making the conference lucrative and the conference commissioners very wealthy and powerful. Conference commissioners have become more powerful than college presidents and athletic directors, or what ESPN's Pat Forde (2011) calls the "commanders-in-chief" (para. 2).

TABLE 10.4.

Correlations between "Winning" (Appearances in BCS and National Championships) and Sources of Football Revenues and Football Expenditures

		Total BCS & championship appearances
Total FB operating budget	Pearson Correlation	0.259
Sig. (2-tailed)		0.202
N		26
Revenue-Budget	Pearson Correlation	0.019
Sig. (2-tailed)		0.927
N		26
Contributions	Pearson Correlation	0.048
Sig. (2-tailed)		0.816
N		26
NCAA distributions	Pearson Correlation	−0.036
Sig. (2-tailed)		0.863
N		26
Athletic scholarships	Pearson Correlation	−0.109
Sig. (2-tailed)		0.595
N		26
FB guarantees	Pearson Correlation	0.196
Sig. (2-tailed)		0.338
N		26
Coaches' salaries	Pearson Correlation	0.355
Sig. (2-tailed)		0.075
N		26
Recruiting costs	Pearson Correlation	0.182
Sig. (2-tailed)		0.374
N		26
Game expenses	Pearson Correlation	−0.136
Sig. (2-tailed)		0.507
N		26
Facilities	Pearson Correlation	0.315
Sig. (2-tailed)		0.117
N		26
Travel	Pearson Correlation	0.168
Sig. (2-tailed)		0.401
N		27

Source: Data based on author's research (Smith 2014).
Note: None of the relationships approached significance.

And, as we argue later in the chapter, this new movement is an attempt on the part of the conference commissioners to effectively remove the influence and power of the NCAA over college football. Also, not surprisingly, any consideration of the impact of conference realignment on athletes or on the students paying to attend these institutions with the goal of earning a college degree is completely absent from the discussion.

In the social sciences, unintended consequences are outcomes that are not the ones intended by a purposeful action (Merton, 1936). The concept has long existed—at least since Adam Smith's *The Wealth of Nations*—but was named and popularized in the twentieth century by the American sociologist Robert K. Merton. This "law" of unintended consequences is what happens when a simple system tries to regulate a complex system, and this is what we see happening with what we call the conference realignment movement.

Using the classic scientific research model for this chapter—that is, ask a question, do background research, construct a hypothesis, test the hypothesis by doing an experiment, analyze the data, draw a conclusion, and communicate the results—we could not find one clearly articulated, peer-reviewed research paper on conference realignment. In other words, we are not able to ground the argument in this chapter in existing scientific literature because there isn't any. As a result, we will be building an argument based on the reading of related literatures, as summarized early on in the chapter.

It is important to point out that the topic of conference realignment is highly charged and can be polarizing. Additionally, the issues are very wide ranging. As a result, we are limiting the discussion in this chapter to the impact of conference realignment on the colleges and universities that are caught in this conference realignment movement, jockeying for position, and in some cases nearly bleeding to death to do so. There are aspects that we are not going to discuss here because they are more appropriate for other forums and we hope that scholars will explore, such as the implications of conference realignment on Title IX or racial disparities (see Smith & Hattery, 2015).

With all this in mind, the following questions drive the focus of our analysis of conference realignment and its impact, intended or unintended, on the institutions that are scrambling to remain relevant in the new conference structure:

1. What impact will conference realignment have on the budgets of athletic departments?

2. What impact will conference realignment have on the larger college and university budgets?

BACKGROUND RESEARCH

The question of whether athletic departments make money is one that has been asked systematically for at least 25 years. And, there is much disagreement on this question. Despite disagreements about the exact number or percentage of athletic programs that turn a profit—which is different from generating revenue—the data indicate that no more than 25 percent of FBS institutions bring in more money than they spend, or in other words, generate a profit (Comeaux, 2015)

This simple fact is important for many reasons. First, it is important to speak the truth. If you walk around in the world, on college campuses or in booster clubs, or even sports bars, the vast majority of people believe that college sports make money. As noted, many football programs do generate revenue, but the majority of athletic programs do not make a profit. This fact provides the backdrop for this chapter.

We turn now to some more provocations. We looked at a variety of sources of information to find the relevant data to answer each of the questions we posed, including digging deeply inside of the budgets reported by public universities.

Q1: *If the majority of athletic programs are not, in fact, making money, and most are running "in the red," where is their funding coming from?*

A1: The majority of athletic programs are receiving funds from the general operating budgets of their universities in two ways: (1) student fees and (2) subsidies.

1. Student fees: If you are a parent who has been or will soon be paying college tuition, be sure to take a very careful look at the tuition bill. Most students in college are paying between $500 and $1,000 *per year* in athletic fees. That might not seem like much, but if you are the one paying the tuition it sure is! Furthermore, across the time a student spends in college, he or she will be assessed $2,000 to $5,000 in fees, which must paid out of pocket or covered with student loans. We know enough about student loan debt to know an extra $5,000 in debt is something no student (nor parent!) wants to incur. Consider the average in-state tuition and fees: a student may find that 10 percent of their tuition and fees are "athletic fees."

2. Subsidies: Nearly all athletic departments receive subsidies from the general operating budgets of the colleges and universities that house them. The amount of the subsidy and the percentage of the athletic budget that is subsidized vary, but the range is from $3 million or so to $20 million *annually*. The median subsidy at FBS programs is $7.5 million to $8 million per year. Again, this might not seem like much out of a billion-dollar budget, but for those of us who live and work in colleges and universities, it is not difficult to imagine the kind of a difference a few million dollars would make in terms of hiring more professors, improving the salaries for faculty and staff, installing updated classroom technology, and increased funds for student aid.

When we think about the cost of intercollegiate athletics this way, a different picture begins to emerge. We tend to talk about college and university budgets, and athletic budgets in particular, as if they are unlimited, when in fact, all budgets are finite. Every dollar a university spends on athletics—and we are not saying they should not spend any money—is a dollar that they are not able to spend elsewhere, including faculty salaries—which have remained relatively flat for the past 30 years—classroom upgrades, funding for research and creative activities, and student aid. This last piece is particularly important when we think about the skyrocketing debt our students and their parents are taking on just to get an education.

Q2: *Okay, then, if athletics is generating some revenue, but rarely any profit, where does the money for the university to operate come from?*

A2: We limit our discussion to public institutions and focus our specific comments on those whose budgets we examined. That said, with few exceptions the budgets of most institutions of higher education come from the same primary sources, though the percentage each contributes to the overall budget will vary from state to state and institution to institution. These sources include: tuition, student fees, state subsidies (for public colleges and universities; private schools do not have this revenue source), research funding (public and private), financial aid (primarily federal), auxiliary services (rent on coliseum space, memberships at the gym, sports and arts camps), athletics (ticket sales, TV contracts, sale on "gear," payouts from the NCAA for postseason play), and fund-raising.

Despite the myth that is perpetuated during March Madness or on football Saturdays, when tens of thousands of people pack stadiums to watch athletic teams battle on fields and courts, the *vast majority* of the funding that comes into colleges and universities is a direct result of the work of faculty and staff who teach classes and conduct research. Put another way, academic pursuits are the revenue generators for colleges and universities. Athletics brings in a fraction of that which is brought in by each of the following sources: tuition, student fees, subsidies from the state, and at many institutions even research dollars. In terms of the overall budget, athletics generates a tiny fraction of the entire operating budget of the university. And, yet, athletic departments are frequently subsidized at percentages significantly greater than the revenue they are generating. For example, at a large public institution in the mid-Atlantic region that belongs to a mid-major conference (not named here), athletics generates a mere 2.4 percent of the entire budget of the university but is subsidized at 83.9 percent (Hoffer & Pincin, 2015).

In contrast, the tuition, student fees, state subsidies, and research dollars generated by the primary college at this same university generate more than two-thirds of the budget for the university and yet keeps only about 75 percent of what it generates, with the remaining funds going back to the central operating budget, which pays administrators, student support services, and *subsidizes athletics*. In an average year, despite generating tuition, student fees, state subsidies, and research dollars, this college begins every academic year with a deficit.

ATHLETICS IS (NOT) A UNIT WITHIN COLLEGES AND UNIVERSITIES

It's quite clear from considering the budget data that athletic departments are, in fact, part of the colleges and universities with which they are associated until it comes to the most important issues: spending and hiring.

1. Spending: At most public institutions there are very strict rules about spending, since these schools are considered stewards of public resources. Let's consider an example from that same large public school. As part of their professional lives, and compulsory for career advancement, faculty travel to conferences to present their work, collaborate on research, stay current in their fields and so on. At this large public university, no matter how much money is available for faculty travel, traveling faculty are not allowed to spend more on their accommodations than the state identifies as the median for the location to which the faculty are traveling. Let's consider an example. In August 2015 the annual meeting of the American Sociological Association took place in Chicago, Illinois. The least expensive room at the conference hotel (advanced payment required) was $265 per night. The maximum the state will allow a traveling faculty member to be reimbursed for accommodations in Chicago is capped at $192 per night, a net difference of $73 per night, or nearly $300 for the average conference stay, *even if the faculty member's department can afford to pay more.* Based on our observation of the kinds of hotels athletes stay in while traveling, athletics appears to be exempted from these kinds of rules.

2. Hiring: At this same large public institution, as is typical of most public institutions, all hiring must go through a stringent search process, including posting the job for 30 days (unless the search is restricted internally), all applications must be reviewed and databases kept that denote the relationship between the requirements posted in the advertisement (e.g., degree, experience, skills) and every candidate's qualifications. Assessments must be collected for every aspect of the candidate's interview (e.g., phone interview, job talk, small group meetings, even interactions at lunch and dinner). Notes on reference checks must be recorded. At the end of this process, all of these pieces of data must accompany the request to hire, which is reviewed by the hiring authority and everyone who supervises him or her. In the best of circumstances, the typical hire takes a minimum of 12 weeks. Yet, at this same institution, head coaches are hired within days of the firing of the former coach.

These illustrations are important because they contribute to our discussion of the relationship between athletics and the rest of the institution and because they are associated with the disproportionate budgets in athletics, travel costs, salaries, and hiring practices.

THE MONEY FLOWS ONLY ONE WAY!

Other than the scholarship that the athletic department pays to the university to educate the college athlete, the money that is generated by athletics is allowed to stay in athletics, yet the money that is generated by the college or university can flow into the athletic department, and as we have shown, it does, at very high rates. Athletics is allowed to keep whatever it gets and spend it without the same restrictions, while all other units in the university are required to turn back any surplus, which is rare, given that many institutions are grossly underfunded and underresourced to begin with, and the money that circulates to athletic departments from the general operating budget only exacerbates this condition.

So, the final question we pose is this: What is the overall cost to the institutions of higher education that insist on providing incredible resources to their athletic departments on the mere dream that they will field national championship teams—in either football or men's basketball—and in doing so receive the financial rewards they wrongly believe will flow into their coffers?

Colleges and universities are paying an increasingly steep price to keep athletic departments afloat. As noted, while coaches' salaries continue to rise—which is justified by invoking marketplace demands and (falsely) the revenue coaches are generating—faculty salaries are flat, in spite of the fact that their collective teaching and research is in fact the biggest revenue generator for the college or university. Many faculty on these same campuses find that the facilities they need to do their jobs are inadequate and there is almost no support for the graduate students they train (table 10.5).

One of the most glaring examples comes from Rutgers University. As a result of several debacles at Rutgers that were quite expensive (including, *paying fired head football coach Greg Schiano's mortgage*) and the costs associated with leaving the Big East Conference and entering the Big Ten Conference, Rutgers cut many programs that are fundamental to the mission of any public university. Similarly, the large public institution we have been using as an illustration, in 2014, paid a $1 million fee to exit one conference and another million dollars to join the new conference. Just a month after the fee was paid, the state, which had serious budget shortfalls, required that same university to turn back $8 million of support. What the dean of the largest college in the university could have done with that $1 million in good times becomes even more real in harsh times, when that same dean turned back that same amount that the university paid to exit the conference.

Here's the conundrum: academics actually brings in the most revenue to our colleges and universities. But the infighting with athletics brings about this type of sentiment, as Dodd (2015) noted: "Academicians can talk all they want to. The American public loves sports, period. It is what it is. We have a sports page, not a math classroom page" (para. 22).

And under the collegiate model athletes are still considered amateur athletes. Hence, they must be educated using professors' human capital, sit in desks in classrooms, and occupy rooms in the residence halls. The cost of their athletic

TABLE 10.5.

Academic and Athletic Spending in Division I Football Subdivision Conferences

Div I Subdivision FBS Conferences	Median academic spending per student, 2010	Median athletic spending per athlete, 2010
Southwestern (SEC)	$13,390	$163,931
Big 12	$13,988	$131,286
Pac-12	$14,217	$102,121
Football Bowl Subdivision Average	*$13,628*	*$91,936*
Atlantic Coast (ACC)	$15,360	$103,384
Conference USA	$11,867	$76,181
Big Ten	$19,225	$116,667
Big East	$17,620	$102,032
Mountain West	$13,690	$74,264
Western Athletic (WAC)	$11,789	$56,180
Sun Belt	$10,012	$41,796
Mid-American	$13,069	$52,537
Div I—No Football	*$11,861*	*$39,201*
Football Championship Subdivision (FCS)	$11,769	$36,665

Source: Knight Commission on Intercollegiate Athletics (2012), http://bit.ly/1RFwtWd.

requirements (e.g., coaching salaries, travel, equipment costs) is often subsidized by student fees of the students sitting next to them in classes, and yet athletics pays no rent (other than scholarship money) back to the institution. In fact, as we have demonstrated repeatedly in this chapter, athletic departments are subsidized at the *cost* of the institution.

RECOMMENDATIONS

It is difficult to generate reasonable policy recommendations, given the polarizing positions that this kind of discussion generates. In our experience, most scholars, activists, and journalists take an all-or-nothing approach: at one end of the spectrum are those who genuinely believe that college athletics generate not only money but also notoriety for colleges and universities, and they generally advocate that athletic programs simply be allowed to continue on the same course. At the other end of the spectrum are those who argue for disbanding college athletics entirely and/or removing it from higher education and establishing professional club systems similar to the structure in many European countries. Neither of these approaches will address our concerns, and neither is practical. To begin with, we recommend that college and university presidents take back control of their institutions and reorient them around their core mission: providing education and research to the citizens in the communities in which they reside. Once control is restored and the institutions are realigned around the missions, goals-based budgeting practices would allow colleges and universities to bring the balance back; athletic departments would be funded and supported adequately—for all athletes, not just members of the football and men's basketball teams—and academic units would once again find that their needs are being met as well, in terms of faculty salaries, classroom technology, and the like. Because intercollegiate athletics is involved in an "arms race" (Smith 2014), this will only work *if all* college and university presidents agree to implement these changes. Additionally, holding athletic departments to the same spending and hiring practices required of all other units would be a good first move in terms of reeling in the out-of-control spending that we currently observe as well as the astronomical salaries associated with the head football coaching carousel—a system that allows coaches with losing records to be fired, have their contracts paid out, and to be rehired within days at even higher salaries. These two approaches would dramatically slow the bleeding that many college and university general operating budgets and academic units are experiencing.

CONCLUSION

What does consference realignment have to do with all of this?

As noted in the example of Rutgers University and the large public institution we mentioned earlier, conference realignment will accelerate the process of defunding the academic mission of colleges and universities. The lure to become a member of the Power Five conferences will grow to massive proportions as this elite group gets to set its own rules and control championship play. Colleges and universities who think they have a chance to get into a Power Five, or are afraid of being kicked out of a Power Five conference—or even those who believe that their status and revenue will improve by moving from a lower mid-major to a higher mid-major conference—will face extraordinary pressure to do so. And, the costs associated with this movement will be too much for many to bear.

What makes all of this interesting is that not even a year has passed since the creation of this Power Five block and already the "winds of change" are blowing, suggesting that among these 65 or so institutions there is talk that several will be kicked out of the Power Five. Finally, this allows us to speculate that many colleges and universities will be bled to death by this arms race to a place they will never arrive. Much like families who bought houses on 100 percent mortgages and who a few years later found themselves in foreclosure, colleges and universities will face a similar fate. The closing of the football program at the University of Alabama, Birmingham in 2015 serves as one recent example. Only time will tell what the total impact on colleges and universities and the system of higher education will be.

QUESTIONS FOR DISCUSSION

1. If you were a college or university president, what strategies would you employ to bring athletic spending back into line with athletic revenue generation?

2. If you were a college or university head football coach, what arguments would you make to your college or university president, to state legislators, and to students paying exorbitant student fees to justify both your salary and your team's operating budget (e.g., recruiting, travel, etc.)?

3. Is there a way to save both college athletics and the larger colleges and universities in which they reside or will a decoupling be the only solution to the problems we pose in this chapter?

References

Bennett, B. (2014). NCAA board votes to allow autonomy. ESPN. Retrieved from http://espn/1FvIKbw

Comeaux, E. (Ed.). (2015). *Introduction to intercollegiate athletics.* Baltimore, MD: Johns Hopkins University Press.

Dodd, D. (2015). Despite UAB debacle, football a must-have for status-hungry schools. CBS Sports. Retrieved from http://cbsprts.co/1K2rr3Q

Durkheim, É. (1982). *The rules of sociological method and selected texts on sociology and its method.* New York: Free Press.

Edwards, H. (1973). *Sociology of sport.* Belmont, CA: Dorsey Press.

Forde, P. (2011). Meet the commanders-in-chief. ESPN. Retrieved from http://espn/1Bx6erI

Guinier, L. (2015). *The tyranny of the meritocracy: Democratizing higher education in America.* Boston: Beacon Press.

Hoffer, A., and Pincin, J. (2015). The effects of conference realignment on NCAA athletic departments. Retrieved from http://ssrn.com/abstract=2578333

Knight Commission on Intercollegiate Athletics. (2012). Retrieved from http://bit.ly/1RFwtWd

Merton, R. K. (1936). The unanticipated consequences of purposive social action. *American Sociological Review, 1*(6), 894–904

Merton, R. K. (1968). *Social theory and social structure.* New York: Free Press.

Morris, A. (2000). Reflections on social movement theory: Criticisms and proposals. *Contemporary Sociology, 29,* 445–454.

Smith, E. (2014). *Race, sport and the American dream* (3rd ed.). Durham, NC: Carolina Academic Press.

Smith, E. (2015). Keeping up with the Joneses: And ending up broke. *Out of Bounds.* Retrieved from http://bit.ly/1CUV5RZ

Smith, E., & Hattery, A. J. (2015). Conference realignment and the demise of the academic Mission. In E. Comeaux (Ed.), *Introduction to intercollegiate athletics* (pp. 219–230). Baltimore, MD: Johns Hopkins University Press.

Therborn, G. (1980). *The ideology of power and the power of ideology.* London: New Left Books.

Competitive Equity

*Can There Be Balance between Athletes' Rights
and a Level Playing Field?*

Andy Schwarz and Daniel A. Rascher

A level playing field. Competitive equity. Balanced competition. All of these terms are used to describe the idea that, without an agreement across Division I as to how much each school's college athletes can be compensated, schools with large fan bases and high revenues will have an "unfair" advantage over schools with smaller fan bases, and that the resulting competitive imbalance will lead to lower fan interest in college sports. This, in turn, will harm or even kill college sports as an institution. The answer, goes this argument, is to impose the college equivalent of an individual-player salary maximum, limiting the value of the grant-in-aid or athletic scholarship each school can provide, in order to ensure the two teams setting foot on the field of play are more or less equally likely to win.[1]

> ## KEY TERMS
>
> ▶ Collusion
>
> ▶ Cartel
>
> ▶ Competitive balance
>
> ▶ Non-price competition
>
> ▶ Invariance Principle

So goes the argument, but virtually none of the above is true. In particular, despite 60 years of study of the topic of competitive balance, across sports in general and including many studies on National Collegiate Athletic Association (NCAA) Division I sports in particular, there has been no economic evidence supporting the theory that the amateurism rules that cap how much a school can pay an athlete have any positive impact on competitive equity. Take, as a simple example, the sport of women's basketball, where, despite having 340 or more teams in Division I and 64 teams in the tournament, the list of national champions from 2007 through 2016 included just four teams: Connecticut (with five championships), Tennessee (with three), Baylor (with one), and Texas A&M (with one).

A word on terminology: while the NCAA has historically focused on the term "competitive equity" and has recently begun to favor "competitive fairness,"[2] the sports economics literature typically refers to the concept as "competitive balance." How these terms differ as far as the goal they seek is not entirely clear. Competitive balance usually refers to evenness in outcomes, whether those be the closeness of a single game, the chance of winning a single-season championship, or the ease/difficulty of winning multiple championships over a short period of time. When pressed to measure "competitive equity" or "competitive fairness," the NCAA has fallen back on these same measures (even though the intent may be the "equity" invested in creating competitive outcomes, e.g., athlete compensation or coaches' pay), and so we treat the terms as synonymous.[3]

In this chapter, we lay out the economic theory and empirical evidence against this false narrative, as well as put the argument in the context of a century-plus of labor/management arguments of competitive balance across the sports industry. We also address the question of whether a search for competitive equity is a just goal. That is, even if there were evidence of an improvement in competitive equity from the imposition of amateurism onto college sports, would this justify extracting profits from a small subset of the population just to ensure collegiate sporting events are more balanced, or are there better ways to do this that are less exploitative?

The chapter is laid out as follows. First, we explain that many of the rules designed to improve competitive balance, such as revenue sharing or limits on individual compensation, have been shown in the empirical sports economic literature not to have any substantial benefit to competitive balance. Then we focus on the authors who have addressed college sports specifically, and we explain how these studies have confirmed and extended the general conclusions that NCAA-specific rules have had little or no benefit to (and sometimes have harmed) competitive balance in Division I sports, especially football and men's basketball. Most of these studies focus on balance based on wins and losses, but we expand the focus to present some of our own evidence on competitive imbalance in recruiting. Then we address the negative economic side effects that the amateurism rules have likely created, primarily an upward spiral of other costs. Finally, we address how a world without limits on athlete pay would likely be one with better competitive balance among teams, and far fewer negative consequences, both economically and from the perspective of the civil and economic rights of the participants.

THE ECONOMICS OF COMPETITIVE BALANCE IN SPORTS

In 1956, the academic field of sports economics was born when Simon Rottenberg published "The Baseball Players' Labor Market" in the *Journal of Political Economy* (Rottenberg, 1956).[4] At the time, Major League Baseball (MLB) required all players to sign a contract that included what was known as a "reserve clause," which prohibited free agency once the contract was over by giving the team the automatic right to renew the contract for another year, and then another, and so on. Rottenberg developed a coherent economic theory for why, despite these strict rules against free agency, competitive balance was very low, with the highest-revenue team, the New York Yankees, seeming to be in the World Series every year (and in fact they were in 15 out of 18 World Series from 1947 through 1964, winning 10. Rottenberg explained that, regardless of rules prohibiting freedom of movement, talent would gravitate toward where it was most highly valued, and therefore, whether free agency were allowed or not, talent would basically be distributed across teams in comparable ways. However, as Rottenberg explained, while the distribution of talent was relatively invariant to rules against free agency, the impact on society was anything but neutral:

> Markets in which the freedom to buy and sell is constrained by the reserve rule or by the suggested alternatives to it do not promise better results than do markets constructed on the postulate of freedom. It appears that free markets would give as good aggregate results as any other kind of market for industries, like the baseball industry, in which all firms must be nearly equal if each is to prosper. On welfare criteria, of course, the free market is superior to the others, for in such a market each worker receives the full value of his services, and exploitation does not occur. (p. 258)

We know this idea today as the "Invariance Principle"—that is, the distribution of talent levels cannot be substantially changed based on rules about whether players have access to a free market or whether owners control player movement. The result is that the primary impact of rules limiting athletes' economic freedom is simply to lower pay and therefore increase exploitation: defined as the difference between the free rate of pay and an imposed cap.

MLB offered its own rival theory as to what free agency would mean. In 1970, Chubb Feeney and Joe Cronin, presidents of the National and American Leagues, issued a dire warning to the public on the perils that would ensue if baseball were ever forced to abandon the reserve clause and allow free agency. According to Feeney and Cronin, (1) free agency would "totally destroy league competition," (2) the minor leagues "would be destroyed," (3) "trades would become impossible," and most ominously (4) "professional baseball would simply cease to exist" (Khan, 2012, pp. 92–93).

Twenty years after Rottenberg published his work, his theory was put to the test when MLB lost a labor review before a federal mediator and was required to end enforcement of the reserve clause for veteran players. Soon the doors to free agency were wide open and the Invariance Principle was proven to be true in practice as well as theory. Consider the Yankees as a simple example. For the decade from 1950 to 1959, the Yankees were in eight World Series, winning six. But in the decade from 2006 through 2015, the Yankees—still the dominant MLB team in terms of revenue—appeared in (and won) just one World Series.[5]

Additional research expanded on Rottenberg's theory, and soon the conclusion was extended across professional sports (Fort & Lee, 2007). But would the same conclusions hold in college, despite the fact that college sports teams don't have a draft, don't have trades, and can't stop an athlete from transferring?[6] Economic research has shown that, yes, even though much of the structure of professional sports differs from college with respect to athlete mobility, rules limiting economic competition for talent—such as the cap on value of a grant-in-aid—have had no beneficial impact on competitive balance (Berri, 2004). These findings span many of the NCAA's rules that are claimed to help competitive equity, including (1) the limit on the value of a grant-in-aid (Baird, 2004), (2) the limits on the number of grants-in-aid (Sutter & Winkler, 2003), and (3) penalties for rules violations (Depken & Wilson, 2004). The findings, for each rule in isolation and for all rules on eligibility and payments taken together (Eckard, 1998; Peach, 2007), are consistent in showing that college sports demonstrate high levels of *imbalance* and that little or no change has taken place in the 60 years in which the grant-in-aid rules have been enforced nationally, even though the structure of college differs from major league sports (Berri, 2004). Economist Rod Fort (Fort, 2011) summarizes the findings across this literature: "Interestingly, many believe that these recruiting restrictions create a level playing field that enables poorer athletic departments to compete with richer ones for talent. Nothing could be farther from the truth. Instead, these restrictions entrench power at departments at the top end of the winning percent distribution" (p. 272).

DOES CAPPING SCHOLARSHIPS RESULT IN BALANCED COLLEGE RECRUITING?

These studies have generally focused their emphasis on the outcomes of games and seasons. For example, James Peach has shown that from 1950 to 2006, 13 schools accounted for 50 percent of the appearances in Final Four games in the NCAA men's basketball tournament (Berri, 2012; Peach, 2007). But rules that restrict economic competition for athletes are supposed to work by making sure a few teams don't hoard all of the talent. So a more direct way to look at whether the rules have helped create competitive equity is to look at recruiting success: have the best athletes been spread throughout college sports, or instead do we find the same few schools consistently recruiting the best athletes year after year?

As is probably obvious to any fan of the University of Alabama football or the University of Kentucky basketball, college sports is just as imbalanced with respect to recruiting as with wins and losses. For example, from 2001 to 2010, there were a total of 1,000 recruits on those ten years' Top 100 lists of recruits. More than 99 percent of those 1,000 recruits went to "Big Six" conferences.[7]

Even within the power conferences, consistently a small number of schools dominate recruiting. In the last decade, recruiting dominance has been remarkably consistent, with the same schools winning over the best athletes, year after year. One measure of the "stickiness" of recruiting success—the same schools winning year after year—is the Spearman rank correlation, which measures this persistence. As can been seen from figure 11.1, which measures the year-to-year rank correlation of football recruiting by team, the tendency for the rich to get richer (in terms of recruiting success) has only magnified over time.

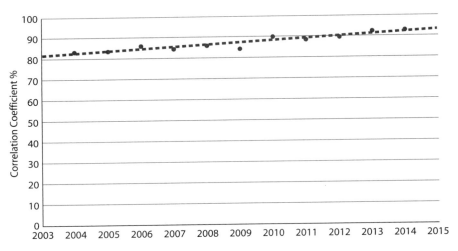

Figure 11.1. FBS Competitive Imbalance: Correlation between Recruiting Ranks.

Notes: Yearly rankings from 247Sports "247Composite Rating" (algorithm that compiles prospect rankings listed in the public domain). The Spearman's Rank Correlation Coefficient ranges from −100% (rankings completely and perfectly reverse each year) to 100% (rankings remain exactly the same each year). Analysis includes 115 NCAA I FBS schools with complete data provided by 247Sports between 2003 and 2014. No ranking ties in the data. Alabama has ranked #1 in recruiting in each year, 2011–2014.

Sources: "The Chase for the Recruiting Champion powered by 247Sports Composite," 247Sports (247Sports.com), last accessed November 10, 2014 (bit.ly/1EFzfT7). "247 Rating Explanation," 247Sports (247Sports.com) (bit.ly/1wTQvQi).

It is easy to see that the relationship between revenue and recruiting success is strong, despite the NCAA rules that supposedly create balanced recruiting. Over time, the schools with the most potential to generate revenue from talent have the most incentive to recruit athletes capable of generating revenue, and that success fuels the process by providing revenue to increase recruiting success. The result is a strong correlation between revenue and recruiting success (figure 11.2).

THE INTUITION BEHIND THE ECONOMICS OF COMPETITIVE BALANCE

Many of the rules common to professional sports-salary caps, drafts, and revenue sharing, as just a few examples—have a surface appeal that by "leveling the playing field," the sport can achieve competitive balance. Unfortunately, this intuition is often incorrect economically. Teams, like all businesses, tend to spend money when they see a strong likelihood of a positive return on investment, and they tend not to spend money if they don't. If two teams have vastly different likelihoods that additional spending will generate additional benefits, almost no set of rules, short of mandatory spending requirements (i.e., salary floors), can force a low-revenue team to keep up with a high-revenue team.[8]

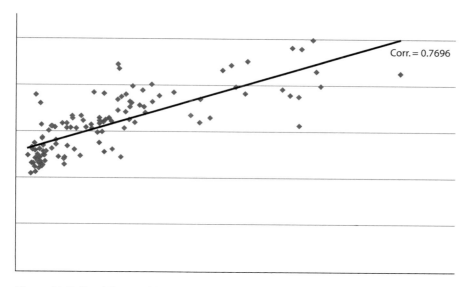

Figure 11.2. Total Count of Stars versus FBS Football Revenue, 2007–2011

The same intuition undergirds the argument for NCAA-style amateurism helping create competitive balance in college sports. And that intuition is equally incorrect. The argument is that by holding the level of athlete pay fixed, financially less-well-off schools can "afford" to compete with the wealthiest. But as this evidence shows, and consistent with basic economic theory, the schools that get the most value out of financial investments in their athletics also tend to keep making those investments, even if athlete compensation is taken out of the mix as one of the vehicles of investment. The result is that, despite a firm cap that can approximate the effect of making direct compensation identical for all schools, schools that are constrained by this cap have economically rational incentives to find other ways to compete. Given that there are no caps on spending by athletic departments on training facilities and coaches, the schools with more to gain financially from winning/recruiting, spend large sums of money on fancy new facilities and name-brand coaches with excellent track records in recruiting star athletes.

For example, the University of Alabama's head football coach, Nick Saban, earned over $7 million in 2015. Duke University's men's basketball coach, Mike Krzyzewski, exceeded $7 million in 2016. The University of Oregon spent $68 million on a "Football Operations Center" complete with expensive wood paneling worthy of a mansion (Averill, 2014). Schools now regularly send recruits a hundred or more recruiting letters and engage in other costly, over-the-top recruiting methods (Kulha, 2013; PostGame, 2013; Ragan, 2013).

Schools for which such investment is not rational may decry the level of indirect spending as an "arms race," but the underlying cause of their "inability" to keep up is that the same investment offers them a far less lucrative return, and so they will rarely be the high bidder factoring in all means of competition.

These investments in facilities and coaches are a form of what economists call "non-price competition," and in the absence of direct competition through pay, they become important points of distinction in recruiting and athlete decision making. For example, as Berri and Peach explain, if every team is constrained to pay the same amount, athletes will seek other forms of compensation, such as a higher chance of winning (Berri & Peach, 2014). The result is that power conferences that have very different economic incentives to spend on sports also generate substantially more resources from those investments and field consistently better teams, and so the cycle of winning perpetuates itself. Short of requiring all schools to spend as much as the dominant schools (perhaps financed by far greater revenue sharing), there is little economic support for the idea that the economic playing field can ever be made level.

There is an important distinction between the NCAA's rules that cap individual athlete remuneration to a grant-in-aid, and the National Football League's rules that cap a team's overall pay. An NFL-style salary cap puts a limit on the aggregate amount the team's athletes can be paid (with some exceptions) but not on the amount an individual athlete within that team cap can be paid. This is different in the National Basketball Association (NBA), which has both a team salary cap and an individual salary cap, which more closely resembles the NCAA system. Given that the amount of money NFL football players earn, their pay is a key factor in their decision on which team to play for, while in the NBA (and in college) a player who will receive the maximum allowed compensation no matter where he goes will tend to choose based on secondary factors, like winning tradition or facilities. Unlike in the NFL, where a lower-quality NFL team with cap space can lure a player using higher pay, in the NBA or NCAA systems,[9] the best players continue to play for the already-best teams/schools, cementing the competitive imbalance in place.

THE NEGATIVE IMPACT OF SCHOLARSHIP CAPS

Economics uses the concept of welfare to capture the net benefits to society from any particular activity.[10] Things that grow total welfare are seen as relatively efficient, things that decrease welfare are relatively inefficient. As we have seen above, caps on the value of individual grants-in-aid to athletes don't have any demonstrated benefit for competitive equity; instead, the rules simply transfer income from athletes to team ownership (see the much smaller athlete surplus in figure 11.3), which in the case of college sports means the schools and employees (like coaches) and contractors of the school (like construction firms) who are able to demand competitive levels of pay. This transfer of wealth is likely in the hundreds of millions or billions of dollars each year,[11] and generally flows from poorer and more heavily minority athletes to better-off and generally fewer minority coaches, staff, and even the shareholders of the firms (including architects, construction, and design firms) the schools hire to push their sports programs forward (Hruby, 2016; Roberson & Austin, 2016).

In addition to this somewhat regressive redistribution of income, the rules against athlete pay are also inefficient in that they reduce total welfare (see figure 11.3, where the cap on the number of scholarships creates a deadweight loss that is not captured by the athletes or the schools). This is because, in the absence of "wage" competition, colleges have resorted to indirect means, or inefficient substitution, to attract athletes to their campuses. Coaches who do the best job of recruiting, year in and year out, can now earn $5 million or more, gobbling up the potential savings from not having to pay athletes. The examples above of $7 million coaches and lavish recruiting palaces result in a distribution of talent that approximates the market distribution but does so far less efficiently. Economic research by Stigler (1968), Douglas and Miller (1974), and Viscusi, Vernon, and Harrington (1997) conclude that non-price competition is likely to be less efficient than price (wage, in this case) competition, and excessive by competing away all of the rents, and then some. Moreover, money is an efficient and divisible means of exchange, as well as allowing the user to buy whatever he/she wants, as opposed to being forced to instead consume a lavish training facility.

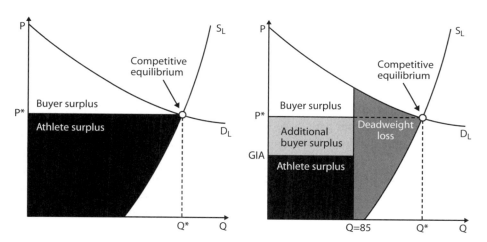

Figure 11.3. Comparison of a Competitive Market (*left*) to a Market with Capped Compensation and Capped Number of Scholarships

IS THERE INDIVIDUAL EQUITY IN A PURSUIT OF COMPETITIVE EQUITY?

With all of that said, assume for a moment that there was good evidence that rules against athlete pay do lead to closer competitive balance, whether on the field of play or in recruiting. Would that make the transfer of wealth inherent in amateurism justified as part of a pursuit of more balanced competition? Of course, since there is little or no support for the premise, this is more of a philosophical than an economic question, but here are some elements to ponder.

Are Sports Outcomes More Important Than Legal Rights?

Generally speaking, in the United States, the presumption is that individual rights, including the right to unencumbered access to the job market, will predominate over an industry's claimed need to abridge those rights for product enhancement. That is, since the antitrust laws serve as a guarantee against collusion among sellers or buyers (including firms hiring athletes), it should require a very important market failure to deny athletes access to the same right to a competitive market for their services. And yet this is what the NCAA and its member schools do—they assert that their need for, *inter alia,* competitive balance, is so important that the baseline rights of athletes must be suspended. Is this consistent with our societal principals?

Whose Rights Matter?

There is more to the question than just competitive equity for fans versus athlete legal equality. Other stakeholders also assert that their needs should be factored in. For example, many argue that, without a cap on the level of pay for athletes who play football and basketball, schools might choose not to provide scholarships to athletes in other sports like lacrosse or wrestling. Often the peril is expressed more starkly: without the money that would go to the football and basketball athletes, schools "could not afford" the cost of a wrestling team.

This argument rests on dubious economic assumptions—is a college with a $100 million or $100 billion annual budget really unable to afford a $400,000 wrestling team without taking the money from its football players? In essence, this argument requires us to accept that the school is not willing to use its own money (from any other source) if the football players' money isn't available. But even if it were true (and the existence of Division II wrestling is strong evidence against this), why would a wrestler's right to receive a scholarship trump the football player's right to access a market free of collusion? Moreover, the revenues in major college sports have been growing at greater than 7 percent per year for decades, and schools continue to clamor to get into the Football Bowl Subdivision and Division I—if they were losing so much money from athletics, they would be leaving in droves. The schools (nonprofits with no shareholders) simply follow Bowen's Revenue Theory of Costs[12] and just spend what they bring in, thus showing no or low profits (table 11.1).

Moreover, does it make ethical sense to impose the obligation to fund a college sports team on other college athletes, when the school itself has made it clear (if we assume the school won't shoulder the cost itself—this could be false) how little value the wrestling team has to the campus community that it won't fund the team itself? Implicit in the idea of this cross-subsidy is an upside down view of equity. In other words, why should wrestling have to rely on a subsidy from football anyway?

TABLE 11.1.

Football Bowl Subdivision Schools Spend 100 Percent of Their Revenue (in millions of dollars)

	2010	2011	2012	2013	2014	2015
FBS Schools Total Athletic Revenues	$5,863	$6,225	$6,617	$7,126	$7,609	$8,205
FBS Schools Total Athletic Expenses	$5,863	$6,225	$6,617	$7,126	$7,609	$8,205
Remaining Revenue	$0	$0	$0	$0	$0	$0

Source: Equity in Athletics Disclosure Act (EADA) Data, Department of Education.

What Role Gender Equity?

In contrast to men, female athletes do have a legal claim, through Title IX, to financial aid in proportion to their level of participation in their college's inter-collegiate sports, and toward some level of parity in participation as well.[13] Here the questions of equities are trickier–does the male athlete's right of access to the market under the Sherman Act trump the female athlete's right to proportional financial aid under Title IX? While this dilemma is a thorny legal and ethical question, it is not one that the college sports community needs to solve. Title IX and the antitrust laws are fully compatible; the market rate that would result were male athlete's compensation untethered by NCAA rules would take each school's Title IX obligations into account, just as professors' wages are set taking into account a school's obligation to pay state and federal payroll taxes.

RECOMMENDATIONS

Given that the theoretical and empirical economic evidence shows no benefit to competitive balance from restrictions on individual athlete compensation, a simple way to achieve today's level of competitive balance without infringing on athletes' rights is to do away with amateurism, at least with respect to rules designed to limit how much compensation a school can provide to its enrolled students who play intercollegiate sports. Gender equity can be maintained by ensuring that all payments to athletes, even above the cost of attendance, be considered "financial aid" and thus legally required to be proportional by gender. These changes would lead to increased spending on male athletes and thus lead to similar increases on spending for women, and they would reduce the indirect forms of competition such as coaches' pay, facilities spending, and administrative bloat. While this might require a phase-in period, once schools adjusted to the new world, the system would be far fairer off the field and court, and no less fair on.

To the extent that college sports want to improve their level of competitive balance, this is a tougher challenge. With some Division I schools willing to spend over $100 million, and others unwilling to spend even $10 million, no set of rules will ever lead to recruiting parity, and without something close to recruiting parity, contests between schools with different levels of spending will never be balanced. To be sure, upsets can and will happen, but few rules can bring spending or recruiting into balance.

One possibility, albeit one that would require a substantial philosophical break from the current system, would be to require far more substantial pooling of revenue, and far stricter spending floors (not caps). To ensure the shared revenue is used on athletics, small schools would be required to spend more than the optimal level for their market, and revenue sharing would lower the incentive for more powerful teams to spend as much as their markets otherwise would merit. Balance would improve, but at the cost of possible inefficiency: overspending in small markets, underspending in big (Rascher, 1997).

Perhaps no one is eager to embrace such a system, because any level of nationwide competitive balance it achieved would come in a way that almost surely would lower total welfare. Remember, competitive imbalance is the outcome we have today, and that has generally resulted in an excellent match between the best talent, the best teams, and the most rabid fans. Forcing talent away from where the market wants it to go may be a recipe for balance but not necessarily in a way that actually pleases fans. It is worthwhile to consider a system that actually did redistribute talent in such a way that made all schools equally likely to win and whether that would be better for the sport as a whole. Because it would fail to match supply and demand, we tend to think it would not.

CONCLUSION

Leaving aside any of the other supposed virtues of amateurism, with respect to improvements in competitive balance, the evidence, like college sports itself, is completely one-sided: limiting athletes' pay by denying them access to a free (or at least freer) market has had no benefit on closeness of competitions, whether measured by balance of game/season outcomes or by equity in recruiting. The primary impact has been to shift income—measured in the hundreds of millions or billions of dollars annually—from athletes to others, in a way that is highly regressive; it functions like an income tax on members of society who are poor and subsidizes the middle class. The secondary impact has been to introduce wasteful, inefficient spending into the system: coaches who earn millions because they can serve as indirect means of recruiting talent, or opulent locker rooms that serve more as billboards and palaces than places to suit up for the game. Athletic department staffs, and budgets, have ballooned over time.

These economic facts are well known, but the misconception that these costs at least bring a benefit—competitive balance—persists. Yet few have stepped back to ask whether, or even if, the myth were fact, would such a trade-off make sense in a country in which our individual rights are generally paramount over such secondary concerns as slight improvements in entertainment products (or perhaps not an improvement at all if competitive balance means that talent and demand end up mismatched). Future leaders of college sports should go in armed with this fact—amateurism doesn't improve competitive balance—but also should be willing to justify why, even if it did, revenue sport athletes alone should be asked to bear the full cost of making the University of Alabama and University of Kentucky slightly less dominant.

QUESTIONS FOR DISCUSSION

1. Do fans really want competitive balance, or are dynasties and blue-blood programs part of what makes college sports special? Can there be exciting upsets without powerhouses?

2. If competitive balance were improved by restraining athlete compensation, should that be given a higher priority than an athlete's right to market access? Is society's desire for exciting football or basketball games a superior claim than the rights of the athletes? What are the foundations of ethics, law, or society that support your position?

3. What might be some approaches to improve competitive balance among college teams that do not involve caps on competitive rates of compensation? If a school or conference is structurally unsuited to spend at a rate commensurate with other schools/conferences, can your rules ensure comparable investments, rather than just having the smaller programs pocket the revenue?

Notes

1. In a public filing in federal court, the Big 12 conference explained the NCAA theory, arguing that caps on scholarships "serve the procompetitive goal of promoting competitive balance between and among NCAA member institutions by encouraging intercollegiate athletic rivalries wherein amateur student-athletes are competing only against other amateur student-athletes, thereby fostering more uncertain outcomes in athletic contests and increasing the prospect that each institution will be competitive both within their conferences and in inter-conference competition."

2. In a January 2013 "Rules Reform," the NCAA formally adopted commitments that "assist[ ] in defining the nature and purposes of Division I and lays foundation for values-based rules, shifting from competitive equity to fair competition": http://www.ncaa.org/governance/reform-efforts.

3. When taken outside the realm of rigorous analysis, the NCAA terms are less clearly defined. For example, the NCAA "acknowledges that variability will exist among members in advantages, including facilities, geographic location and resources and that such variability should not be justification for future [bylaws]." NCAA President Mark Emmert explained competitive fairness meant that "when student-athletes step on the field, they know that the other team's got the same number of players, they've got the same number of coaches, they've got the same number of scholarships. They may have a fancier stadium, they may have other resource advantages, but we've got a chance to beat these guys because there's competitive fairness" (Associated Press, 2013).

4. It is important to note that Rottenberg uses the term "exploitation" in the standard economic sense (which we follow), by which a laborer is exploited if he or she is denied a competitive rate of pay for his or her services.

5. Across each decade, regardless of the rules on free agency, between 40 percent and 50 percent of all MLB teams have appeared in at least one World Series (Schwarz, 2011).

6. NCAA rules do impose high costs on transfers, such as requiring an athlete to sit out up to two years before competing for a new school, but nevertheless, the NCAA and its members cannot stop an athlete from switching schools.

7. Of the seven who didn't, one went to junior college, one went to a MAC (Mid-American Conference) school because a Big Ten school revoked his scholarship prior to entry, and four were Mormons who attended Brigham Young University. The seventh, a wide receiver, went to Texas Christian University (at the time, a pass-heavy offense), which has since moved up to the Power Five. See Schwarz (2011).

8. In the NFL, which is often seen as the most balanced of professional North American sports, teams have a strong salary floor and also play unbalanced schedules, which allows weaker teams to have easier chances to win games by playing weaker opponents. As shown in Rascher, Nagel, Brown, and McEvoy (2011), the minimum team salary in the NFL is an attempt to prevent some teams from spending less on player payroll than they would like to.

9. Specifically in so-called counter sports, where partial scholarships cannot be shared, including football and men's and women's basketball.

10. Don't confuse this use of the term *welfare* with the political sense of cash assistance to the poor.

11. The most recent relaxation of the NCAA Division I limits on grants-in-aid led to an immediate shift of income of $50 million or so in one year in just the sports of football and basketball, as schools leapt at the chance to increase athlete compensation.

12. Howard Bowen (1980) explained that spending by colleges and universities is driven by the amount of revenue available to be spent. In such a system, new revenue generated causes new spending to emerge, giving the appearance of ever-upward spiraling costs.

13. Title IX is a complex law that is frequently misunderstood. There are several different ways a school can meet its participation goals; proportionality is just one of the three "prongs" for compliance. But regardless of how a school meets that element of the regulation, the school is also required to provide financial aid in proportion to participation. See a letter of clarification regarding Title IX from the US Department of Education (O'Shea, 1998).

References

Associated Press. (2013, January 20). NCAA takes first steps to simplify, deregulate complex rulebook. Retrieved from http://www.ncaa.com/news/ncaa/article/2013-01-20/ncaa-takes-first-step-simplify-deregulate-complex-rulebook

Averill, A. (2014, November 25). University of Oregon football facility floors were a gamble. Retrieved from http://www.hardwoodfloorsmag.com/articles/university-of-oregon -football-facility-floors-were-a-gamble.html

Baird, K. (2004). Dominance in college football and the role of scholarship restrictions. *Journal of Sport Management, 18*(3), 217–235.

Berri, D. (2004). Is there a short supply of tall people in the college game? In J. Fizel (Ed.), *Economics of college sports.* Westport, CT: Greenwood Publishing Group.

Berri, D. (2012, March 15). Would paying college players really destroy competitive balance? *Freakonomics.* Retrieved at http://www. freakonomics.com/2012/03/15 /would-paying-college-players-really-destroy-competitive-balance/

Berri, D., & Peach, J. (2014). Impact of wage controls on competitive balance in the NCAA. Presented at the Western Economic Association. Denver, CO.

Bowen, H. R. (1980). *The cost of higher education.* San Francisco: Jossey-Bass.

Depken, C., & Wilson, D. (2004). The impact of cartel enforcement in Division I-A football. In J. Fizel & R. Fort (Eds.), *Economics of college sports.* Westport, CT: Praeger.

Douglas, G., & Miller, J. (1974). Quality competition, industry equilibrium, and efficiency in the price-constrained airline market. *American Economic Review, 64,* 657–669.

Eckard, W. (1998). The NCAA cartel and competitive balance in college football. *Review of Industrial Organization, 13*(3), 347–369.

Fort, R. (2011). *Sports economics* (3rd ed.). San Francisco: Pearson Education.

Fort, R., & Lee, Y. (2007). Structural change, competitive balance, and the rest of the major leagues. *Economic Inquiry, 45*(3), 519–532.

Hruby, P. (2016, April 4). Four years a student-athlete: The racial injustice of big-time college sports. Vice Sports. Retrieved at https://sports.vice.com/en_us/article/four -years-a-student-athlete-the-racial-injustice-of-big-time-college-sports

Khan, A. K. (2012). *Curt Flood in the media: Baseball, race, and the demise of the activist-athlete.* Oxford: University Press of Mississippi.

Kulha, A. (2013, July 1). Kentucky goes all out, sends 182 letters in one day to 5-star recruit Matt Elam. Retrieved at http://bleacherreport.com/articles/1690601-kentucky -goes-all-out-sends-182-letters-in-one-day-to-5-star-recruit-matt-elam

O'Shea, M. (1998). Dear colleague letter: Bowling Green State University. Retrieved at http://www2.ed.gov/about/offices/list/ocr/docs/bowlgrn.html

Peach, J. (2007). College athletics, universities, and the NCAA. *Social Science Journal, 44*(1), 11–22.

The PostGame. (2013, March 19). Football recruit receives 102 letters in one day. Retrieved at http://www.thepostgame.com/blog/dish/201303/football-recruit-receives-102 -letters-one-day

Ragan, Z. (2013). 2014 Tennessee Volunteers recruiting: Dillon Bates receives over 100 letters from Vols. Retrieved at https://allfortennessee.com/2013/04/30/2014-tennessee -volunteers-recruiting-dillon-bates-receives-over-100-letters-from-vols/

Rascher, D. (1997). A model of a professional sports league. In W. Hendricks (Ed.), *Advances in the economics of sport 2.* Westport, CT: JAI Press.

Rascher, D., Nagel, M., Brown, M., & McEvoy, C. (2011). Free ride, take it easy: An empirical analysis of adverse incentives caused by revenue sharing. *Journal of Sport Management, 25*(5), 373–390.

Roberson, J., & Austin, T. (2016, June 20). Player sanctuaries become newest recruiting tool for colleges. *Sports Business Journal.* Retrieved at http://www .sportsbusinessdaily.com/Journal/Issues/2016/06/20/Opinion/

Rottenberg, S. (1956). The baseball players' labor market. *Journal of Political Economy, 64*(3), 242–258.

Schwarz, A. (2011). Excuses, not reasons: 13 myths about (not) paying college athletes, *Selected Proceedings of the Santa Clara University Sports Law and Ethics Symposium.*

Stigler, G. (1968). Price and non-price competition. *Journal of Political Economy, 76*(1), 149–154.

Sutter, D., & Winkler, S. (2003). NCAA scholarship limits and competitive balance in college football. *Journal of Sports Economics, 4*(1), 3–18.

Viscusi, K., Vernon, J., & Harrington, J. (1997). *Economics of regulation and antitrust.* Cambridge, MA: MIT Press.

PART FOUR

Personal and Educational Well-Being of Athletes

Identifying ways to sustain or improve the quality of experiences for college athletes has been an ongoing challenge. Part four brings to light these concerns. In chapter 12, Jamel K. Donnor examines the educational experiences of African American college athletes in high-profile football programs. Next, in chapter 13, Joseph N. Cooper and Eddie Comeaux spotlight various challenges facing college athletes at historically Black colleges and universities and present innovative intervention strategies designed to improve their positive developmental outcomes. In chapter 14, Keali'i Troy Kukahiko and Mitchell J. Chang explore one-year renewable athletic scholarship arrangements, especially as they relate to the educational opportunities of Pacific Islander college football players. In chapter 15, C. Keith Harrison, Leticia Oseguera, Jean Boyd, and Monica Morita discuss campus climate issues associated with African American and Pacific Islander / Polynesian male college athletes. And finally, in Chapter 16, Emmett Gill Jr. explores two examples of activism by the Student-Athlete's Human Rights Project to ensure athletes' rights and well-being. ■

Looking underneath the Helmet

Learning How African American Football College Athletes Navigate Sports, Education, and Expectations

Jamel K. Donnor

Sports occupy a precarious space in the lives of African Americans. From the colonial slave masters' use of sport as an "oppressive instrument and diversionary device to occupy the minds and energies of slaves" (Sammons, 1994, p. 216) to African Americans' collective interpretation of individual African American athletic achievement as progress for the race as a whole during Jim Crow, Black peoples' relationship to sports is complex (Olsen, 1968). A particularly perplexing issue regarding African Americans' relationship to sports is the academic underachievement of African American males participating in major college football. Central to the disparities in the education of African American male college athletes is race. According to professor emeritus Harry Edwards (1984), once an African American male is identified as athletically talented, he is labeled as "something really special" (p. 9). Meaning, other than excellence in athletics, little else is expected of him (Edwards, 1984).

> **KEY TERMS**
>
> ▶ African American male college athletes
>
> ▶ College football
>
> ▶ Critical race theory
>
> ▶ Academic achievement
>
> ▶ Academic advancement

An often-used method of explanation for why African American college athletes in high-profile intercollegiate athletics are academically underachieving at a greater rate than White student-athletes is conflict theory (Donnor, 2005). Citing the hypercommercialization of the sport, conflict theorists argue that the sums of money associated with college football has created a programmatic culture that places greater emphasis on winning than academics. Specifically, highlighting the contradiction between the low graduation rates and sums of money involved in operating a major college football program, conflict theorists posit that African American males are exploited for their athletic prowess. Indeed, when one compares the "effective wage" of college athletes in major sports—that is, the value of (1) an athletic scholarship, (2) room and board, and (3) allowance to purchase books—to the revenue a solvent athletic program receives from merchandising, corporate sponsorship, and boosters, then assertions of exploitation possess more than a modicum of credibility (Brown, 1993, p. 671).

Although conflict theory has been useful for pointing out the contradictions of student involvement in intercollegiate athletics at a macrolevel, scant information exists on how African American male college athletes make sense of the relationship between low academic achievement and sports (Comeaux & Harrison, 2007; Singer, 2005). Hughes, Satterfield, and Giles (2007) point out that most studies on African American male college athletes contain "very little qualitative insight to help explain why an athlete's academic performance may differ from a non-athlete's academic performance" (p. 113). Similarly, Gaston-Gayles (2004) notes that "poor graduation rates and academic performance associated with various groups of college athletes warrant investigation that goes beyond merely examining the influence of traditional variables," such as high school grade point average and standardized test scores (p. 75).

The purpose of this chapter is to discuss how African American college football players at the Football Bowl Subdivision level (FBS) make sense of the interrelationship between athletics, academic achievement, and race using critical race theory (CRT) as an analytical lens. The goals of this chapter are twofold. The first is to present African American male college athletes' capacity to think critically about sports, education, and race; the second is to illustrate how African American male student-athletes manage their postsecondary education in light of the pressure to compete athletically.

BLACK MALE ACADEMIC PERFORMANCE IN MAJOR COLLEGE FOOTBALL: AN OVERVIEW

According to Benson (2000), the marginal academic performance of African American college athletes in major college football is a phenomenon created by a "series of interrelated practices" involving key education stakeholders, including coaches, academic advisors, and the student-athletes (p. 226). Structurally, many major college football programs are organized to "maximize the athlete role and minimize the academic role" (Eitzen, 2001, p. 203). Unlike, low-profile intercollegiate sports, such as golf, the athletic experiences of FBS college athletes consist of a system of formal mechanisms and informal practices that shape the basis of their existence during the season and off-season (Bilberry, 2000; Harris, 2000). For example, during the season an FBS college athlete spends approximately 12 hours in class, 24 hours preparing for class, and approximately 28 hours to his sport a week in the form of practice, weight training, team and position meetings, and/or travel (Eitzen, 2001). Conversely, during the off-season FBS college athletes are involved with voluntary strength and conditioning, programs and unsupervised practice in order to ensure the renewal of their athletic scholarship. In short, being an FBS college athlete is a year-round phenomenon.

As such, this particular group of college athletes is vulnerable to academic misconduct, such as cheating, in order to remain eligible to participate in athletics. Interestingly, African American college athletes are at the center of most academic misconduct scandals (Gragg, 2000). While the National Collegiate Athletic Association (NCAA) does not officially record the racial composition of college athletes involved in academic violations, anecdotally, many former NCAA employees indicate that the overwhelming majority of academic misconduct cases involve African American males (Gragg, 2000). Gragg suggests that when an African American male becomes an FBS college athlete, unlike with his White counterpart, his college education no longer solely serves his interests.

Instead, an African American FBS athlete's education converges with the interests of other individuals and his educational institution. For example, in addition to an annual base salary of "no less than $270,000," Mark Richt, the former head football coach at the University of Georgia, is eligible to earn an academic bonus if the football team is ranked in the "top 33% of Southeastern Conference teams in both Graduation Success Rate (GSR) and Academic Rate of Progress (APR)" (Berkowitz, Bohn, & Upton, 2007). Interestingly, the overall GSR for the University of Georgia men's football team for the 2008–09 academic year was 48, while its APR was 965 (Lapchick, 2008, p. 4). A disaggregation of the statistics reveals that the graduation success rate for African American football college athletes at the University of Georgia was "38 percent" compared to "76 percent" for White football student-athletes (Lapchick, 2008, p. 4). Placing the football program's statistics in a broader context, the overall graduation percentage of White college athletes attending universities with programs at the Football Subdivision level (120 in all) was 76, while the percentage for African American male football college athletes was 59 (Lapchick, 2008, p. 1).

On the surface, the financial incentivizing of academic achievement for football coaches appears to be a win-win situation; however, this inducement negatively influences the educational experiences of FBS college athletes, because they are likely to be steered toward academic courses and majors that are less rigorous. In other words, participants of major college football, particularly African American males, may be tracked into undereducation or educational inequity under a statistical veneer of academic achievement.

THEORETICAL FRAMEWORK

CRT challenges mainstream notions of race, racism, and racial inequality in America by rejecting the following entrenched positions on racism: "[color]'blindness' to race will eliminate racism . . . racism is a matter of individuals, not systems . . . one can fight racism without paying attention to sexism, homophobia, economic exploitation, and other forms of oppression or injustice" (Valdes, Culp, & Harris, 2002, p. 1). Critical race theory situates race at the center of its critique through the following analytical and methodological strategies: (1) history and context (Crenshaw, Gotanda, Peller, & Thomas, 1995), (2) rejecting paradigmatic notions of objectivity and neutrality, (3) acknowledging that racism is endemic (Bell, 1995), (4) utilizing an interdisciplinary perspective to provide a more complete understanding of experiences of people of color (Matsuda, Lawrence III, Delgado, & Crenshaw, 1993), and (5) incorporating "experiential knowledge" to articulate that reality is situational and socially constructed (Ladson-Billings, 1998, p. 11).

In essence, race is more than differences in skin color, motivation, aptitude, or social class. Critical race theory treats race as a social construct that is situated in the lived experiences of a group of people with a common history of marginalization and oppression (Haney López, 1996). It is the reliance upon a group's historical and current social standing that is central to explaining racial inequity collectively and individually. Finally, CRT provides an entrance into how large political and cultural institutions, such as schools, universities, and sports, influence opportunity without minimizing the role of individuals as important actors in the access and opportunity process (Tate, 2003).

RESEARCH METHOD

The data discussed in this chapter comes from a larger study exploring the educational experiences of 17 African American college athletes at three Midwestern universities with football programs at the FBS level. The young men in this study were asked a series of semistructured ethnographic interview questions focused on obtaining their understanding of the relationship between race and athletics on their secondary and collegiate education, respectively. By suggesting that the college education of African American FBS athletes is a convergence of interests, the author was interested in identifying a set of attitudes, interactions, and outcomes within a particular setting. Thus, the information discussed in this chapter addresses the extent to which football-related responsibilities, pressure from coaches, and actions by academic support staff led African American college athletes to select courses (and academic majors) more conducive to maintaining athletic eligibility than their expressed educational interests.

RESEARCH SITES

Fieldwork for this study was conducted at the following universities that met the NCAA's institutional criteria to participate at the FBS level: Big State University (BSU), Crimson University (CU), and Tech University (TU).[1] Similar in academic reputation, research tradition, and level of athletic competition, these three institutions represent the proverbial ideal site to conduct a study on the impact of participation intercollegiate football on the education of African American male college athletes. For example, at the time of data collection, both Big State

University and Crimson University were ranked in the top 10 public national universities according to *U.S. News and World Report,* while Tech University, a private institution, ranked among the top 15 institutions of higher education for undergraduate students.

SELECTION OF PARTICIPANTS

Participants were both purposely and randomly selected for this study. For example, first-year and sophomore participants were intentionally sought for their ability to render a rich description of the difference in athletic and academic expectations between high school and college, while second-year college athletes were selected for their ability to explain how advanced participation in FBS football has and has not shaped academic-related decisions. Conversely, senior college athletes were identified through snowball sampling. The information provided by these young men was particularly illuminating because of their advanced involvement with intercollegiate football, and they were best positioned to offer a comprehensive assessment of the attitudes, institutionalized practices, and actions on the part of education stakeholders and themselves.

DATA COLLECTION PROCESS

All interviews were conducted face to face and varied in length. While a formal interview protocol was used to interview participants, the questions were open ended in order to allow the participants to share additional information. In addition to the research literature and theoretical framework, the interview questions were shaped by three pilot studies. All three pilot studies were instrumental to the design, development, and refinement of the formal data-generating instrument used in the larger study.

DATA ANALYSIS

Three analytic strategies were used throughout the course of this study. The first data analysis method was pattern matching. The second data analysis method used in the study was triangulation. Three types of triangulation took place to address internal validity (Merriam, 1998; Stake, 2000). The first triangulation method used was member checking. Here, the data was presented to the interviewees through informal follow-up sessions to confirm their responses and findings. The second method of triangulation was peer examination (Merriam, 1998). The aim of this approach was to corroborate the emergence and convergence of data points. The third triangulation method used, and a corollary, was theoretical proposition. In utilizing a CRT perspective to frame this study, specifically its context tenet, I was able to formulate a richer understanding of the rules, institutionalized behaviors, and practices that marginalize African American male athletes. In addition, the use of critical race theory helped to situate the findings as systematic. The third method of data analysis was analytical memo writing and analyzing field notes, which also occurred throughout the data collection process.

MAKING SENSE OF BLACK MALE COLLEGE ATHLETES IN FBS FOOTBALL

The literature on the academic experiences of African American college athletes frames their collegiate educational processes as static and linear and often positions them as passive participants. The findings from this study suggest the contrary. In fact, the findings reveal that there are two distinct competing sets of interests in the education of African American FBS athletes. The first set of interests, which are athletic and academic, belong to the football program. The football department is preoccupied, in terms of athletics, with its ability to compete regularly at the highest level and to appear in postseason bowl games. In contrast, the football program's academic interests are rooted not in student achievement but, according to the participants, in the coaches' interest in ensuring that student-athletes remain eligible to participate in the sport. Academic eligibility as defined by the NCAA is a requirement for participation in intercollegiate athletics. The data suggests that academic counselors in the athletic department encouraged college athletes to enroll in classes that were less likely to interfere with their eligibility to play football than in those that would advance their academic achievement.

The second set of interests belonged to the college athletes, whose interests are also athletic and academic. In terms of athletics, the participants had to balance sport-related responsibilities with personal aspirations of playing professional football and graduating from college. In terms of academics, these college athletes discussed how they negotiated the football program's expectations of retaining their eligibility in conjunction with their personal interests and intellectual desire to have a meaningful educational experience. More important, the findings revealed that a majority of African American football college athletes are interested in receiving a quality education and graduating from college. In many instances, the participants cited academic reputation as a factor in their decision to attend their particular university. The following section describes the 17 participants' involvement with major college football and its impact on their college education.

Learning to Work: Understanding the Football Program's Interests
When asked to describe a typical day during the football season, all of the participants used the word "work" to define the experience of being a college athlete

and to differentiate between high school and intercollegiate football in terms of athletic expectations and experiences. In fact, all of the participants reported that high school football was less structured than intercollegiate. In short, weight lifting, team practice, and team meetings composed the bulk of the participants' existence at the college level. When asked, "What does your morning consist of?" one participant remarked, "You have a 6:00 a.m. [weight] lift, which means you get up at 4:45 to get to the weight room by 5:00 a.m., because there is no telling what time the coaches are going to go in and check, [and] there is a 15-minute [late] rule. Then we go to class." When asked to distinguish the athletic experience at the collegiate level from the scholastic level, this individual stated that "in high school you practiced for two hours, and that was it. There wasn't film study, two-hour meetings before practice, meetings after practice and on weekends, like there is in college." The concept of work helps to debunk the widely held point of view that football college athletes in general, and African American college athletes in particular, receive preferential treatment because of their athletic status.

Work helped to contextualize the experience of the college athlete by giving the researcher an operational framework for thinking about how athletes and their lives are structured. Moreover, defining their involvement as work helped the college athletes to distinguish their experiences with major college football from those of traditional undergraduate students. Darryl explained the conundrum of being a scholarship college athlete:

> People wouldn't have jobs if it wasn't for college football, whether it's the stadium workers or the coaches. They have their jobs, because people come to see us play. People want to be entertained by us. It's hard not to think about football the majority of the time because it is our job. That's the reason why we are here. People like to say that I get a free education, [and] to an extent I do and to an extent I don't. I got to pay for it by putting the majority of my time in college football. The coaches tell us to put the majority of time in education, but it's not true. The majority of time goes to college football because you are making money for other people.

Darryl's comments bring to light an implicit and complex message regarding participation in college football at the FBS level. Although the message does not convey an explicit directive to deemphasize education in favor of athletics, having to fulfill duties uncommon at the secondary level, such as film study, extra practices, and conditioning, does convey the fact that football-related activities are the focal point of the college experience for the student-athlete.

Remaining Eligible

When I inquired about the issue of race in their collegiate experiences, participants acknowledged that it was a factor, but it was subtle. According to the participants, African American college athletes are encouraged more than their White counterparts to enroll in courses that are (1) more conducive to their athletic responsibilities, (2) intellectually less rigorous, and (3) divergent from personal and career interests. For instance, when I broached the topic of whether African American college athletes are steered toward courses they might not be interested in, Garland remarked that some of the academic advisors in athletics "don't care, the main reason we are here is to play football, they want us to be able to play. And if the academic advisors do not think a college athlete is going to do the work, they are going to put them in something so they can stay eligible. I think they [athletic advisors] want to see us succeed, but they usually have a college athlete take a class they know he can make it in, instead of trying to push him."

Julian, a senior, talked about how the culture of playing at a school with a strong football tradition, which his had, created a "system":

> The academic support staff [in the athletic department] has a system. They want what the coaches want. They know what they are doing. If we graduate, then it reflects positively on the head coach. He [head coach] has to say, "Get your degree," [but] the truth is he does not care what you get your degree in, the staff could care less. It is more for his job's sake that they preach graduating and things like that, because if he's not graduating athletes then that does not look good on him. He is doing what he has to do. He is a football coach first.

Julian's description of the influence the ethos of big-time college football has on the actions of some academic advisors also speaks to the experiences of the majority of participants at Big State University and Tech University.

CONCLUSION

This chapter presents a rich portrait of the educational experiences of African American males participating in college football at the FBS level. In doing so, it creates a conceptual space for rethinking the relationship between sports, educational opportunity, and academic achievement. Although the popular perception of intercollegiate athletics in the United States is that they foster higher academic aspirations and a positive self-conception, the empirical information presented in this chapter suggests otherwise. In fact, one might infer that, based on the accounts presented here, involvement in major college sports for the majority of African American male athletes is counterproductive for their educational interests.

Using critical race theory to understand the underlying motivations informing the academic choices of African American FBS athletes allows for a reevaluation of the factors informing their decisions. This approach includes viewing African American college athletes as active agents in the schooling process, which suggests that they not only have the capacity to make sense of their experience as a highly structured phenomenon but also to develop and implement strategies for their educational advancement. Unlike more conventional theories used to examine the impact of intercollegiate sports on college athletes, this study, through critical race theory, affirms their agency as a resource for making meaning of the interrelationship between educational opportunity, sports, and academic advancement.

In demonstrating how African American, male college athletes navigate their college experience, new epistemologies and ways of thinking about them and their experiences are constructed. Thus, what might be construed as a fixation on the athletic achievement of African American male college athletes who "select" a less rigorous major might instead be a reflection of the accumulated obstacles in their particular situation. Therefore, it is important that future analyses consider how academic choices are influenced by institutionalized practices that can create divergent experiences. For instance, one policy recommendation derived from this study is for universities to develop formal mentoring programs for African American college athletes with African American faculty on campus as means of checks and balances. In addition to serving as potential role models for the college athletes, African American faculty serving in this capacity can also serve as advocates for this traditionally marginalized student population.

A second policy and practice recommendation is requiring college athletes to declare an academic major at the beginning of their sophomore year in college. Currently, the NCAA requires college athletes to declare a major by their third year in college, which makes them susceptible to "choosing" academic majors based on the classes completed, instead of unobstructedly following an outlined programmatic or departmental sequence in advance. Thus, declaring a major early would require football college athletes and their academic advisors to plan sooner, rather than later, by organizing and identifying academic options in advance. Also, this would allow college athletes to develop a contingency plan in the event that they change their area of study, as most undergraduates do.

QUESTIONS FOR DISCUSSION

1. Should college athletes be required to have an academic advisor outside the athletic department?

2. Are FBS college athletes exploited with universities now covering the full cost of attendance?

3. Should first-year college athletes be prohibited from participating in sanctioned activities in order to develop a strong academic foundation and acclimate to the culture of FBS football?

Note

1. The names of the institutions discussed in this chapter are pseudonyms.

References

Bell, D. A. (1995). Who's afraid of critical race theory. *University of Illinois Law Review, 893.*

Benson, K. F. (2000). Constructing academic inadequacy: African American athletes' stories. *Journal of Higher Education, 71*(2), 233–246.

Berkowitz, S., Bohn, P., & Upton, J. (2007, December 4). Compensation for Division IA college football coaches. *USAToday.* Retrieved from http://www.usatoday.com/sports/graphics/coaches_contracts07/pdfs2007/georgia_fb.pdf

Bilberry, D. (2000). The myth of athletics and educational opportunity. In J. R. Gerdy (Ed.), *Sports in school: The future of an institution* (pp. 91–101). New York: Teachers College.

Brown, R. W. (1993). An estimate of the rent generated by a premium college football player. *Economic Inquiry, 31,* 671–684.

Comeaux, E., & Harrison, C. K. (2007). Faculty and male student-athletes: Racial differences in the environmental predictors of academic achievement. *Race, Ethnicity & Education, 10*(2), 199–214.

Crenshaw, K. W., Gotanda, N., Peller, G., & Thomas, K. (1995). Introduction. In K. W. Crenshaw, Gotanda, N., Peller, G., & Thomas, K. (Eds.), *Critical race theory: The key writings that formed the movement* (pp. xiii–xxxii). New York: New Press.

Donnor, J. K. (2005). Towards an interest-convergence in the education of African American football student athletes in major college sports. *Race, Ethnicity and Education, 8*(1), 45–67.

Early, G. (1998/2002). Performance and reality: Race, sports and the modern world. In P. J. Giddings (Ed.), *Burning all illusions: Writings from* The Nation *on race* (pp. 439–460). New York: Thunder's Mouth Press / Nation Books.

Edwards, H. (1984). The Black "dumb jock:" An American sports tragedy. *College Board Review* (131), 8–13.

Eitzen, D. S. (2001). Big-time college sports: Contradictions, crises, and consequences. In D. S. Eitzen (Ed.), *Sport in contemporary society: An Anthology* (6th ed., pp. 201–212). New York: Worth.

Eitzen, D. S., & Sage, G. H. (1997). *Sociology of North American sport* (6th ed.). Boston: WCB McGraw-Hill.

Gaston-Gayles, J. L. (2004, January/February). Examining academic and athletic motivation among student-athletes at a Division I University. *Journal of College Student Development 45*(1), 75–83.

Gragg, D. (2000). Race in athletics: Integration or isolation? In J. R. Gerdy (Ed.), *Sports in school: The future of an institution* (pp. 79–91). New York: Teachers College Press.

Guinier, L. (2004). From racial liberalism to racial literacy: *Brown v. Board of Education* and the interest-divergence dilemma. *Journal of American History, 91*(1). Retrieved August 8, 2007, from http://www.historycooperative.org

Haney López, I. (1996). White by law. *Critical race theory: The cutting edge.* New York: NYU Press (pp. 542–550).

Harris, O. (2000). African American predominance in sport. In D. Brooks, & Althouse, R. (Eds.), *Racism in college athletics: The African American athlete's experience* (pp. 37–52). Morgantown, WV: Fitness Information Technology.

Harrison, C. K. (2000). Black athletes at the millennium. *Society, 37*(3), 35–39.

Harrison, C. K., & Lawrence, S. M. (2003). African American student athletes' perception of career transition in sport: A qualitative and visual elicitation. *Race, Ethnicity and Education, 6*(4), 373–394.

Hartmann, D. (2000). Rethinking the relationships between sport and race in American culture: Golden ghettos and contested terrain. *Sociology of Sport Journal, 17,* 229–253.

Hoberman, J. (1997). *Darwin's athletes: How sport has damaged Black America and preserved the Myth of Race.* Boston: Houghton Mifflin.

Hughes, R. L., Satterfield, J., & Giles, M. S. (Fall 2007). Athletisizing Black male student-athletes: The social construction of race, sports, myths, and realities. *NASAP Journal.*

Ladson-Billings, G. (1998). Just what is critical race theory and what's it doing in a nice field like education? *Qualitative Studies in Education, 11*(1), 7–24.

Lapchick, R. (2008). Keeping score when it counts: Assessing the 2008–09 bowl-bound college teams—Academic performance improves but race still matters. Retrieved from http://www.tidesport.org

Lawrence, S. M. (2005). African American athletes' experiences of race in sport. *International Review for the Sociology of Sport, 40*(1), 99–110.

Matsuda, M. J., Lawrence III, C. R., Delgado, R., & Crenshaw, K. W. (1993). *Words that wound.* Boulder, CO: Westview Press.

Merriam, S. B. (1998). *Qualitative research and applications in education.* San Francisco: Jossey-Bass.

Olsen, J. (1968). *The black athlete: A shameful story: The myth of integration in American sport.* Time-Life Books.

Sammons, J. T. (1994). "Race" and sport: A critical, historical examination. *Journal of Sport History, 21*(3), 203–278.

Singer, J. N. (2005). Understanding racism through the eyes of African American male student-athletes. *Race, Ethnicity, and Education, 8*(4), 365–386.

Stake, R. E. (2000). Case studies. In N. K. Denzin, & Lincoln, Y. S. (Eds.). *Handbook of qualitative research* (pp. 435–454). Thousand Oaks, CA: Sage.

Tate, W. (2003). The "race" to theorize education: Who is my neighbor? *Qualitative Studies in Education, 16*(1), 121–126.

Valdes, F., Culp, J. M., & Harris, A. (2002). *Crossroads, directions and a new critical race theory.* Philadelphia: Temple University Press.

13

Athletic Scholarship Arrangement

Maximizing Educational Opportunities for Pacific Islanders in College Football

Keali'i Troy Kukahiko and Mitchell J. Chang

KEY TERMS

▶ Pacific Islanders

▶ One-year renewable contracts

▶ NCAA

▶ Retention

▶ Athletic scholarship

For a disproportionately high number of Pacific Islander (PI) males, playing football has provided a pathway into US higher education. Their growing participation by way of active recruitment into college football is associated with the rising prominence and visibility of PI professional athletes (Uperesa, Kukahiko, Wright, Markham, Roxbury, & Semaia, 2015). These players are regularly stereotyped by college football recruiters as being "genetically gifted, with size, girth, and quickness suitable for football, as well as with a violent impulse that can be channeled into success on the field" (Uperesa, 2014, p. 283). Besides gaining access to college, talented PI players are also seduced by playing at the professional level. Indeed, PIs are 56 times more likely to play professional football than players from any other racial background (Pelley, 2010; Uperesa & Mountjoy, 2014).

Gaining such educational opportunities through athletics is a double-edged sword. On the one hand, high interest in recruiting PI athletes to play college football provides both educational and professional opportunities that would not otherwise be available to those young men. On the other hand, it discourages PI males from pursuing traditional academic pathways into higher education, which subsequently constrains their career opportunities. According to Hokowhitu (2004), limiting educational pathways through athletics further positions PIs as eternal laborers in a neocolonial society.[1] While the bigger issue here is to expand and enhance multiple pathways for PIs into higher education, we recognize that an increasing number of them are entering colleges and universities through the athletic pipeline and will continue to do so into the foreseeable future (see, e.g., *In Football We Trust*).[2] Thus, the question for us is not whether we should restrict or confine this pathway but how to maximize the educational opportunities for PIs who enter such athletic arrangements.

Receiving an athletic scholarship to attend college can be very educationally rewarding for those recipients and perhaps should be, as their institutions also stand to benefit in stature from their athletic performance. The National Collegiate Athletic Association (NCAA, 2015) regularly celebrates the fact that college athletes typically graduate at higher rates than their peers. This rosy academic picture, however, does not apply for PIs who play college football, as they are among the least likely of any group to receive an undergraduate degree (NCAA, 2015; US Department of Education, 2013). Why? This chapter examines one major impediment for PIs, which compromises the educational opportunity of receiving a football scholarship. We then offer suggestions on how to address this impediment and improve college athletic opportunities for PIs to advance their degree attainment.

THE EVOLUTION OF ATHLETIC SCHOLARSHIPS

Curiously, athletic scholarships were initially designed to discourage "the offering of inducements to players to enter colleges and universities because of their athletic abilities or maintaining players while students on account of their athletic abilities, either by athletic organizations, individual alumni, or otherwise directly or indirectly" (NCAA, 1906, p. 4). Because the NCAA's previous guidelines to protect amateurism were being widely violated through a range of surreptitious means, Byers (1995) notes, the NCAA approved in 1956 the offering of athletic scholarships to cover commonly accepted educational expenses. Yet in doing this, the NCAA was concerned that athletic scholarships might constitute a "pay for play" arrangement, which would expose its membership to worker's compensation claims. To avoid such problems, Byers (1995) maintains, the NCAA mandated that financial aid be awarded for four years and not be "reduced (gradated) or canceled on the basis of an athlete's contribution to team success, injury, or decision not to participate" (p. 75). By requiring four-year support, the NCAA hoped that a scholarship would be perceived as a gift to further an athlete's education rather than as a contractual quid pro quo (Barnes, 1964).

In 1973, however, the NCAA made a total break from its original four-year scholarship model and allowed athletic scholarships to be renewable on an annual basis. This shift enabled the cancelation of an athlete's scholarship at the end of one year for virtually any reason, including injury, lack of contribution to team success, the need to make room for a more talented recruit, or failure to fit into a coach's style of play (Byers, 1995; Sack & Staurowsky, 1998; Yasser, 2012). Shifting to one-year "athletic scholarships" also gave coaches greater control over their players, mimicking the power dynamics of an employment contract. For football players, it created greater pressure to provide immediate returns on the financial investments made by their football programs by excelling on the field or risk having their enrollment and financial support terminated (McCormick & McCormick, 2006).

In 2012, the NCAA "revived" the multiyear scholarship (Sack, McComas, & Cakan, 2014).[3] It is important to note, however, that multiyear scholarships were revived, not reinstituted, which would have made it mandatory for NCAA member institutions to provide four-year guaranteed scholarships. Multiyear scholarships[4] were simply made available for member institutions to use at their discretion, making them the exception, not the standard. Kukahiko (2015b) suggests that even though multiyear scholarships have been made available, a majority of NCAA member institutions continue to favor one-year renewable scholarships. Sack, McComas, and Cakan (2014) explain that one-year renewable contracts are not simply cost containment strategies, but they give coaches control over their players like employers have over their employees.

IMPACT ON PACIFIC ISLANDERS

The shift away from guaranteeing four-year scholarships continues to have disparate impact on college football players. In 2012, for example, 55 percent of college football players were college athletes of Color. This population of players is made even more vulnerable by the racial imbalance among the coaching staff: 89 percent of the head football coaches, 84 percent of offensive/defensive coordinators, and 77 percent of assistant football coaches in 2012 were white. Climbing further up on the food chain, we find in 2012 that whites also made up 87.5 percent of college athletic directors, 100 percent of all conference commissioners, and 90 percent of those who sit on the NCAA Division I Board of Directors (Lapchick, 2012). Such a "White-topped racial hierarchy," Ulluci and Battey (2011) argue, is likely to reinforce culture and color blindness that make invisible the negative impact of one-year renewable contracts on college athletes of Color. While the problems with such athletic scholarships for PI college football players may not get the attention they deserve, the issues are becoming increasingly more pressing, and we highlight below two major ones.

First, one-year renewable contracts tend to be misleading, and many PI athletes do not fully grasp their implications, nor can they anticipate how such limitations will affect their academic success. One of the authors of this chapter recently interviewed current and past PI college football players (Kukahiko, 2015a). Below are two excerpts from those interviews:

> When I entered college football in 1974, I didn't know I was on a 1-year scholarship. When I was recruited they told me I would be receiving a full scholarship, and I assumed that meant for the duration of the 4 to 5 years needed for me to get my degree. Given the low graduation rates of our PI college football players, it is a crime that these are sold to our communities as full scholarships. It's fraud and outright exploitation. —Jack Thompson[5]

Most players aren't educated that scholarships are 1-year scholarships. Most of us just sign the scholarship paper, not knowing that it's only for a year . . . As a freshman you don't really care about things like this, but as you get older these things become important. Because if you're not performing, or not getting along with the coaches, that scholarship could be gone the next year.
—Tongan college football player

Based on his interviews, Kukahiko concluded that "full" athletic scholarships can be easily misrepresented as "education for play" with long-term support but are actually only one-year contracts with no guarantee of renewal. Even if recruiters and coaches were to honestly represent those offers, another problem that Kukahiko notes is that they may be dealing with recruits from economically vulnerable and poorly informed communities, who cannot anticipate the long-term implications of those scholarship limitations and have few other educational options. Such conditions place PI football players at great risk, because when they arrive on campus, it becomes increasingly clear to them that the priority is to improve "play" and not to improve their "education," which subsequently decreases their chances for academic success.

Indeed, a major problem with one-year renewable contracts is that this arrangement has not consistently enabled PI football players to leverage their athletic scholarships in ways that enable them to graduate from college. This problem is most apparent when PI college athletes who play in Division I college football programs are further disaggregated. In 1978, the NCAA split Division I football into two divisions: the I-A level, which is now the Football Bowl Subdivision (FBS), and I-AA, which is the Football Championship Subdivision (FCS). The FBS consists of 128 teams and allows a maximum of 85 full athletic scholarships per team, whereas the FCS consists of 124 teams and allows a maximum of 63 full athletic scholarships per team. The FBS is considered the more competitive and higher-revenue division of the two, and the FBS teams are eligible to play in the annual College Football Playoffs, for the National Championship.

Table 13.1 shows the four-year graduation rate (or on-time graduation rate) for different groups of students who entered college in 2007.[6] Specifically, this table compares the percentage of students who graduate within four years of starting college by ethnicity and by football divisions. Looking across those divisions, we see that PIs are significantly less likely to receive a degree in four years if they play in the FCS, with only an alarming 17 percent graduating within that time frame. This rate is three times lower than their football counterparts within the FCS, with the next lowest rate at 52 percent for African Americans. While PIs fare better in the FBS—60 percent graduate in four years—they still do worse than their Latino (69 percent) and white (70 percent) counterparts. The rates tend to be generally more consistent both within and across divisions for other groups of players. Overall, PI athletes have not leveraged their participation in college football into

TABLE 13.1.

Four-Year "On-time" Graduation Rates of 2007
Freshman Cohort by Ethnicity and Football Division

| | Percentage graduating in four years | |
Ethnic group	College football players in FCS	College football players in FBS
Pacific Islander	17	60
Latino	56	69
African American	52	53
White	64	70

Source: NCAA (2015).

the same rate of academic success as their counterparts, although the rates for those in FBS programs are encouraging. Most troubling, PIs who play in the FCS are the least likely of any group of Division I football players to graduate within four years.

Given that one-year renewable contracts can be very misleading and that such arrangements do not consistently contribute to degree attainment for PI college football players, we offer suggestions in the next section for improving the application of athletic scholarships to maximize educational opportunities for PIs.

MOVING FORWARD

Although the current athletic scholarship arrangement for PI football players is not the only problem that impedes their capacity to maximize their educational opportunities, eliminating one-year renewals is a good starting point, because its alternatives have the potential to enhance other areas that contribute to academic success. Therefore, our first recommendation would be to transition the one-year renewable contracts to guaranteed four-year scholarships. Since the current multiyear scholarships can be rescinded if a player becomes ineligible or quits the team for personal reasons (NCAA, 2016), a guaranteed four-year scholarship would mean that, even if a player becomes ineligible or quits the team, the player has a guaranteed four years to complete his degree. This is important because (1) many football players are strategically recruited to elite universities that would not otherwise admit them due to GPA requirements (Go, 2008; Lederman, 2008), (2) the *O'Bannon v. NAACP* case originally ruled that athletes will only receive compensation for the use of their likenesses as trusts upon successful college graduation, and (3) the institutions are more likely to accommodate cultural aspects of learning to improve transition and retention if policies made it more difficult to redistribute athletic scholarships. These guaranteed four-year scholarship contracts should include living stipends (Boren, 2014; Hruby, 2014) and extended medical care after graduation for injuries that necessitate long-term care. To improve academic success, we would also add other institutional provisions that support PI students' academic achievement as identified by one of the authors (Kukahiko, 2015a), which include (1) ensuring that the sport work-load does not overwhelm and dominate the college experience, so that college athletes maintain focus on academics and on-time graduation; (2) hiring institutional agents (staff, faculty, administrators, etc.) who can provide culturally relevant curriculum and programs (i.e., Polynesian studies, critical service learning courses, internships, etc.) that assist PIs with transition, persistence, degree attainment, and matriculation to graduate school; and (3) use the four-year on-time graduation rate as the standard measure for degree attainment.[7]

We are not naïve, and we fully understand that the recommendation to eliminate one-year renewable contracts for guaranteed four-year scholarships with expanded benefits are meaningless unless organizations recognize that the system is broken and are committed to either fixing or transforming it. One pivotal organization that can realize broad-level change is the NCAA, yet making such moves may run up against its competing interests. Economists often refer to the NCAA as the joint marketing organization designed to advance the economic interests of its membership schools (DeBrock & Hendricks, 1996). For example, the NCAA has brokered television rights and shared in the billions of dollars of revenue that has created the industry that is now college athletics. In 2014 alone, the NCAA made nearly $1 billion, with $80.5 million in surplus, which was $20 million more than what it made in 2013 (Berkowitz, 2014). Why would such a powerful and profitable conglomerate want to change its current practices? Although the NCAA has governed college athletics for over 100 years, it is now under a great deal of scrutiny and pressure that threaten its very existence. We will point to three trends that have already changed how the NCAA operates and may well determine its future.

On August 8, 2014, the federal courts ruled against the NCAA in *O'Bannon v. NCAA*. The plaintiff charged that the NCAA and its institutional members violated antitrust laws by profiting from college athletes' images and likenesses in perpetuity, while placing a ceiling for their compensation at zero dollars (Holthaus, 2011). This ruling would have allowed college athletes to share in broadcasting revenue, approximately $16 billion in 2014, for the use of their names and likenesses (Gallo, 2014). Per the court decision the compensation would have been paid out as trusts when players graduate, but in the fall of 2015 the Ninth Circuit Court of Appeals overruled the US District Judge Claudia Wilken's decision to pay college athletes up to $5,000 annually (Solomon, 2016). At the same time, however, the Court of Appeals upheld the decision that NCAA rules restricting payments to players violate antitrust laws, a decision that currently enables NCAA members to pay "cost of attendance stipends" to college athletes, since they are tied to education. The *O'Bannon* plaintiffs have submitted their case to the US Supreme Court, and the case continues to raise many questions about how the NCAA operates and its obligations to athletes. Until those questions are settled, we will likely see more legal challenges that can potentially unsettle the NCAA's authority and oversight.

Additionally, college athletes are not passively waiting on the sidelines for the NCAA to improve their circumstances, and some have organized to pursue collective bargaining. On March 26, 2014, the National Labor Relations Board (NLRB) in Chicago ruled that the Northwestern football team could unionize, a ruling that was overturned by its full board in August of 2015. Interestingly, the NLRB did not state in its overruling decision that players are not employees, and this opens the door for future petitions by college players (Strauss, 2015). Any future success by labor unions in reclassifying college athletes as employees rather than students (McCormick & McCormick, 2006) could undermine the oversight of the NCAA, since it governs *student* athletics. Thus, more widespread efforts to unionize will force the NCAA to improve circumstances for college players, or the organization risks becoming irrelevant.

Lastly, the top five college football conferences, also known as the Power Five, have already formed self-governing structures that can fill the managing and governing roles that the NCAA currently plays (Solomon, 2014). Those institutional members of the Power Five belong to the most profitable athletic conferences, and perhaps anticipating the decline of the NCAA, they developed the capacity to create their own rules and regulations. If more of the decision making shifts over to the Power Five and other NCAA member institutions follow their lead or organize their own governing bodies, this trend will greatly diminish the capacity of the NCAA. So, the NCAA is under increasing pressure to take a stronger stance on key collegiate athletics issues or concede its leadership to other forms of oversight.

While these trends point to the vulnerability of the NCAA's future, it is unclear if and how they will support and enhance college players' experiences and success in higher education (Boren, 2014; McCann, 2014), particularly for PIs. The Power Five conferences have begun to advocate for policies aimed at providing more support and resources to college athletes, including transitioning to multiyear scholarships. Although some might suggest that the NCAA should make this the standard, not the exception, many institutions within non–Power Five conferences claim they lack the revenue to provide multiyear scholarships at parity with top revenue-generating college football programs. Certainly what constitutes a "scholarship" would change considerably if college athletes were to be reclassified as employees, altering the meaning of a college athlete. Whatever the case, the NCAA is now under greater pressure to change the way it operates and is being forced to pay more attention and respond to the welfare of college athletes.

CONCLUSION

I think that the NCAA has rules and regulations that capitalize on these athletes while giving them the bare minimum of an education. The "take" is far more than the give.

Tony Vainuku, Director of *In Football We Trust*

A popular story consistently told about athletic scholarships is one in which the main actors are the philanthropist (the institution) and the pauper (the college player). Here, college athletes are cast as the sole beneficiary of such scholarships, but the transition away from four-year scholarships approved by the NCAA in 1973 stain that characterization. Moreover, some institutions have actually profited handsomely from participating in revenue-generating sports such as football. PI athletes have not leveraged their participation in college football with the same rate of academic success as their counterparts. In fact, those PIs who play for a set of 124 football programs that make up the FCS are at least three times less likely to graduate in four years than any other group of Division I football players. Given that an alarmingly large number of PI players do not earn a degree, it is especially disingenuous to cast those athletes as the sole, or even primary, beneficiaries of athletic scholarships.

Even harsher criticisms have been leveled on this athletic pathway into higher education for PIs. They include the charge that the treatment of PIs in college football is a form of colonization and exploitation of PI communities (Grainger, 2006; Hokowhitu, 2004; Ulluci & Battey, 2011) because those football programs are nearly always overseen by an all-white leadership and tend to (1) treat PIs as if they were natural resources, (2) exercise ownership of those resources by profiting from their names and likenesses in perpetuity, (3) discard those resources with impunity, and (4) employ education as a mechanism to assimilate PIs. Because many PI males still view football as one of the few options to improve their life circumstances, they are especially vulnerable to being exploited in this system. Although the above criticisms cast an especially dark shadow on college football, they will gain even more traction if athletic programs fail to improve the educational opportunities for PI athletes, especially those who play for one of those FCS football programs.

To maximize athletic scholarships as educational opportunities, we recommend the elimination of one-year renewable contracts that have defined "athletic scholarships" for 40 years. In their place, we recommend an expanded guaranteed four-year scholarship, which would enhance the academic success of college athletes and provide a socially just framework to realize any financial compensation available to them per the trusts set up by the *O'Bannon* decision. While this would not necessarily address important campus cultural issues (Chang, 2000; Chang, Milem, & Antonio, 2011) that can derail PI students' academic goals, elevating support through scholarship is a good starting place to begin improving educational success for those students. We are optimistic that athletic scholarships can be leveraged in ways that provide fulfilling educational experiences that can advance the circumstances of our nation's most vulnerable populations, who would not otherwise have the opportunity to obtain a four-year college degree. Certainly, the four-year degree attainment rates for PIs in FBS football programs are encouraging. Those players, however, are in programs that have higher profiles and generate more revenue than FCS programs, which might subsequently afford FBS players better academic support. Still, the four-year attainment rates for PI players in FBS programs lag behind their white and Latino counterparts, and 40 percent of them are still failing to obtain their undergraduate degrees in four years. Taken all together, the problems for PI athletes highlighted in this chapter amplify the charges that the college football system is deeply flawed and instead of helping the most vulnerable, it appears to be further exploiting them for the interests of the most powerful.

QUESTIONS FOR DISCUSSION

1. Considering that a majority of college football players are student-athletes of Color, how do one-year renewable scholarships maintain the white hegemonic leadership of US higher education? Or inhibit their professional matriculation within the academy?

2. What is the purpose of one-year renewable athletic scholarships, and whose interests do they serve?

3. How does policy influence the interpretation of college football players as students or employees, and how does this impact their ability to leverage "access" to higher education?

Notes

1. Hokowhitu (2004) argues that the characterization of the PI identity as "the natural sportsman" who is inherently physical and academically inept is a dominant discourse "constructed to limit, homogenize, and reproduce an acceptable and imagined" Polynesian masculinity, one that is rooted in the colonial context and meant to be internalized by the colonized to solidify the working caste (p. 262).

2. Tony Vainuku directed the movie *In Football We Trust,* which debuted at the 2015 Sundance Film Festival. Mr. Vainuku explained to one of the authors of this chapter that the movie was intended to tell a story about the challenges of Polynesian immigrants in the United States who pursue football as a "way out."

3. The NCAA Board of Directors' decision to revive the multiyear scholarship was nearly overruled by an online referendum. Of the 330 NCAA members, 62.12 percent voted to override the legislation, "falling just short of the 62.5 percent majority needed to kill the legislation" (Sack, McComas, & Cakan, 2014, p. 210).

4. It should be noted that a multiyear scholarship can be rescinded if a player becomes ineligible, commits fraud or misconduct, or quits football for personal reasons.

5. Jack Thompson was nicknamed the Throw'n Samoan, and until the 2015 NFL draft, was the highest drafted PI in NFL history (he is now the fourth). Washington State has only retired two jerseys in its entire history as a football program. Jack Thompson's was one of them. He is now a successful businessman who also coaches and mentors youth in the PI community.

6. Although the NCAA favors using six-year rates to measure "Graduation Success," we report four-year rates because they more closely mirror the terms of athletic aid (or scholarship options). Beyond four years, those student athletes are at greater financial and academic risk.

7. While the NCAA's Academic Success Rate (ASR) calculates graduation of college athletes who transfer out of their original institutions within six years, this methodology attributes the academic success, or degree completion, to the original institution, and does not hold those institutions accountable for improving transition and persistence of their own athletes.

References

Barnes, E. D. (1964). Letter to Walter Byers, 6 July 1964, Walter Byers Papers, Workman Compensation Folder, NCAA Headquarters, Overland Park, Kansas.

Berkowitz, S. (2014, March 11). NCAA nearly topped $1 billion in revenue in 2014. *USA Today*. Retrieved from http://www.usatoday.com/story/sports/college/2015/03/11/ncaa-financial-statement-2014-1-billion-revenue/70161386/

Boren, C. (2014). Five key things to know about O'Bannon vs. NCAA. *Washington Post*. Retrieved from http://www.washingtonpost.com/blogs/early-lead/wp/2014/08/09/five-key-things-to-know-about-obannon-vs-ncaa/

Byers, W. (1995). *Unsportsmanlike conduct: Exploiting college athletes*. Ann Arbor: University of Michigan Press.

Chang, M. J. (2000). Improving campus racial dynamics: A balancing act among competing interests. *Review of Higher Education, 23*(2), 153–175.

Chang, M. J., Milem, J. F., & Antonio, A. L. (2011). Campus climate and diversity. In S. R. Harper & J. Schuh (Eds.), *Student services: A handbook for the profession* (5th ed.). San Francisco, CA: Jossey-Bass.

DeBrock, L., & Hendricks, W. (1996). Roll call voting in the NCAA. *Journal of Law, Economics, and Organization, 12*(2), 497–517.

Gallo, K. (2014). *College athletes win piece of $800 million NCAA broadcast revenue*. *Newsmax*. Retrieved from http://www.newsmax.com/US/NCAA-court-ruling-paid-athletes/2014/08/08/id/587808/

Go, A. (2008, December 30). Athletes show huge gaps in SAT scores. US News. Retrieved from http://www.usnews.com/education/blogs/paper-trail/2008/12/30/athletes-show-huge-gaps-in-sat-scores

Grainger, A. (2006). From immigrant to overstayer: Samoan identity, rugby, and cultural politics of race and nation in Aotearoa / New Zealand. *Journal of Sport & Social Issues, 30*(1), 45–61.

Hokowhitu, B. (2004). Tackling Maori masculinity: A colonial genealogy of savagery and sport. *Contemporary Pacific, 16*(2), 259–284.

Holthaus, W. (2011). Ed O'Bannon v. NCAA: Do former NCAA athletes have a case against the NCAA for its use of their likenesses? *Saint Louis University School of Law Journal, 55*, 369–394.

Hruby, P. (2014, January 27). The ulterior motives behind four-year scholarships. *Sports on Earth*. Retrieved from http://www.sportsonearth.com/article/81801184/why-schools-suddenly-support-four-year-scholarships-for-college-athletes

Kukahiko, K. T. (2015a). Racial diversity deficit in college football: Fixing the pipeline. *Journal of Critical Race Inquiry, 2*(2), 25–53.

Kukahiko, K. T. (2015b, May). Pacific Islanders in college football: Exploitation of brown bodies as natural resources. Paper presented at Coral Bell School of Asia Pacific Affairs Series. Australian National University, Canberra.

Lapchick, R. L. (2012). Mixed progress throughout collegiate athletic leadership: Assessing diversity among campus and conference leaders for Football Bowl Subdivision (FBS) schools in the 2012–13 academic year. Informally published manuscript, College of Business Administration, University of Central Florida, Orlando. Retrieved from http://www.tidesport.org/RGRC/2012/2012_D1_Leadership_Report.pdf

Lederman, D. (2008, December 29). The admissions gap for big-time athletes. *Inside Higher Ed*. Retrieved from https://www.insidehighered.com/news/2008/12/29/admit

McCann, M. (2014, August 9). What the NCAA's loss in court means moving forward. *Sports Illustrated*. Retrieved from http://www.si.com/college-basketball/2014/08/09/ed-obannon-ncaa-claudia-wilken-appeal-name-image-likeness-rights

McCormick, R. A., & McCormick, A. C. (2006). The myth of the student-athlete: The college athlete as employee. *Washington Law Review, 8*, 71–157.

NCAA. (1906). Formerly the Intercollegiate Association of the United States. Proceedings of the First Annual Convention, 29 November 1906, p. 4.

NCAA. (2015). Diversity research. Retrieved from http://www.ncaa.org/about/frequently-asked-questions-about-ncaa#schola

NCAA. (2016). Frequently asked questions about the NCAA: Scholarships. Retrieved from http://www.ncaa.org/about/frequently-asked-questions-about-ncaa#schola

Pelley, S. (2010, January 14). American Samoa: Football Island. *60 Minutes*, CBS.

Sack, A. L., McComas, A. E., & Cakan, E. (2014). The revival of multiyear scholarships in the twenty-first century: Which universities supported and opposed this legislation and why? *Journal of Issues in Intercollegiate Athletics, 7*, 207–223.

Sack, A. L., & Staurowsky, E. J. (1998). *College athletes for hire: The evolution and legacy of the NCAA's amateur myth*. Westport, CT: Praeger.

Smith, J. M., & Willingham, M. (2015). *Cheated: The UNC scandal, the education of athletes, and the future of big-time college sports*. Lincoln: University of Nebraska Press.

Solomon, J. (2014, August 7). NCAA adopts new Division I model giving Power 5 autonomy. *CBS Sports*. Retrieved from http://mweb.cbssports.com/ncaaf/writer/jon-solomon/24651709/ncaa-adopts-new-division-i-model-giving-power-5-autonomy

Solomon, J. (2016, March 15). Ed O'Bannon plaintiffs ask Supreme Court to take NCAA case. CBS Sports. Retrieved from http://www.cbssports.com/college-football/news/ed-obannon-plaintiffs-ask-supreme-court-to-take-ncaa-case/

Strauss, B. (2015, August 17). N.L.R.B. rejects Northwestern football players' union bid. *New York Times*.

Ullucci, K., & Battey, D. (2011). Exposing color blindness/grounding color consciousness: Challenges for teacher education. *Urban Education*. doi: 10.1177/0042085911413150

Uperesa, F. L. (2014). Fabled futures: Migration and mobility for Samoans in American football. *Contemporary Pacific, 26*(2), 281–301.

Uperesa, F. L., Kukahiko, T. K., Wright, E. K., Markham, J. K., Roxbury, T., & Semaia, P. (2015). Addressing hyper/in-visibility: Preliminary research with Pacific Islander student-athletes." *Amerasia,* Special Issue: Sport in Asian America, Rachael Joo and Sameer Pandya (Eds.).

Uperesa, F. L., & Mountjoy, T. (2014). Global sport in the Pacific: A brief overview. *Contemporary Pacific, 26*(2), 263–279.

US Department of Education, National Center for Education Statistics. (2013). *Digest of Education Statistics.* Table 326.10. Retrieve from http://nces.ed.gov/programs/digest /d14/tables/dt14_326.10.asp

Yasser, R. (2012). Case for reviving the four-year deal, *Tulsa Law Review, 86,* 987–1016.

14

Intervention Strategies for Improving College Athletes' Academic and Personal Development Outcomes at Historically Black Colleges and Universities

Joseph N. Cooper and Eddie Comeaux

A critical examination of the structure and outcomes (both athletic and academic) associated with intercollegiate athletic programs in the United States

KEY TERMS

▶ Historically Black colleges and universities

▶ College athletes

▶ Educational equity

▶ Excellence Beyond Athletics

▶ Model

▶ Career Transition Scorecard

reveals widespread inequities along racial lines, which are also prevalent in society at large (Cooper, Cavil, & Cheeks, 2014). More specifically, within the National Collegiate Athletic Association (NCAA), the largest and most recognizable governing body of intercollegiate athletics in the United States, there has been persistent Graduation Success Rate[1] (GSR) and Academic Progress Rate[2] (APR) gaps between historically Black colleges/universities (HBCUs) and historically White colleges/universities (HWCUs). For example, despite constituting less than 7 percent of all NCAA member institutions, HBCUs accounted for nearly two-thirds (10 out of 16) of the schools that received postseason bans for the 2015–16 season due to low academic performance in accordance with NCAA metrics (Grasgreen, 2013). Unfortunately, these disturbing trends are not a recent phenomenon. Ever since the NCAA implemented its academic performance program in 2003, HBCUs have been disparately impacted. In 2007 (one of the first years the NCAA began issuing penalties for low APRs), HBCUs accounted for 13 percent of the schools penalized for low APRs despite only constituting roughly 6 percent of all NCAA Division I institutions (Associated Press, 2007). A widely cited reason for HBCUs' underperformance based on NCAA academic standards is the lack of financial resources associated with these institutions (Cooper et al., 2014; Hosick, 2011; Johnson, 2013; Lillig, 2009).[3] Although, financial resources are one major factor associated with these trends, there are additional areas of improvement at HBCUs that should also be addressed. In the next section, the authors highlight a brief literature review on college athletes at HBCUs specifically related to professional sport aspirations, time spent on athletics, and related support programs at these institutions. Following this section, the authors explicate the need for innovative intervention strategies at HBCUs and propose two models for college athletes' academic and personal development.

LITERATURE REVIEW

Despite the fact that HBCUs possess fewer resources than many of their HWCU counterparts, research on HBCUs has found the athletic programs and college athletes at these institutions encounter similar challenges in balancing competitive athletic interests with college athletes' academic and holistic development outcomes. As previously mentioned, HBCUs consistently graduate their college athletes at lower rates than HWCUs within the same athletic classification (Hosick, 2011). Although, limited resources have been cited as the primary reason for these lower academic outcomes, there is some research to suggest additional areas of improvement are needed to shift the focus from athletic success to a more academic-focused and culturally responsive intercollegiate athletic culture (Charlton, 2011; Cooper, 2013). For example, Sellers and Kuperminc (1997) found that college athletes at Division I HBCUs who were nontraveling members of their athletic teams were more likely to report professional sport aspirations than their peers at Division I HWCUs. The authors described this occurrence as goal discrepancy, whereby individuals possess strong professional sport aspirations that are not consistent with their current status/positions on their athletic teams. Along the same lines, in a mixed-methods study at a Division II HBCU, Cooper and Hawkins (2012) found that over half of the survey participants (27 out of 48; 56.3 percent) and all seven of the focus group participants (three football and four men's basketball players) cited attending a Division I HWCU as their primary college choice prior to college enrollment. The authors surmised that the increased exposure and resources associated with Division I HWCUs, as well as the related possibilities of pursuing a professional sports career in the National Football League (NFL) or National Basketball Association (NBA) by attending these institutions, served as motivating factors for these Black, male college athletes. Within the same study, all seven of the focus group participants cited pursuing a professional sport career as a viable occupational path for them despite the reality that less than 1 percent of all college athletes will achieve this feat (Cooper & Hawkins, 2012; Sailes, 1998). Both the aforementioned studies underscore the reality that many college athletes who attend HBCUs are not immune to the myopic focus on professional sport career attainment, which is particularly problematic, because it can lead to negative transitional outcomes after their athletic careers are over (e.g., identity foreclosure, depression, resentment, unemployment, etc.) (Edwards, 2000).

In a related vein, many HBCUs who are members of the NCAA's Division I and II are susceptible to engaging in practices that prioritize academics over athletics, like their HWCU counterparts (Gawrysiak, Cooper, & Hawkins, 2013; Lillig, 2009). For example, Lillig (2009) outlined how many Division I HBCUs participate in guarantee games with larger, more well-funded Division I HWCUs in order to receive large payouts. Guarantee games are "nonconference matches, usually between high-profile, high-ranking Division I schools from BCS [Bowl Championship Series] conferences and low-profile, low-ranking schools from non-BCS conferences" (Lillig, 2009, p. 46). The fact that these games usually result in embarrassing losses for HBCUs reflects the extent to which athletic revenue generation is prioritized at the expense of institutional reputation and college athletes' psychosocial well-being. Aside from these games, some HBCUs like their HWCU peer institutions require their college athletes to spend extensive amounts of time on their sport to the detriment of their academic performance. For example, Gawrysiak et al. (2013) found that Black baseball athletes at two Division II HBCUs expressed how their intercollegiate athletic participation generated both benefits and detriments for them in terms of attaining their overall educational goals. Among the detriments cited were a lack of free time and energy due to the significant time commitments associated with being a college athlete. Consequently, this time spent on athletics minimized the time and energy they could put forth toward their academics or participation in educationally purposeful activities aside from athletics. The fact that these findings were identified at Division II HBCUs further illustrated how the emphasis on athletics is not limited to the Division I level or only to athletically competitive HWCUs.

In spite of the aforementioned trends, previous research has also found that HBCUs excel at cultivating positive academic support programs through partnerships with campus-wide retention efforts that enhance the academic performance and personal development of its college athletes (Charlton, 2011; Cooper, 2013; Cooper & Hawkins, 2012; Person & LeNoir, 1997). More specifically, Cooper (2015a) outlined five key components of effective support programs at HBCUs: (1) early intervention programs, (2) purposefully designed study halls, (3) institution-wide academic support services, (4) public recognition of college athletes' academic achievement, and (5) nurturing familial campus climates. Despite the presence of strong support programs at HBCUs, the attrition rates of college athletes at these institutions remain an alarming issue (Hosick, 2011). Thus, in an effort to build on current support programs and address the issues of poor academic outcomes and the broader trend of athletic success over academic and personal development (Lillig, 2009), the authors offer two models for college athletes' holistic development that seek to bridge the gap between theory and practice. Both the Excellence Beyond Athletics model (Cooper, 2015b) and the Career Transition Scorecard (Comeaux, 2013, 2015) are grounded in data-driven research on college athletes. It is our hope that the adoption of these models and appropriate modification for each institutional culture at HBCUs could lead to improved academic, psychosocial, and postcollege career outcomes for college athletes at these institutions.

EXCELLENCE BEYOND ATHLETICS MODEL

The Excellence Beyond Athletics (EBA) model is a comprehensive holistic development strategy designed to empower Black college athletes[4] as they navigate a society, athletic spaces, and educational contexts that often marginalize them (Cooper, 2015b). Influenced by previous models on college student development, college athlete academic success, and African American cultural values, experiences, and identity development, the EBA approach serves as a data-driven and culturally responsive model for fostering positive developmental outcomes for Black college athletes (figure 14.1). The EBA approach is particularly appropriate for HBCUs because it centralizes racial and cultural empowerment and emphasizes the role of institutional and community partnerships in enhancing college athletes' developmental outcomes. The purpose of the EBA approach is to empower, educate, and inspire Black college athletes to maximize their full potential as holistic individuals both within and beyond athletic contexts. The key components of the EBA approach include the following six holistic development principles (HDPs): (1) self-identity awareness, (2) positive social engagement, (3) active mentorship, (4) academic achievement, (5) career aspirations, and (6) effective time management skills.

The EBA approach posits that holistic self-identity awareness is integral to combat the threat of athletic role engulfment and underpreparation for life after athletic careers come to an end. Specific exercises that HBCUs should consider incorporating within their college athlete support programs include the writing of personal mission statements and core values, self-identity awareness assessments (e.g., personality, values, and skills), and critical reflexive group discussion sessions. Personal mission statements could be written and discussed with an academic counselor on a semester by semester basis and include information regarding the college athletes' personal goals, values, and beliefs. An emphasis on goals both within and beyond sport should be encouraged. Self-identity assessments could be coordinated with career development services on campus to enable college athletes to explore their multiple identities and identify areas of interest they possess that they may not have previously explored.

Figure 14.1. Excellence Beyond Athletics (EBA)

Culturally relevant group discussions could include: small groups of college athletes focused on topics related to self-identity perceptions and salience (e.g., race, gender, athletic identity, etc.); behaviors related to fostering the growth of these various identities; photo elicitation activities to explore the presence, impact, and productive responsiveness to stereotypes associated with their race (i.e., Black) and institutional affiliation (i.e., HBCUs) (Comeaux, 2010a); and personal brand management strategies. Within these activities, concepts such as racial microaggressions (Sue et al., 2007), critical race theory (Crenshaw, Gotanda, Peller, & Thomas, 1995), and community cultural wealth (Yosso, 2005) could be introduced to expand college athletes' lexicon around their experiences within society and more specifically the significance of their presence as students at an HBCU in a US culture that privileges Whiteness and devalues Blackness. The EBA approach posits that enhancing Black college athletes' holistic consciousness, internalized empowerment, and engagement in counteractions is pivotal to their personal development and life after college (Cooper & Cooper, 2015). More specifically, the self-identity awareness HDP requires Black college athletes to understand the historic legacy of HBCUs and how their enrollment, performance in college, and subsequent career outcomes are deeply connected to the collective uplift of the Black community.

The second HDP associated with the EBA approach is positive social engagement. This involves Black college athletes' active involvement in student organizations that perform community outreach in communities of color. Outreach activities could include mentoring, tutoring, general volunteering, physical fitness/sport tasks, clothing/food drives, and many other related endeavors. The underlying purpose behind this culturally relevant strategy would be to increase the social ties between Black college athletes, HBCUs, and local Black communities. In addition, their increased involvement with organizations aside from athletics could foster stronger and more positive relationships with non-athlete peers.

The third HDP of the EBA approach is active mentorship. The EBA approach recommends the establishment of a formal faculty–college athlete mentorship program. Within these routine meetings, topics such as holistic identities, goal setting and attainment, productive responses to negative stereotypes, and positive coping skills could be discussed. In addition to this formal mentorship program, HBCUs should consider formalizing a constellation mentoring program (Kelly & Dixon, 2014), whereby college athletes identify a range of individuals on and off campus who can assist them with their various needs, including psychosocial well-being, career advancement, relationship development, academic achievement, and so on. According to Kelly and Dixon (2014), constellation mentoring asserts that multiple mentors are more beneficial than a single mentor. Hence, formalizing the "village" culture at HBCUs could bode well for Black college athletes' holistic development and postcollege career preparation.

The fourth HDP of the EBA approach is academic achievement. Within the EBA approach, comprehensive retention models that operate year-round and have oversight by a group of faculty, administrators, student affairs personnel, and psychological services staff should be considered (Person & Lenoir, 1997). Core areas of focus should include precollege transition assistance, intense academic support throughout the year, graduate school workshops, career development activities, and counseling services. A culturally relevant aspect of this academic achievement program would involve the consistent exposure to HBCU alumni and successful Black collegians who have not only graduated from college but moved forward to accomplish great feats in a range of disciplines (e.g., education, medicine, law, politics, science, technology, engineering, etc.). This exposure could be archival via images, records, and videos as well as personal contact with those available through in-person meetings or remote communications. Another strategy within the academic achievement HDP for HBCUs to consider is to reestablish the first-year ineligibility standard for academic preparation. Comprehensive academic support could focus on developing specific remediation, effective study habits, setting and attaining academic goals, enhancing academic self-efficacy, and engaging in productive academic behaviors.

The fifth HDP associated within the EBA approach is career aspirations. The EBA approach involves exposing Black college athletes to professionals in various fields beyond athletics while in college. A formal career exploration program could involve a concerted effort between the athletic department, career services office, academic advising staff, academic departments, alumni associations, and various off-campus organizations. Using career assessments from the campus career services office as a foundational tool, professionals from specific occupational fields could be recruited to share their experiences and advice for the college athletes. Former HBCU athletes should also be targeted to foster a positive role model effect for the current college athletes. Another strategy associated with the career development HDP is the requirement of HBCU athletes to meet with a career development counselor at least once a month from their initial enrollment through graduation to map out a plan of action for their success after college. Having this consistent interaction and support throughout their college tenure would allow college athletes to explore their various interests and pursue careers with confidence and relevant knowledge.

The final HDP associated with the EBA approach is effective time management skills. As previously noted, many HBCU athletes encounter challenges managing the intense time commitments associated with being a college athlete (Gawrysiak et al., 2013). Therefore, a recommended strategy HBCUs should consider is stricter enforcement of the NCAA 20-hour-per-week rule. Along the same lines, once time spent on athletics is reduced and/or properly managed, HBCU athletes should be expected to be involved in educationally purposeful activities. Creating a system whereby college athletes report their hours spent on academics and social development could foster a culture where holistic development is prioritized.

CAREER TRANSITION SCORECARD FOR ATHLETES

Influenced by the Diversity Scorecard (Bensimon, 2004), the Career Transition Scorecard (CTS), an action-oriented approach to accountability and change, is designed to help bridge the chasm between research and practice in academic support centers for athletes and to enhance the quality of school-to-career transitions of athletes across race/ethnicity, gender, and type of sport (see Comeaux, 2015). This critical action research approach to practice (i.e., practitioner-as-researcher model) is a departure from a traditional research methodology of knowledge production. In the practitioner-as-researcher model, an outside researcher works closely with a team of practitioners in participating athletic departments to build a professional learning community and to help create a version of the CTS that is specific to their needs and interests. During this inquiry process, the team of practitioners conducts the actual research and assumes responsibility for working with the outside researcher to compile, analyze, and interpret existing data on the athlete campus experience and outcomes as well as to develop and implement intervention strategies. As such, a basic premise of the CTS is that examination of data about the state of equity in campus experiences and subsequent outcomes of college athletes by race/ethnicity, gender, and type of sport can raise awareness of their potential strengths and inequalities, which can then lead to collective action by the team of practitioners.

ACCESS, RETENTION, INSTITUTIONAL RECEPTIVITY, EXCELLENCE, AND ENGAGEMENT

The CTS consists of five performance perspectives deemed important for quality career transition of college athletes: access, retention, institutional receptivity, excellence/high achievement, and engagement (figure 14.2). The *access* perspective commonly refers to college athletes' access (or lack thereof) to internship opportunities and certain majors, which can influence both their learning and desirable outcomes (see Kuh, 2008). The *retention* perspective might focus on the completion rates and levels of success in basic skills courses among athletes. Under the *institutional receptivity* domain, athletic departments might use existing data to answer questions about the extent to which coaches, staff, and administrators reflect the diversity of the athletes they recruit (see Comeaux & Fuentes, 2015). *Excellence/high achievement* indicators typically include, for example, athlete participation in high-demand programs of study, career placement postgraduation, and the types and magnitude of academic honor and awards received. Lastly, the *engagement* perspective is focused on the purposeful engagement activities of athletes in campus learning environments (Comeaux & Harrison, 2011). Engagement activities can include, but are not limited to, preparing for class, interaction with non-athlete peers, reading and writing, meaningful interactions with faculty, and collaboration with peers on problem-solving

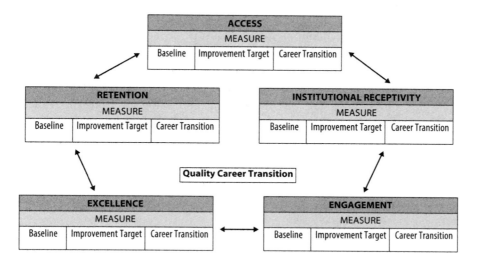

Figure 14.2. Career Transition Scorecard (CTS)

tasks (Gaston-Gayles & Hu, 2009; Kuh, 2001). With a better understanding of the frequency and quality of athletes' interactions with faculty, for example, practitioners would be more likely and better able to take actions that could lead to positive gains in learning (Comeaux, 2010b).

Athletic departments might have different circumstances, needs, and interests within the CTS framework, and they might select specific domains on which to focus. Thus, the outside researcher works closely with the team of practitioner researchers in the participating athletic department to create the Scorecard. After intentional selection of performance perspectives, the outside researcher and team of practitioners can identify strengths and problem areas and construct tailored goals and measures (defined as indicators of strengths and problem areas that impact quality career transitions of athletes) as well as baselines (defined as the current status of or initial information about a measure) and improvement targets (or markers of progress for given measures) under each selected performance perspective. Through the ongoing process of creating the CTS and examining the data disaggregated by subgroups, practitioners, while reflecting on their own practices, essentially become knowledge *makers* rather than merely knowledge *users*. As well, they have the opportunity to learn to think from a data-driven standpoint and to address inequalities in athlete experiences and outcomes.

CONCLUSION

In an era of increasing prioritization of athletic revenue generation and persistent academic underperformance, HBCUs are in a precarious situation. In order to stay true to their founding educational missions and principles, innovative educational practices must be considered. Within this chapter, the authors offer the Excellence Beyond Athletics model and the Career Transition Scorecard as useful tools to increase the academic performance and personal development outcomes for college athletes at HBCUs. Each of these approaches can and should be modified to fit each institution's unique circumstance. However, the overarching focus and structure around holistic development is pivotal for meaningful progress to transpire. It is our hope that, with the adoption of the aforementioned strategies, HBCUs will reverse the trend of academic underperformance as measured by NCAA metrics, increase the quality of college athletes' experiences at HBCUs, and better equip them for success in careers after college.

QUESTIONS FOR DISCUSSION

1. What role do administrators, faculty, coaches, and support staff at HBCUs play in influencing HBCU athletes' academic and personal development outcomes?

2. Beyond the NCAA's academic performance measures, what additional standards should HBCU athletic programs consider implementing to increase the effectiveness of their support services?

3. To what extent can both the EBA model and the CTS be viewed as tools for social justice?

Notes

1. Graduation Success Rate (GSR) is an NCAA team-based metric that calculates the percentage of total college athletes within a six-year cohort at a school by the total college athletes within a six-year cohort who graduate from the school while accounting for transfer college athletes. The six-year cohort is derived from the US Department of Education (http://www.ncaa.org/about/resources/research/graduation-success-rate).

2. Academic Progress Rate (APR) is an NCAA team-based metric created in 2003 that measures academic performance by dividing the total eligibility and retention points possible for a team by the total eligibility and retention points earned by a team (http://www.ncaa.org/about/resources/research/division-i-academic-progress-rate-apr).

3. See Cooper, Cavil, & Cheeks (2014) for an extensive discussion on the multilayered challenges HBCUs face including macrolevel/societal, mesolevel/structural, and microlevel/intra-institutional challenges.

4. The model was initially created for Black, male college athletes, but the concepts are applicable for Black college athletes across gender groups.

References

Associated Press. (2007). HBCUs, Katrina-area schools struggle with APR. 1. *ESPN.* Retrieved from http://sports.espn.go.com/ncaa/news/story?id=2857999

Bell, D. A. (1992). *Faces at the bottom of the well: The permanence of racism.* New York: Basic Books.

Bensimon, E. M. (2004). The diversity scorecard: A learning approach to institutional change. *Change, 36*(1), 44–52.

Charlton, R. (2011). The role of policy, rituals, and language in shaping an academically focused culture in HBCU athletics. *Journal of Issues in Intercollegiate Athletics, 4,* 120–148.

Comeaux, E. (2010a). Racial differences in faculty perceptions of collegiate student-athletes' academic and post-undergraduate achievement. *Sociology of Sport Journal, 27,* 390–412.

Comeaux, E. (2010b). Mentoring as an intervention strategy: Toward a (re)negotiation of first year student-athlete role identities. *Journal for the Study of Sports and Athletes in Education, 4*(3), 257–275.

Comeaux, E. (2013). Rethinking academic reform and encouraging organizational innovation: Implications for stakeholder management in college sports. *Innovative Higher Education, 38*(4), 281–293.

Comeaux, E. (2015). Organizational learning in athletic departments: Toward an anti-deficit and data-driven approach to academic support for division I athletes. In E. Comeaux (Ed.), *Making the connection: Data-informed practices in academic support centers for college athletes* (pp. 1–16). Charlotte, NC: Information Age Publishing.

Comeaux, E., & Fuentes, M. V. (2015). Cross-racial interaction of division I athletes: An examination of the campus climate for diversity. In E. Comeaux (Ed.), *Introduction to intercollegiate athletics* (pp. 179–192). Baltimore, MD: Johns Hopkins University Press.

Comeaux, E., & Harrison, C. K. (2011). A conceptual model of academic success for student-athletes. *Educational Researcher, 40*(5), 235–245. doi: 10.3102/0013189X11415260

Cooper, J. N. (2013). A culture of collective uplift: The influence of a historically Black college/university on Black male student athletes. *Journal of Issues in Intercollegiate Athletics, 6,* 306–331.

Cooper, J. N. (2015a). Strategies for athlete success at historically Black colleges and universities (HBCUs). In E. Comeaux (Ed.), *Making the connection: Data-informed practices in academic support centers for college athletes.* Charlotte, NC: Information Age Publishing.

Cooper, J. N. (2015b). Excellence beyond athletics: Best practices for enhancing Black male student athletes' educational experiences and outcomes. Paper presented at the Black Student Athlete Conference, University of Texas at Austin.

Cooper, J. N., Cavil, J. K., & Cheeks, G. (2014). The state of intercollegiate athletics at historically Black colleges and universities (HBCUs): Past, present, & persistence. *Journal of Issues in Intercollegiate Athletics, 7,* 307–332.

Cooper, J. N., & Cooper, J. E. (2015). "I'm running so you can be happy and I can keep my scholarship": A comparative study of Black male college athletes' experiences with role conflict. Paper presented at the College Sport Research Institute, Columbia, South Carolina.

Cooper, J. N., & Hawkins, B. (2012). A place of opportunity: Black male student athletes' experiences at a Historically Black University. *Journal of Intercollegiate Sport, 5,* 170–188.

Crenshaw, K., Gotanda, N., Peller, G., & Thomas, K. (1995). *Critical race theory: The key writings that formed the movement.* New York: New Press.

Edwards, H. (2000). Crisis of Black athletes on the eve of the 21st century. *Society, 37*(3), 9–13.

Gawrysiak, E. J., Cooper, J. N., & Hawkins, B. J. (2013, June 28). The impact of baseball participation on the educational experiences of Black student-athletes at historically Black colleges and universities. *Race, Ethnicity and Education* (696–722). doi: 10.1080/13613324.2013.792795

Gaston-Gayles, J., & Hu, S. (2009). The influence of student engagement and sport participation on college outcomes among Division I student athletes. *Journal of Higher Education, 80*(3), 315–333. doi: 10.1353/jhe.0.0051

Hosick, M. B. (2011). Resources crux of HBCU challenges: Schools faces uphill battle in meeting academic standards. NCAA. Retrieved from http://www.ncaa.com/news/ncaa/2011-05-24/resources-crux-hbcu-challenges

Johnson, M. N. (2013). Financial and related issues among historically Black colleges and universities. *Journal of Intercollegiate Sport, 6,* 65–75.

Kelly, D. D., & Dixon, M. A. (2014). Successfully navigating life transitions among African American male student-athletes: A review and examination of constellation mentoring as a promising strategy. *Journal of Sport Management, 28*(5), 498–514.

Kuh, G. D. (2001). Assessing what really matters to student learning: Inside the national survey of student engagement. *Change, 33*(3), 10–17. doi: 10.1080/00091380109601795

Kuh, G. D. (2008). *High-impact practices: What they are, who has access to them, and why they matter.* Washington, DC: Association of American Colleges and Universities.

Lillig, J. (2009). "Magic" or misery?: HBCUs, guarantee contracts, and public policy. *Journal of Sports Law & Contemporary Problems, 6*(41), 41–71.

Grasgreen, A. (2013, June 12). Postseason bans on the rise. Inside Higher Ed. Retrieved from https://www.insidehighered.com/news/2013/06/12/ncaa-postseason-bans-poor-academic-performance-continue-rise-especially-hbcus

Person, D. R., & LeNoir, K. M. (1997). Retention issues and models for African American male athletes. *New Directions for Student Services, 80*, 79–91.

Sailes, G. (1998). A comparison of professional sport career aspirations among athletes. In G. Sailes (Ed.), *African Americans in sport: Contemporary themes* (pp. 261–269). New Brunswick, NJ: Transaction Publishers.

Sellers, R. M., & Kuperminc, G. P. (1997). Goal discrepancy in African American male student-athletes' unrealistic expectations for careers in professional sports. *Journal of Black Psychology, 23*(1), 6–23.

Sue, D. W., Capodilupo, C. M., Torino, G. C., Bucceri, J. M., Holder, A. M. B., Nadal, K. L., & Esquilin, M. (2007). Racial microaggressions in everyday life: Implications for clinical practice. *American Psychologist, 62*(4), 271–286.

Yosso, T. J. (2005). Whose culture has capital? A critical race theory discussion of community cultural wealth. *Race, Ethnicity and Education, 8*(1), 69–91.

Revisiting African American Males and Highlighting Pacific Islander/Polynesian Male Experiences

C. Keith Harrison, Leticia Oseguera, Jean Boyd, and Monica Morita

Campus climate is broadly defined as the "current attitudes, behaviors and standards and practices of employees and students of an institution" (Rankin & Reason, 2008, p. 264).

KEY TERMS

▶ Campus climate

▶ African American male

▶ Pacific Islander/ Polynesian American male

▶ Cultural stereotypes

Campus climate and well-being issues on college students attending American higher education have been long documented (Chang, 2001; Hurtado, Milem, Clayton-Pederson, & Allen, 1999). Scholars in the North American Society for Sport History as well as the North American Society for Sport Sociology have addressed athletic departments' climates on colleges and universities from both a historical and contemporary perspective (Harrison, 1996; 2007). In 2015, contemporary campus climate issues related to race surfaced at the University of Oklahoma and University of Missouri and continue on our campuses (Winkle-Wagner & Locks, 2013). These issues related to racial macro- and microaggressions have a historical context. The following quote from Paige Smith (1990), former chancellor at the University of California, Los Angeles seems to capture the dynamics of the African American male (AAM) experience with a mirror cultural reflection for their Pacific Islander/Polynesian[1] American (PAM) male peers and colleagues:

This chapter is dedicated to Johnny Nansen, Washington State University alumnus, and Byron Hurt, Northeastern University alumnus, with a special shout out to Junior Seau, posthumously inducted into the Pro Football Hall of Fame on August 8, 2015.

The crowning irony is that, in states where blacks were only a few years ago barred from voting, the majority of football and basketball players are black. When Georgia, let's say, plays Alabama in football or basketball, black players dominate—if not in numbers, in performance (of course, collegiate basketball has become virtually a black monopoly from Mississippi to Arizona and points north and south). On every campus I visit I see a little band of black students (they are especially conspicuous on campuses in states where there are few black residents, such as Utah, Nevada, Nebraska, Colorado). There are the mammoth black students—basketball forwards and centers, the football tackles, linebackers, and defensive ends—and the small black students— the fleet backs and pass receivers. They mix very little with white students. They are the classic black entertainers. It is for their exploits that arenas of white students shout themselves hoarse. The cultural discontinuity is staggering, the irony beyond articulation. (pp. 12–13)

This quote eloquently articulates how ethnic minority college athletes are, and continue to be, positioned at many predominantly White institutions (PWIs) in American higher education. These campuses are the reason, in part, that climate has been studied by so many higher education scholars and other scholars interested in how human identities navigate the college experience.

Despite years of studying AAMs in sport, higher education has yet to create campus climates that are conducive to holistic AAM success, and even less has been focused on PAM college athlete success on campus (Comeaux & Fuentes, 2015; Morita, 2013; Oseguera, 2010; Tengan & Markham, 2009). Both AAM and PAM college athletes are significant contributors to the landscape of college and professional football. In the most recent NFL Draft, the first two overall picks were Jameis Winston and Marcus Mariota—an AAM and a PAM. Thus, it is timely to examine the context of these two pan-ethnic groups' campus climate issues in the twenty-first century.

We offer a brief profile of AAM and PAM athletes, then synthesize the broader literature on campus climate and well-being and present how existing research relates to AAM and PAM college athlete experiences. The chapter then presents ways in which these populations have unique dimensions to consider, as both face overt and covert racism on campus and are expected to maintain rigorous academic, athletic, and social commitments. We conclude with recommendations for ways to improve the campus climate for AAM and PAM college athletes.

AAM AND PAM INTERSECTING PROFILES

AAMs and PAMs are positively and negatively stigmatized while simultaneously being valued and recruited across American higher education on athletic scholarships (Beamon, 2014; Harrison, 1996). Both ethnic groups that serve as the focus of this chapter are often recruited from urban and rural communities, where their identities to access higher education are most often prioritized on athletic pursuits. The literature on ethnic minorities in sport and education has focused primarily on African American college athletes, namely males, yet the intersection of both AAM and PAM athletes seems to be in the context of their imagery as large gladiators who are physical specimens simply present to make money for Whites in power (Hawkins, 2013). Both groups face stereotypes and limited perceptions by the campus-at-large in regard to their academic and athletic motivations for attending universities, which are usually majority campuses with fewer people of color (Morita, 2013; Oseguera, 2010). Both groups are recruited heavily to compete in major-college sports, primarily in the high-profile sports of football and basketball, while the overall student representation of African American and Pacific Islander / Polynesian American students is underrepresented on these same campuses (Harper, Williams, & Blackman, 2013). While undergraduate fall enrollment numbers have increased for most minority racial and ethnic groups from 1976 to 2008, the enrollment figures are still significantly less than their White peers, who still represent over 60 percent of the student body population at higher education institutions. In 2008, African American students represented 14 percent, while Asian / Pacific Islander students represented 7 percent (Aud, Fox, & Kewal Remani, 2010) of the student body. Generally, in comparison to White, male college athletes, college athletes of color in the sport of football are less prepared academically; score lower on standardized tests (SAT/ACT); graduate at lower rates; and come from lower socioeconomic backgrounds and family origins that are more often urban or rural, compared to suburban and more affluent White athletes (Lapchick, 2014; Upthegrove, Roscigno, & Zubrinsky, 1999). Many of these factors influence AAM and PAM college football players aspiring to compete at the next level in the NFL, as research has shown that students from lower socioeconomic families are more likely to view professional sports as their main career goal (Charleston, Jackson, Adserias, & Lang, 2015). Competing in the NFL and playing professional football is not a negative career goal, when things are kept in perspective, but the reality is that without a college degree or a professional contract after four or five years in college, AAM and PAM football athletes face a rough and challenging transition from sport to life and the workforce (Harrison, 1996; Harrison & Lawrence, 2003).

DIFFERENCES BETWEEN AAM AND PAM ATHLETES IN THE CONTEXT OF CLIMATE

Graduation rates for AAMs and PAMs are vastly different. While it should be noted that African Americans are just under half of all football players in Division I or Football Bowl Subdivision (FBS), Polynesian Americans represent less than 3 percent of all college football athletes at this competitive level (Lapchick, 2014).

AAM collegiate football athletes graduate at a higher rate than PAM football players. For AAMs, some of this slight advantage is that there is some representation of African Americans in the general student body. Paradoxically, at many of these same campuses African American non-athletes graduate at a lower rate than AAM college athletes in any sport (Lapchick, 2014). Among PAMs, there are few Pacific Islander / Polynesian students attending these institutions, except for those participating in athletics. This is a powerful reality and a much broader issue that says a lot about the recruitment and retention of students of color at PWIs.

In terms of athleticism, AAM football athletes are typically given access to virtually any position during the collegiate recruitment process. This plays in part to sport stereotypes in which African American males are more apt for athletic roles such as cornerback and running back instead of kicker (Rhoden, 2011). Conversely, PAM football athletes are routinely recruited to select positions such as quarterback, lineman, linebacker, and defensive back. PAM football athletes are also perceived to be more of a risk to stay eligible and matriculate. PAM football college athletes are perceived to have intensified issues of underperformance in academics when compared to many AAMs in terms of their identity as players in this major revenue-producing sport. Harrison (1996), in his qualitative investigation of Samoan American football athletes, inquired about the academic, athletic, and social experiences of this ethnic population. In regard to the negative perception of his ethnic heritage in the context of their perceived college athlete experience, one Samoan American football player in the study expressed: "I asked one of our assistant coaches and defensive coordinators why our football program does not recruit more Samoans. He told me that we can't keep them eligible. With the Black players we can at least keep them eligible" (p. 6). This type of stereotyping is negative, regarding the intellectual abilities of Samoan and other Pacific Islander / Polynesian college athletes. However, there are other, less pernicious perceptions about PAM athletes. Coaches often recruit Polynesian athletes because of their footwork; their upbringing, which stresses hard work and discipline; and their ability in hard-hitting, combat-like situations. And they don't have "some of the issues of other kids like drinking or getting into trouble" (Corbett, 2013; Sager, 2015).

In this section, we also highlight the findings of one of the few studies specifically on PAM experiences to demonstrate some of the possible differences between AAMs and PAMs. Morita (2013) conducted a qualitative study at one PWI to better understand the academic, athletic, social, and career transition issues faced by Polynesian male college athletes. The study included interviews with current and former college athletes, Polynesian football coaches, non-Polynesian coaches, and Polynesian community leaders. The findings most relevant to the context of climate are related to athletic capital as well as social and cultural capital. In particular, one of the findings suggests that the NFL plays an important part of an individual's decision to attend a specific institution. The second finding was connected to the NFL, through the decision to attend an institution based on the national exposure that an individual perceives he may receive there and the historical success other Polynesian college athletes have had by attending that particular institution. The third finding related to how the Polynesian culture had a strong influence on the college athletes' identities and the lens they used to view their experience in the higher education setting and their relationships with institutional agents such as teachers, counselors, administrators, and coaches. Lastly, the community leaders and coaches described the differences of the college athletes who were raised in the island nations, compared to those from the continental United States. The majority of these differences relate to the discipline and value of respect that is ingrained in the lives of those athletes raised in the island nations. The rich culture incorporated into everyday activities teaches a high level of respect, which relates to how others are treated and communicated with. Football athletes raised on the islands are not as westernized as those raised in the United States, who often have cultural backgrounds that are considered "watered down" or more assimilated. Levels of assimilation and acculturation are historically a challenge for all immigrant groups. This work signals how disconnected PAM students must feel on college campuses, when much of the motivation to attend college has less to do with the actual college experience or fit with the institution than with external stimuli. In many instances, athletes of color face added challenges on majority campuses because of the juggling act of academics with athletics and the isolation that many high-profile sports such as football often impose (Harrison, 1996), and this gulf may be exacerbated for certain racial and ethnic groups. The research highlighted in this section reminds us that much more work needs to be undertaken to understand the similarities among AAMs and PAMs, but it also reminds us of the nuances of their campus experiences. The reality is that with the emerging demographics of Polynesians in football on campus and the stability of AAMs on athletic scholarships in football, there will be numerous opportunities to assess those best practices for both populations to succeed. The next section presents a review of the campus climate literature more broadly and integrates commentary by practitioners on AAMs and PAMs.

CAMPUS CLIMATE, ACADEMIC SUCCESS, AND STUDENT WELL-BEING

It is important to note that college athletes view campus climate through a different lens because of athletics. There are tremendous time demands when participating in collegiate athletics and an unwavering media scrutiny on significant college athletic programs (Carodine, Almond, & Gratto, 2001). College athletes also must deal with sport-specific stereotypes, such as the stigma of being a "dumb jock" (Harrison, 2007). College athletes who participate in featured sports, such as football and basketball, generally show less academic achievement and choose less rigorous majors (Richards & Aries, 1998; Upthegrove et al., 1999). Upthegrove and colleagues (1999), drawing from the 1987–88 National Study of Intercollegiate Athletes, examined 2,921 student-athletes, with 1,327 representing men's basketball and football, and concluded that the athletes most likely to repeat courses and go on academic probation were male basketball and football players. These sports tend to recruit exceptional athletes, despite the athletes' low academic standings. This initial disadvantage increases the number of athletes in revenue-generating sports who require more classroom support for their academic hardships.

Chang (2001; 2002) and Hurtado and colleagues (1999) have written a great deal on racial and ethnic diversity campus climate issues. Other scholars have also contributed to this area of inquiry, in attempts to create positive educational experiences for all students (Museus & Jayakumar, 2012; Oseguera & Rhee, 2009; Winkle-Wagner & Locks, 2013). Some of the conclusions from this growing body of research reveal interesting patterns, in terms of students of color on campus in American higher education. Chang (2001), in a study examining links between racial diversity on college campuses and positive educational outcomes, found that the extent to which students interact across racial lines is an important factor for producing positive educational outcomes. Campus diversity had a small but significant positive impact on students' college experiences. Interacting and socializing across racial and ethnic lines and dialogue about issues of race were reported as positive educational experiences. Oseguera and Rhee (2009) found that the institutional retention climate independently determined whether a student would persist or not. These same researchers also indicated that university faculty and peer groups are important constructs to consider when evaluating campus climate effectiveness.

A comfortable campus climate environment in which professors are able to work with the athletes will produce better results. Athletes are often faced with the task of disproving the "dumb jock" stereotype that pervades sport. College athletes report more difficulties than non-athletes in being taken seriously by professors (Oseguera, 2010; Richards & Aries, 1998). Situations regarding athletes receiving full scholarships and admittance with lower SAT scores elicited stronger feelings of anger and disapproval (Engstrom, Sedlacek, & McEwen, 1995). This negative perception of faculty can harm the college athlete, and it lends credibility to the self-fulfilling prophecy of underperformance discussed in the sociopsychological approach that combines macrofactors of the education system with microfactors of individual socioeconomic status (Lam, 2014). However, Comeaux and Harrison's (2007) work on the quality of faculty interaction with athletes of color indicates that ethnic minority populations bring a different perspective to the environment and that faculty engagement is a key predictor of success for all students. College athletes in general must see faculty as allies and key mentors, just like coaches who facilitate learning on the field. Engaging in the academic process with faculty and student peers on campus has a stronger positive impact on well-being and cultural development as a human being of college athletes (Comeaux & Harrison, 2007).

Lawrence (2005) conducted a qualitative study of male and female African American college athletes' campus experiences at a PWI. In particular, the African American college athletes' stories of race and racial discrimination focused on specific incidents that occurred while they were each on athletic scholarship. Five themes were identified: (1) being hurt, (2) outrage and shock, (3) team togetherness, (4) being empowered, and (5) differences. While there were some positive coping techniques used to respond to racial discrimination, these findings remind us of the negative impact racial discrimination and bias can have on college athletes in addition to the already challenging juggling act of academics, athletics, and social life. The potential negative impact of African American college athletes experiencing the above realities on campus contributes to the challenges experienced by the African American college athlete as he navigates campus life.

Morita (2013) offers three themes pertinent to Polynesian American athletes and their potential to impact how this group experiences climate on campus: respect, family, and religion. Respect emerged as a theme under social and cultural capital, and it suggests that the relationship of family upbringing, the importance of family hierarchy, and not talking out of turn or without having earned the right to speak out must be accounted for when working with Polynesian American college athletes. Family was an indicator related to athletic capital that played a part in an individual's decision to attend an institution because of its proximity to the family, the Polynesian legacy, and the opportunity for continued family and community support. Religion, also under social and cultural capital, was noted as critical, suggesting the importance of faith-based institutional agents and the value the Polynesian community places on faith as the foundation of family and for strengthening an individual's character. These three themes highlight the need for campuses to attend to the ways in which they interact with the cultural practices and beliefs that PAM students bring to campus.

Singer (2005) has also found that AAM college athletes' experiences are much better understood when researched from their cultural perspective. He utilized critical race theory (CRT) in his in-depth qualitative case study of four African American male football players in a big-time college sport program at a PWI in the Midwestern United States. An African American scholar conducting this research in a single focus group revealed that "these African American males felt that racism manifested itself in terms of African Americans 1) being denied access to leadership and major decision-making opportunities in college and professional sport, and 2) being treated differently than their White counterparts" (Singer, 2005, p. 365).

As the research above illuminates, negative and hostile campus climates continue to be part of the lived experiences of African American and Pacific Islander populations. Further, there are employees of color, in addition to students, who describe campus climates as racist (Harper & Hurtado, 2007; Rankin & Reason, 2005). Public discourse on race relations, however, implies that racism is a thing of the past. More recently, Bimper (2015) explored the theoretical notion of postracial narratives and colorblind racism in a case of Black intercollegiate athlete experiences at PWIs. In this study, participants also indicated that racial beliefs and racial inequities abound among their campus climate realities as both students and athletes. These same Black college athletes expressed that colorblind racism has indirectly impacted their perceptions as college athletes. While not tested, it is likely that colorblind ideologies also impact the PAM college athlete experience as well.

The key to understanding the dynamics of campus climate with football athletes of color is that they are embraced for their physical talents while at the same time having to effectively navigate a campus where they are in the minority. The intellectual capacity of AAMs and PAMs is rarely at the forefront of campus perceptions about their academic prowess. One related issue with climate pertains to the presence, or lack thereof, of AAM or PAM university leadership. Hodge's (2015) work presents the continued reality of racial and ethnic leadership imbalances on college campuses and shows that among key university leadership positions: 90 percent are White men and women; nearly 100 percent of conference commissioners are White men, across all Division I football programs; 85 percent of coaches are White men; and 90 percent of athletic directors are White men. The low representation of African American or Pacific Islander men or women in these key leadership areas likely contributes to poor perceptions of AAM or PAM college athletes and thus poorer campus climate experiences.

In the next section we examine some practical strategies offered by two leaders who have worked in the field of academic support services and college athlete development for nearly two decades. We include empirical evidence from the literature that supports these recommendations. We spotlight the perspective of two practitioners in the field of higher education and athletics for one major reason. Daily, these practitioners have access to mentor athletes in the academic support and athlete development world on campus. Their voices complement the campus climate literature on ethnic minorities, as these two practitioners routinely interact with ethnic minority athletes.

POLICY RECOMMENDATIONS FROM A PRACTITIONER PERSPECTIVE

The following are recommendations for how AAMs and PAMs can maximize their campus experiences across the constructs of academics, athletics, social life, and career transition. We begin with specific recommendations primarily for PAMs, as we want to engage in a conversation about the need to better understand the PAM experience and then offer recommendations applicable to both groups. According to Morita (2013), there are several important aspects to consider with the recruitment of PAMs to an athletic program. First, there is a need to understand the Pacific Islander / Polynesian family values and what will help the Pacific

Islander / Polynesian college athlete navigate through the institution to obtain a degree and successfully transition to the NFL if the opportunity presents itself. Second, there needs to be emphasis on all aspects of the academic and athletic needs for these students. It will be helpful for institutions to utilize institutional agents to provide the necessary support in all areas: athletics, academics, and socially integrating into an institution of higher education. There needs to be balance in all areas of an athlete's life and career. The insight of former college athletes currently in the NFL and pursuing other career avenues could give the prospective and current college athletes relevant information on what to expect in the transition to college and a career. Lastly, in support of a unique population such as this, an institutional agent who is Polynesian or who understands the Polynesian culture would aid in support of a Pacific Islander / Polynesian college athlete experience at an institution of American higher education. Someone with an understanding of the Pacific Islander / Polynesian cultures and/or who understands the importance of family, religion, and respect to this collegiate athlete group would better serve as a mentor or someone to whom these individuals could relate. Research done on barriers and bridges to success for Pacific Islanders attending a university have focused on the success of outreach initiatives including mentorship of students with the same cultural background (Kearney & Donaghy, 2010). Since the Pacific Islander / Polynesian college athlete population consists largely of first-generation college students, it is important to provide support in order to foster successful student development.

One of the cornerstones of effective programming and support for African American and Pacific Islander / Polynesian football athletes is creating an environment of cultural competency. Some coaches, administrators, faculty, and so on refer to a "colorblind" approach. The flaw here is that disparities in graduation, retention, and experience do exist, and a response to the factors that impact these groups necessarily has to have a race component (Donnor, 2005). The following are both policy and practical recommendations to work toward providing an optimum environment for success:

- Acknowledge and show respect for both historical and contemporary cultural contexts of these young men. This does not mean that coaches, administrators, faculty, and academic professionals should try to speak in "Ebonics." However, seeking to be informed and relatable on the issues and concerns that these groups share goes a long way in building trust (Bennett, Hodge, & Graham, 2015; Comeaux, 2010; Gayles, Crandall, & Jones, 2015).

- Implement structured discussion about college athletes' multiple identities inclusive of ethnicity. As freshmen and transfer students enter the intercollegiate framework, discussions about identity and values between players, coaches, and staff are important. Studies have shown the importance of establishing identity, especially an identity separate from athletics (Kimball, 2007; Settles, Sellers, & Damas, 2002).

- Establish value for education. Because of the historical, cultural and socioeconomic context of sport participation, there is often a disparity in perceived value toward educational attainment. Incentives and rewards for college athletes and coaches tied to academic achievement is a productive strategy to demonstrate that athletic programs value educational accomplishment (Harrison & Boyd, 2007).

- Partner with campus and community organizations and professionals to create targeted, culturally relevant programming. These types of programs not only address ethnic group–specific challenges but create natural mentoring opportunities (DeCuir-Gunby, Taliaferro, & Greenfield, 2010) so that AAM and PAM college athletes have access to individuals who share similar experiences and have succeeded beyond their sport (NCAA, 2006).

- Commit to investing in human resources that are representative of the populations of college athletes on campus. African American and Polynesian athletes should see coaches and support staff members who "look like them" and share life experiences (Council, Robinson, Bennett, & Moody, 2015; Comeaux & Fuentes, 2015; Rhodes, 2005).

- Incorporate family structure so that college athletes of color have support from that cultural unit (Morita, 2013; Oliver, 1980).

- Provide resources to minimize social adjustment issues (Winkle-Wagner & Locks, 2013) that college athletes of color face so that they can be productive in academic and athletic pursuits (Bennett, Hodge, & Graham, 2015).

CONCLUSION

This chapter focused on some of the major campus climate issues that AAM and PAM football athletes face in higher education and contemporary society. It is important that we conclude this chapter by highlighting the academic and athletic success of AAMs and PAMs. During the 2014 FBS season, two male athletes emerged as superstars and competed heavily for the Heisman Trophy and the number one overall pick in the 2015 NFL Draft. One of these young men happened to be African American, and the other, Polynesian American. Jameis Winston left school early to enter the NFL Draft, and despite having off-the-field character issues while attending Florida State University (FSU), he was lauded by FSU head football coach Jimbo Fisher, who said, "Jameis, in football intellect, intelligence level, is as smart as anybody" he'd been around (Wilson, 2015). Marcus Mariota, a Polynesian American, earned his degree and also demonstrated his academic and athletic identity excellence by earning the Scholar-Baller Award[2] along with over 30 other teammates at the University of Oregon in 2012. AAM and PAM athletes will continue to be recruited by PWIs with major college football programs that compete at the NCAA level, so attention to their experiences with the campus climate and their well-being is necessary. While many of the issues and challenges on campus could be aided by better K–12 preparation of these individuals' academic and athletic identities, stakeholders in American higher education must address the challenges discussed in this chapter. The synergy between scholarship and practice was highlighted in this chapter by two scholars and two practitioners collaborating on the topics of campus climate and student well-being. We suggest this type of partnership at various PWIs, with academic scholars and athletic department practitioners seeking to empower all their college athletes.

QUESTIONS FOR DISCUSSION

1. What are some of the common stereotypes that AAM and PAM football athletes face in terms of academics, athletics, and social life at PWIs, and how can these stereotypes be minimized?

2. How does the presence of the NFL, in concert with competing in Division I football, impact the perceptions and aspirations of AAM and PAM football athletes, and what steps can be taken to improve the college athlete experience while on campus?

3. In what ways might the cultural identities of AAM and PAM football athletes differ from one another in American higher education, and how should higher education institutions respond to these nuances?

Notes

1. For purposes of this chapter, we do not distinguish between continental-US-born versus non-continental-born in the Pacific Islander / Polynesian population and primarily refer to the entire group originating in the Pacific Islands as Pacific Islander / Polynesian. In football, the majority of Pacific Islander / Polynesian athletes identify as Samoan, Hawaiian, or Tongan. We also use "Pacific Islander" interchangeably with "Polynesian," as the pan-ethnic term "Pacific Islander" is found in academic literature and the pan-ethnic term "Polynesian" is more often utilized in sport.

2. This award recognizes college athletes with a B or better grade point average

References

Aud, S., Fox, M. A., & Kewal Ramani, A. (2010). Status and trends in the education of racial and ethnic groups. Washington, DC: National Center for Education Statistics.

Beamon, K. (2014). Racism and stereotyping on campus: Experiences of African American male student-athletes. *Journal of Negro Education, 83*(2), 121–134.

Bennett, R. A., Hodge, S. R., & Graham, D. L. (2015). *Black males and intercollegiate athletics: An exploration of problems and solutions.* UK: Emerald Group Publishing. Retrieved from http://www.eblib.com.

Bimper, A. (2015). Lifting the veil: Exploring colorblind racism in Black student-athlete experiences. *Journal of Sport and Social Issues, 39*(3), 225–243.

Carodine, K., Almond, K. F., & Gratto, K. K. (2001). College student-athlete success both in and out of the classroom. In M. F. Howard-Hamilton & S. K. Watt (Eds.), *New Directions for Student Services* (vol. 93, pp. 19–33). San Francisco, CA: Jossey-Bass.

Chang, M. (2001). The positive educational effects of racial diversity on campus. *ERIC* (ED456198).

Chang, M. (2002). Preservation or transformation: Where's the real educational discourse on diversity? *Review of Higher Education, 25*(2) 125–140.

Charleston, L. J., Jackson, J. F. L., Adserias, R. P., & Lang, N. M. (2015). Beyond the game™: Transforming life outcomes of Black male collegiate student athletes. In R. A. Bennett, S. R. Hodge, & D. L. Graham (Eds.), *Black males and intercollegiate athletics: An exploration of problems and solutions* (pp. 285–306). UK: Emerald Group Publishing. Retrieved from http://www.eblib.com

Comeaux, E. (2010). Mentoring as an intervention strategy. *Journal for the Study of Sports and Athletes in Education, 4*(3), 257–275.

Comeaux, E., & Fuentes, M. V. (2015). Cross-racial interaction of division I athletes: An examination of the campus climate for diversity. In E. Comeaux (Ed.), *Introduction to intercollegiate athletics* (pp. 179–192). Baltimore, MD: Johns Hopkins University Press.

Comeaux, E., & Harrison, C. K. (2007). Faculty and male student-athletes: Racial differences in the environmental predictors of academic achievement. *Race, Ethnicity and Education, 10*(2), 199–214.

Corbett, J. (2013). Polynesian players bring passion, power. *USA Today*. Retrieved from http://www.usatoday.com/story/sports/nfl/2013/02/03/polynesian-super-bowl /1882001/

Council III, M. R., Robinson, L. S., Bennett III, R. A., & Moody, P. M. (2015). Black male academic support staff: Navigating the issues with black student athletes. In R. A. Bennett, S. R. Hodge, & D. L. Graham (Eds.), *Black males and intercollegiate athletics: An exploration of problems and solutions* (pp. 69–89). UK: Emerald Group Publishing. Retrieved from http://www.eblib.com

DeCuir-Gunby, J., Taliaferro, J., & Greenfield, D. (2010). Educators' perspectives on culturally relevant programs for academic success: The American Excellence Association. *Education and Urban Society, 42*(2), 182–204.

Donnor, J. K. (2005). Towards an interest convergence in the education of African American football student athletes in major college sports. *Race, Ethnicity, and Education, 8*(1), 45–67.

Engstrom, C., Sedlacek, W., & McEwen, M. (1995). Faculty attitudes toward male revenue and nonrevenue student-athletes. *Journal of College Student Development, 36*(3), 217–227.

Gayles, J. G., Crandall, R. E., & Jones III, C. R. (2015). Advising Black male student athletes: Implications for academic support programs. In R. A. Bennett, S. R. Hodge, & D. L. Graham (Eds.), *Black males and intercollegiate athletics: An exploration of problems and solutions* (pp. 45–68). UK: Emerald Group Publishing. Retrieved from http://www.eblib.com

Harper, S. R., & Hurtado, S. (2007). Nine themes in campus racial climates and implications for institutional transformation. *New Directions for Student Services* (120), 7–24. doi: 10.1002/ss.254

Harper, S. R., Williams, C. D., & Blackman, H. W. (2013). *Black male student athletes and racial inequalities in NCAA Division I college sports.* Center for the Study of Race and Equity in Education. University of Pennsylvania, Philadelphia.

Harrison, C. K. (1996). Samoan-American and African American male student-athletes: Any common themes? Paper presented at the North American Society for Sport Sociology Annual Meeting in Birmingham, Alabama.

Harrison, C. K. (2007). "Drop it like it's hot": Releasing Scholar-Baller voices and changing the "character of the discourse" in North American post-secondary institutions. *Journal for the Study of Sports and Athletes in Education, 1*(1), 77–88.

Harrison, C. K., & Boyd, J. (2007). Mainstreaming and integrating the spectacle and substance of Scholar-Baller: A new blueprint for higher education, the NCAA, and society. In D. Brooks & R. Althouse (Eds.), *Diversity and social justice in college sports: Sport management and the student-athlete* (pp. 201–231). Morgantown, WV: Fitness Information Technology.

Harrison, C. K., & Lawrence, S. M. (2003). African American student athletes' perceptions of career transition in sport: A qualitative and visual elicitation. *Race, Ethnicity and Education, 6*, 373–394.

Hawkins, B. (2013). *The new plantation: Black athletes, college sports and predominantly white NCAA institutions*. Reprint edition. New York: Palgrave Macmillan.

Hodge, S. R. (2015). Black male student athletes on predominantly white college and university campuses. In R. A. Bennett, S. R. Hodge, & D. L. Graham (Eds.), *Black males and intercollegiate athletics: An exploration of problems and solutions* (pp. 121–149). UK: Emerald Group Publishing. Retrieved from http://www.eblib.com

Hurtado, S., Milem, J., Clayton-Pederson, A., & Allen, W. (1999). Enacting diverse learning environments: Improving the climate for racial/ethnic diversity in higher education. *ASHE-ERIC higher education report, 26*(8).

Kearney, J., and Donaghy, M. (2010, June 27–30). Bridges and barriers to success for Pacific Islanders completing their first year at an Australian university. Proceedings of the 13th Pacific Rim First Year in Higher Education Conference, Adelaide, Australia.

Kimball, A. C. (2007). "You signed the line": Collegiate student-athletes' perceptions of autonomy. *Psychology of Sport and Exercise, 8*, 818–835.

Lam, G. (2014). A theoretical framework of the relation between socioeconomic status and academic achievement of students. *Education, 134*(3), 326–331.

Lapchick, R. (2014). Racial and gender report card on college football graduation rates. Institute of Diversity and Ethics in Sports. University of Central Florida, Orlando.

Lawrence, S. (2005). African American athletes' experiences of race in sport. *International Review for the Sociology of Sport, 40*(1), 99–110.

Morita, M. (2013). A study of Pacific Islander scholarship football players and their institutional experience in higher education. PhD diss., School of Education, University of Southern California, Los Angeles.

Museus, S. D., & Jayakumar, U. M. (2012). *Creating campus cultures: Fostering success among racially diverse student populations*. New York: Routledge.

NCAA. (2006). *Best hiring practices. Partnering for a better tomorrow manual*. Overland Park, KS: NCAA.

Oliver, M. L. (1980). The transmission of sport mobility orientation in the family. *International Review for the Sociology of Sport, 15*(2), 51–75.

Oseguera, L. (2010). Success despite the image: How African American male student-athletes endure their academic journey amidst negative characterizations. *Journal for the Study of Sports and Athletes in Education, 4*(3), 297–324.

Oseguera, L., & Rhee, B. S. (2009). The influence of institutional retention climates on student persistence to degree completion: A multilevel approach. *Research in Higher Education, 50*, 546–569.

Rankin, S. R., & Reason, R. D. (2005). Differing perceptions: How students of color and white students perceive campus climate for underrepresented groups. *Journal of College Student Development, 46*(1), 43–61. doi: 10.1353/csd.2005.0008

Rankin, S. R.?, & Reason, R. D.? (2008). Transformational tapestry model: A comprehensive approach to transforming campus climate. *Journal of Diversity in Higher Education, 1*(4), 262–274.

Rhoden, W. (2011, December 11). At some N.F.L. positions, stereotypes create prototypes. *New York Times.* Retrieved from http://www.nytimes.com/2011/12/12/sports/football/at-some-nfl-positions-stereotypes-reign.html?_r=0

Rhodes, J. E. (2005). A model of youth mentoring. In D. L. DuBois & M. J. Karcher (Eds.), *Handbook of youth mentoring* (pp. 30–43). Thousand Oaks, CA: Sage.

Richards, S., & Aries, E. (1998). The Division III student-athlete: Academic performance, campus involvement and growth. *Journal of College Student Development, 40*(3), 211–218.

Sager, M. (2015, November 19). The Samoan pipeline: How does a tiny island, 5,000 miles from the U.S. mainland, produce so many professional football players? *California Sunday Magazine.*

Settles, I. H., Sellers, R. M., & Damas Jr., A. (2002). One role or two? The function of psychological separation in role conflict. *Journal of Applied Psychology, 87,* 574–582. doi: 10.1037//0021-9010.87.3.574

Singer, J. (2005). Understanding racism through the eyes of African American male student-athletes. *Race, Ethnicity and Education, 8,* 365–386.

Smith, P. (1990). *Killing the spirit.* New York: Penguin Group.

Tengan, T. P. K., & Markham, J. M. (2009). Performing Polynesian masculinities in American football: From "rainbows to warriors." *International Journal of the History of Sport, 26*(16), 2412–2431.

Upthegrove, T., Roscigno, V., & Zubrinsky, C. (1999). Big money collegiate sports: Racial concentration, contradictory pressures, and academic performance. *Social Science Quarterly, 80,* 718–737.

Wilson, R. (2015). Jimbo Fisher: Jameis Winston "is as smart as anybody I've been around." *CBS Sports.* Retrieved from http://www.cbssports.com/nfl/eye-on-football/25081104/jimbo-fisher-jameis-winston-is-as-smart-as-anybody-ive-been-around

Winkle-Wagner, R., & Locks, A. (2013). *Diversity and inclusion on campus: Supporting racially and ethnically underrepresented students.* Core Concepts in Higher Education. New York: Routledge.

16

Activism in College Athletics

A Case Study of the Student-Athletes Human Rights Project

Emmett Gill, Jr.

The idea that the opportunity to participate in sports is a human right is fairly well established (Kaufman & Wolff, 2010; Kidd & Donnelly, 2000), but that is not the type of human rights to be discussed here. When a senior athletic department administrator was informed about a panel discussion on college athletes' rights at the 2014 National Collegiate Athletic Association (NCAA) convention, she smirked and blurted: "Student-athletes don't have any rights." Human rights refer to moral principles and norms on the way humans should behave and should be treated. Barnes (1996) notes that a right is a recognized interest and a matter of moral and legal entitlement that others, like sport organizations, universities, and businesses who sponsor sports, are duty-bound to respect. In the United States, there are only two formal policies that guarantee student-athletes specific rights. First, in 2012 the state of California passed Senate Bill No. 1525—a college athlete bill of rights that requires continuing education for players attending institutions of higher education with graduation rates under 60 percent. Additionally, this bill requires colleges and universities to provide coverage for insurance premiums and medical expenses for players up to two years after they exhaust their eligibility (SB-1525, 2012). The only other policy guaranteeing college athletes specific rights is at the institutional level; Indiana University (IU) is the only Division I athletic department that has developed a college athlete bill of rights. The bill includes multiyear scholarships to full scholarship athletes, increases in healthcare commitments, a lifetime opportunity to earn a degree, an iPad, and a blazer for all IU athletes. Although college athletes have gained some rights, most notably, multiyear scholarships, their human rights are violated on a weekly, if not daily, basis.

When using traditional human rights terminology, some of the substantive human entitlements that apply to college athletes include freedom from torture (e.g., physical, emotional, and sexual abuse), the right to a fair trial (due process when accused of an NCAA violation), and freedom of movement (in the case of a

KEY TERMS

▶ Activism

▶ Human rights

▶ Confrontation

▶ Collaboration

▶ College athletes

request to transfer and play immediately) (United Nations Human Rights, 2014). The purpose of this chapter is to explore two college athletics human rights issues—abusive coaching and cultural racism and how one nonprofit organization attempted to address these issues with the NCAA and two NCAA member institutions.

THE STUDENT-ATHLETES HUMAN RIGHTS PROJECT

The Student-Athlete's Human Rights Project is a 501(c)(4) organization committed to ending the exploitation of college athletes while promoting their development and overall well-being. The Project provides real-time advocacy and activism for college athletes in cases where they are treated unjustly. In the Project's developmental stages, we realized there was a great need for work "in between the hedges." Less global, but more fundamental individual rights violations continue to prevail in the college athletics systems, because the NCAA and its member institutions profit from exploiting college athletes. The Project has challenged several human rights issues, involving the right to transfer expeditiously and without limitation; new and cultural racism; verbal, physical, sexual, and emotional abuse; lack of due process; sudden scholarship loss; unequal/miseducation; and dangerous "working conditions." Nonetheless, the Project also gathered that the complexity and high-stakes nature of college sports activism required a unique and largely incomparable model.

Activism can include collaboration, confrontation, negotiation, and co-optation (Homan, 2010). Of these four, the Project focused on collaboration and confrontation. When reaching out to an NCAA member institution about an alleged violation of a college athlete's rights, our first option or approach is collaboration. Collaboration is the Project's priority strategy and is a result of conversations with Dr. Harry Edwards. Of course, Edwards (1969) was the architect of the Olympic Project for Human Rights, which was an effort to protest against racial segregation in the United States and racism in sports generally (Zirin, 2012). Collaboration is when two or more parties share resources to accomplish a goal important to them both and they each perform work toward that goal. Collaboration is the desire to work together. Yet, we quickly learned that athletic departments are more closed and somewhat resistant to being open to outsiders, which makes collaboration challenging. To date not one institution has welcomed the Project with open arms. Given this reality, our next option is typically confrontation. Confrontation is a strategy used when trying to compel a target to change its behavior, position, policies, procedures, or some aspect of the way it does business (Homan, 2010). In the early stages of the Project's work, confrontation was our second option and, unfortunately, also our last resort when universities were unresponsive. In the process of "calling out" schools, our efforts can become complex simply because athletic departments do not like the attention or to be questioned. "Calling out" schools included "truth exposure," which consisted of providing the facts of the case to stakeholders (e.g., athletes, alumni, and local media) of the university's athletic department. To date, the Project has been involved in 17 cases ranging from racism to miseducation.

RACISM AT COLORADO STATE UNIVERSITY

This section will explore the Project's first of two college athlete human rights cases. The first case involves the Project's response to racist comments made by the Colorado State University (CSU) athletic director and head football coach to a group of Black CSU football alumni. In addition to supplying a timeline of the CSU case, this section will integrate key principles of activism that the Project learned and/or implemented during the CSU case, including making a choice between collaboration and confrontation.

On April 23, 2013, a former CSU Black football college athlete alumnus contacted Dr. Harry Edwards, who in turn notified the Project of allegations against CSU. Allegedly Jack Graham, the CSU athletic director, and Jim McElwain, the CSU head football coach, made the following comments in a heated exchange with Black former football players during a meeting at the home of the CSU vice president of student affairs:

> "Culturally Black people teach their kids to smoke weed @ 10/11 yrs old."
> —Jack Graham

> "I've never seen a solid family structure in a home of a player I recruited"
> —Jim McElwain

Over the next several days, the national coordinator of the Project and the CSU Black football college athlete alumnus had several conversations about the Black athlete experience at CSU. The members of the Project were notified of the case and encouraged to provide input and during our electronic interactions, we learned that Drs. David Ridpath and Albert Bimper attended CSU as undergraduate students.

On May 2, the Project received a call from Dr. Bimper, and he affirmed Graham and McElwain's comments. After days of consultation, the Project leadership determined that it would open a case concerning CSU and that our communiqué should be directed to the university president. The initial goal of our interface with CSU was to collaborate with the university by helping it understand the detrimental nature of the comments, craft strategies to repair the harm, build programming to understand new and cultural racism, and prevent future race talk. Much of our direction was charted after mentoring from Dr. Edwards.

On May 4, the Project received a call from Dr. Bimper, who is now the leader of the newly formed Black Student-Athletes Alumni Association (BSAAA) (Bimper,

2013). Dr. Bimper asked that the Project allow the BSAAA to handle engaging CSU in strategies to make amendments for the racist comments and other past transgressions related to its Black athletes.

On May 6, the Project contacted Danny Mattie, CSU assistant director of public relations, to affirm the alleged comments. Mr. Mattie expressed that he would research and communicate with the Project later. Mattie never returned the phone call. On May 10, and via email, the Project sent correspondence to the BSAAA and CSU president Dr. Tony Frank. On May 20, Frank responded via email to the Project. Dr. Frank acknowledged something had happened and that Graham and McElwain would be dealt with internally.

On May 29 and 30, the Fort Collins *Coloradoan* newspaper emailed the Project and inquired about Graham and McElwain's comments and asked to speak with the Black former CSU football athlete who first reported the comments (Novey, 2013). The *Coloradoan* refused to run a story on the incident, because opinions varied on whether the comments were offensive. On May 31, the Project sent a second letter to President Frank; asking Graham and McElwain's supervisor to hold them accountable for their comments. On the same day, CSU announced the hiring of Albert Bimper as the senior associate athletic director for diversity and inclusion.

On June 12, President Frank responded to the Project's second letter inquiring about the inappropriate comments by senior athletic administrators and their accountability. President Frank reiterated that he wanted to keep the door open with regard to working with the Project but that he would leave that decision to the vice president of student affairs, Dr. Blanche Hughes, and vice president for diversity, Mary Ontiveros. Neither CSU official reached out to the Project. And as of August 2013, CSU had not provided any information on McElwain or Graham's discipline or any information on what steps the university would take to prevent future cultural and new racism in athletics or to intervene in cases that escaped prevention efforts.

Line between Collaboration and Confrontation

Our first major lesson pertained to the most productive way to proceed once collaboration was not feasible, and confrontation began because repeated attempts to engage in dialogue were unsuccessful. In the Project's early cases, we would share potentially antagonistic strategies with universities. Despite our best attempts to soften our message, most times our revealing was construed as a threat. The Project had to rethink that tactic. It was the Project's hope that by sharing alternative avenues, universities would see that there are other streams of accountability and be more responsive. Regrettably, that did not happen until our fifteenth case. Now, our strategy is not to reveal combative tactics; we "just do it."

After three months of phone and letter exchanges with CSU and with the onset of the college football season near, the Project decided to engage in some "truth exposure" about the CSU incident by reaching out to CSU recruits and players. First, the Project secured a list of CSU recruits and then secured their Facebook and Twitter accounts and addresses. Next, we began to contact current CSU football athletes, CSU recruits, and CSU football enthusiasts via Twitter and Facebook. We sent messages that included McElwain and Graham's quotes with no other content or commentary. The aim of the truth exposure was to inform. There was no return communication from current athletes, but one CSU recruit contacted our organization, three CSU contacts retweeted our tweets, and another recruit communicated that he was reconsidering his CSU commitment.

On August 9, 2013, Madeline Novey of the *Coloradoan* published "CSU Athletics Boosts Diversity Efforts after Allegations of Racial Insensitivity." The 145-line story incorporated the following five lines about the incident: "Upset by comments made by CSU Athletic Director Jack Graham and head football coach Jim McElwain that some attendees deemed to be racially insensitive, the alumni continued to push for changes in emails sent in the days following the meeting" (Novey, 2013). And on August 9, 2014, ESPN reported that Jack Graham was fired (Frei, 2014). Then, the University of Florida Gators hired McElwain on December 4, 2014 (Low, 2014). On April 21, 2015, the Project met with University of Florida (UF) senior administrators and McElwain to discuss our continuing concern about how he might impact UF college athletes.

Members of the Project believe it would have been appropriate for CSU to (1) rely on the Project or some other entity familiar with cultural competence in sports to provide an independent assessment of diversity and inclusion within CSU's athletic department; and (2) disclose any disciplinary actions and mandates (e.g., cultural humility training) for Jack Graham and Jim McElwain. The Project believes the disclosure of this information would have provided a measure of social justice for the Black former athletes involved in the meeting and a blueprint for other athletic departments that might be challenged by issues of racism. The Projects' case involving Jim McElwain remains open.

PHYSICAL, VERBAL, AND EMOTIONAL ABUSE AT RUTGERS UNIVERSITY

This section will explore the widely publicized case of abuse of college athletes within the Rutgers University (RU) men's basketball program. The Rutgers occurrence was the Project's second case, and it was very challenging because of its notoriety and the fact that there was no athletic director in place in the aftermath of the controversy. In addition to supplying a timeline of the case, this section will integrate key principles of activism that the Project learned and/or implemented during the case, including utilization of the media and of public policy in the pursuit of social justice for college athletes.

On April 2, 2013, the video of Rutgers men's basketball coach, Mike Rice, physically and verbally abusing players was revealed. As well, on April 5, the Project sent correspondence to the Rutgers university secretary, board of governors, board of trustees, and university president regarding the video. And on April 10, the Newark *Star-Ledger* published parts of the Project's April 5 letter to RU. In the letter, the Project asked the RU Board of Governors to dismiss university president Robert Barchi, in part because of athletic department mismanagement and the reality that Barchi didn't bother to watch the tape of Rice's abuse months prior to the public revelation.

On April 18, the Project sent correspondence to the RU interim athletic director, Carl Kirschner, regarding the welfare and needs of the college athletes touched by the verbal, physical, and emotional abuse. The electronic correspondence was followed with three phone calls. The same correspondence was sent via certified mail on May 1 to the interim athletic director and the university president. On May 31, the Project delivered an email letter to new RU men's basketball coach, Eddie Jordan, expressing concern for the "abused" men's basketball college athletes' well-being. Tom Stephens, the RU faculty athletic representative was also copied on the letter. On the same day, the Project forwarded an email to Richard Edwards. Edwards is the RU executive vice president for academic affairs, a member of the Academic Oversight for Intercollegiate Athletics committee, and a co-chair of the RU athletic director search committee. Not one representative from Rutgers responded to the Project's outreach. On June 4, the Project followed up on its email to Coach Jordan with a phone call. Neither representative from the men's basketball team returned our calls or messages. In mid-June, the Project sent a fifth letter to Rutgers regarding the treatment of the student-athlete victims. The Project sent the letter to RU in part because one student-athlete transferred out and then back in to the RU program, and that was concerning.

Emerging Activism Strategies, Part I

Once the Project decided on confrontation, acquiring some media exposure became paramount. In the Rutgers case, the willingness of the *Newark Star-Ledger* to post one of our letters garnered the attention of the Rutgers University athletic department and demonstrated that we had at least one ally. In the Colorado State University case we desperately tried to harvest some media coverage but were unsuccessful. Since the Rutgers case, media exposure has not been included in our arsenal. The Project looks to return to strategies to secure media exposure, because this tactic is not a labor-intensive task. Media exposure can be extremely beneficial in terms of the audience it reaches. In terms of group dynamics, some favor more media, but others prefer a more modest approach. The Project's aim is to make athletic programs uncomfortable and help them understand that college athletes have another organization trying to ensure their rights.

On an August 13, 2013, the Project sent a request to the NCAA asking it to open an investigation into the abuse by Mike Rice and the response by the NCAA member institution. In late August, Julie Hermann, the new Rutgers athletic director, contacted the Project regarding its August 13 NCAA letter. The Project never talked with Hermann but did dialogue with Rutgers associate athletic director, Kate Hickey. The Project did understand that Rutgers was going through a significant transition with its move to the Big Ten and believed that this might delay its responses, but we believed it was important to reserve our place in line to discuss RU college athlete abuse. On September 10, 2013, the Project received correspondence from NCAA president Mark Emmert. Emmert acknowledged concerns over the situation at Rutgers, expressing that there are bylaws to address abusive coaching. He offered as well the opportunity for a member of the Project to serve on the newly formed NCAA Mental Health Task Force.

Emerging Activism Strategies, Part II

A strategy that became a derivative of confrontation was the use of public policies, laws, and systems that could be used to hold universities accountable for violations of college athletes' rights. The first use of public systems was the use of state child welfare systems in the Rutgers University student-athlete abuse case. The use of state and federal systems and policies has great promise and is as close to a legal strategy that an advocacy organization can come without dipping into the legal realm. When speaking of abuse, neglect, and mistreatment of college athletes, state and federal provisions regarding child abuse are relevant. In general the provision protects adolescents under the age of 18, and the average age of a college freshman is 18. However, a meaningful number of college athletes also enter college before they are 18; moreover, the perception of accountability that state child abuse laws provide can act as a deterrent. In addition, state child abuse officials informed the Project that filing a complaint with law enforcement officials is another avenue for college athletes who are 18 or older and abused, neglected, or mistreated by coaches. The enforcement structure established by the NCAA also falls within the boundaries of this strategy. The scheme that Rutgers most disliked was the Project asking the NCAA to investigate the abuse and lumping Rutger's abuse with the Jerry Sandusky case at Penn State.

On November 13, 2013, the Project reached out to the New Jersey Department of Children and Families (DCF) Division of Child Protection and Permanency (DCP&P) and Institutional Abuse Investigative Unit (IAIU) to report the abuse of RU coach Mike Rice. On November 6, Robyne Jiles (2013), the university secretary, responded that, in regard to "the situation concerning the Rutgers' basketball coach, the coach did not have any caretaking responsibilities of the 17 year old college students. As such, there's no exchange of caretaking responsibilities for any professor or coach whom [sic] works for the university" (para 2). On February 15, 2014, the Project received an email from a local reporter covering RU sports. The following is the opening of the letter: "I have a sincere respect for who you are and what you do, for your organization in general and you in particular have done in following the Mike Rice controversy and the ensuing fallout" (Duggan, 2014). From a collaborative standpoint, the Project hoped that Rutgers would consult with our scholars with expertise in college athlete development and abuse (1) to assess the athletic department's efforts to prevent abuse and (2) to develop a system, external to athletics, for reporting abusive and neglectful coaching. Lastly, the Project maintains that President Barchi should have been dismissed and that his successor appoint a vice president to provide strict oversight over athletics. To help address concerns about the rights and well-being of college athletes, six recommendations for change are suggested:

RECOMMENDATIONS FOR CHANGE

- Increase the number of college athletes on the NCAA 80-member autonomy panel from 15 to 40.

- Develop an amateur sport-governing body, with higher education accreditation (e.g., the Southern Association of Colleges and Schools Commission on Colleges) to produce policy regarding physical, verbal, and emotional abuse of college athletes that includes penalties for athletic departments and their universities.

- Develop a national caucus supported by the US Senate Commerce, Science and Transportation Committee and the Congressional Black Caucus to develop a national agenda for college athletes' human rights.

- Pursue the reintroduction of the Collegiate Athletics Due Process Act of 2000. The proposed act requires the institution to provide (1) any accused student-athlete with separate independent legal counsel at the institution's expense immediately upon any investigation or alleged violation or infraction, and through the entire investigation, until all matters and facts of the pending case have concluded to the satisfaction of all parties involved; and (2) the accused college athlete with one notice and opportunity to be heard before an arbitrator not associated with the NCAA.

- Create a national new racism advisory board that includes diversity and inclusion experts, college athletes, social workers, psychologists, sociologists, and other related professional disciplines.

- Create a penalty structure in which federal funds are withheld from NCAA member institutions found to be involved in racism, abuse, or violations of college athletes' due process and human rights.

Indicators of Success

The Colorado State University case did not yield any direct measurable results. Some Project members suggested that the pressure we exerted contributed to the hiring of CSU's associate athletic director for diversity and inclusion. As a result of our "truth exposure" campaign, one CSU recruit reconsidered his decision to include CSU in his college choice and ultimately signed with another university.

For the Rutgers University case, the only evidence that the Project's efforts made an impact was based on an email received from a local reporter. The Rutgers case, because the institution was in the midst of a move to the Big Ten, was unusually challenging. Rutgers University is also unique in that the school is constantly involved in athletic scandals. For instance, during our interface with Rutgers over the Mike Rice abuse, it was revealed that the new athletic director had a history of abusive coaching, a defensive coach bullied a football player, and the newly hired head basketball coach misrepresented his educational accomplishments. Months later the Project received a call from a Rutgers women's sports team about alleged neglect of Rutgers athletes.

CONCLUSION

What the Project learned, in terms of new strategies and a renewed focus, is invaluable. In order to more clearly define our collaborative intentions, we added one new strategy to our arsenal because of the changes, such as the pursuit of college athletes' name and likeness rights, in the college athletics landscape. One change is that athletic departments are more seriously considering collaborating with outside resources as they seek resolutions to college athlete and athletic department controversies. One strategy enhancement was taking a summary of the Project's assets and developing information on them for the schools with which we interacted. Our summary of assets communicated to athletic programs what the Project could offer.

Moving forward, the Projects' two primary foci will be due process and mobilizing college athletes. The number one matter in college athletes' human rights is due process. Some of the critical due process elements include the ability to confront witnesses, the full disclosure of the facts, the right to suppress illegally obtained evidence, the right to counsel, a formal and public hearing, and the ability to impose liability for damages. Foremost, college athletes deserve the right to be heard before being banned from practicing their trade. It is plausible that, because due process is a legal issue that has been ignored by the court, it will require more serious forms of confrontation, such as work stoppages. The Project's pursuit of college athlete due process will require partnering with the small number of lawyers practicing civil rights in college sports law. Nonetheless, the most viable, and ironically related, strategy that the Project will work toward in subsequent years is mobilizing college athletes. The oppression of college athletes continues, because they remain separated from one another and from activists. The Project will try to work directly with college athletes affected by or interested in college athletes' rights.

QUESTIONS FOR DISCUSSION

1. Should independent organizations be involved in college athlete human rights issues?

2. Can you name three local, state, or federal policies that can be used to enforce college athletes' human rights?

3. In each case study presented in this chapter, what might you do differently in terms of pursuing collaborative efforts or confronting schools who refuse to engage in constructive dialogue?

References

Barnes, J. (1996). *Sports and the Law in Canada*. Toronto: Butterworths.

Bimper, A. (2013, May 4). Personal communication.

Duggan, D. (2014, June 12). Personal communication.

Edwards, H. (1969). *The revolt of the Black athlete*. New York: Free Press.

Frei, T. (2014, August 8). Jack Graham fired as CSU athletic director, calls decision "surprising," "disappointing." *Denver Post*. Retrieved from http://www.denverpost.com/colleges/ci_26302027/jack-graham-fired-csu-athletic-director

Homan, M. (2010). *Promoting community change: Making it happen in the real world*. Cengage Learning.

Jiles, R. (2013, November 3). Personal communication.

Kaufman, P., & Wolff, E. A. (2010). Playing and protesting: Sport as a vehicle for social change. *Journal of Sport & Social Issues, 34*(2), 154–175.

Kidd, B., & Donnelly, P. (2000). Human rights in sports. *International Review for the Sociology of Sport, 35*(2), 131–148.

Low, C. (2014, December 4). Jim McElwain to coach Florida. ESPN. Retrieved from http://espn.go.com/college-football/story/_/id/11977425/jim-mcelwain-becomes-florida-gators-coach

Novey, M. (2013, August 21). CSU athletics boosts diversity efforts after allegations of racial insensitivity. *Coloradoan*. Retrieved from http://archive.coloradoan.com/article/20130808/NEWS01/308080055/CSU-athletics-boosts-diversity-efforts-after-allegations-racial-insensitivity

SB-1525. Postsecondary education: Student athlete bill of rights. California State Legislature. (2011–2012). Retrieved from http://leginfo.legislature.ca.gov/faces/billNavClient.xhtml?bill_id=201120120SB1525

United Nations Human Rights. (2014). *What are human rights?* Retrieved from http://www.ohchr.org/en/issues/pages/whatarehumanrights.aspx

Zirin, D. (2012, June 28). Resistance: the best Olympic spirit. *International Socialism*. Retrieved from http://www.isj.org.uk/index.php4?id=823&issue=135

Restoring Balance

Putting the "Student" and "Collegiate"
Back in Intercollegiate Athletics

Scott N. Brooks

This volume is a necessary text. The "Sports Industrial Complex" is ever-expanding and so are the inequality gaps in participation, wages, opportunities, and experiences. The authors have done an outstanding job by addressing the most pressing concerns for today's college athletes. We all are encouraged to think and act differently. And, some student athletes have already begun to do so.

Saturday, November 7, 2015, at about 8 pm: The *Tweet sent around the world* by Anthony Sherrills pictured 30-plus Black members of the University of Missouri football team. Under the picture read, "We're black. Black is powerful. Our struggle may look different, but we are all *#ConcernedStudent1950*." The players announced that they were boycotting all football activities until Johnathan Butler was eating again. This was it, the proverbial game changer. The following morning, head coach, Gary Pinkel, his staff, and all of the members of Mizzou's football team took a photo and tweeted that they were all together. Sherrills wrote: "WE ARE ONE!!!! The coaches and administration are behind us!!!! *#ConcernedStudent1950*." This action by some of Missouri's Black football players was the match that lit the whole situation aflame. On November 9, the University of Missouri's system president resigned and the Columbia campus chancellor was demoted.

Missouri is only a canary in the mine; there is a huge problem in our collegiate system, where millions of dollars are at stake each and every kickoff. It is clear the business of the university is football. Because of this, Black football players, as the "preferred workers" and cornerstones of the workforce, can bring that business to a halt by saying that they won't play.

The Missouri Black football player strike is an example of class consciousness. Class consciousness develops through a process of self- and collective awareness of conditions vis-à-vis others (i.e., athletes in relation to the figure or organization of power, or in this case, administration), sharing information, and then coordinating an action. The result is always some change, but this is what is left to be figured out. However, the University of Missouri strike reveals some key fissures in the team: the protest was not unanimous, a total collective effort of the football team. Only Black players were in the picture, and only about half of the Black players were included. Not only might this signal a racial division in the team but also a division among Black players—those who were "down" and those were not. What are the other possible divisions, the teams within the team? And, how might this reflect what exists broadly in athletics and on campus as a whole? As the tweet read, the student and student-athlete experiences are connected. What are we to do when our campus is so divided, when some feel alienated and therefore alienate others? Is this healthy for an athletics department and a campus?

These are important questions, and yet there are even more troublesome potential issues of crime in intercollegiate athletics to be worked out in the near future: cyberbullying and cybersexual assault and harassment; gender equity; violations of privacy; freedom of speech; policing and surveillance; mental health issues and corporate responsibility; wrongful termination and hostile management of athletes; long-term health care for athletes and the university's responsibility; and unethical educational practices. Athletics has long been decried as the "front porch of the University," as a positive marketing and advertising arm that increases applications for admissions and therefore revenues, selectivity, and possible prestige. But the current media-driven sports climate has clearly also brought the underbelly to light, showing that breaking the rules and exploitation are more commonly the rule than the exception. Athletics can be the front porch but also the back porch or the outhouse of the university as well.

As critical researchers and onlookers of the collegiate arms race and its exploitation of specific athletes—those who are predominantly Black and male and participating in cash sports—we might understandably conclude that the whole thing be scrapped and begun anew, strive for the creation of a totally different intercollegiate athletic model. However, this is improbable, if not unreasonable; what would happen to those student-athletes currently on the conveyor belt and in the pipeline. It is not only the institutions of higher education that would be affected. Athletic administrators need to seize this opportunity to progress. How can an athletic department be a leader for change and resolution? It is not only time for the *student* to be emphasized in "student-athlete," but for the *collegiate* to be priority in "collegiate athletics."

I recall a few years back reading responses to Taylor Branch's analysis of collegiate athletics in the *Chronicle of Higher Education*. One hefty thread of discussion was sparked by a comment that universities should give a degree in athletics to those athletes who are not really going in order to earn a degree but are clearly contributing to university life and potential revenues. Some agreed, even outlining a rough curriculum that would offer course credit for weight lifting and practice, identify coaches as professors, and award degrees early, to those who excelled on their respective playing field. The logic was: let's stop pretending that we don't know about the exploitive relationship between intercollegiate athletics and athletes and just give the athletes degrees for their athletic participation—something that universities are uniquely in the position to give and already give, for far less work. This seemed crazy: a degree in football or basketball. Initially, I could not put my finger on exactly why this idea was so wrong. Of course, this would be only a Band-Aid; this would not change "business as usual" and would drag down the worth of all degrees. Still, it was addressing the basic issue of inequity: athletes weren't given enough by universities, and guaranteeing athletes degrees would ensure that they get something that they could hold on to. But then it dawned on me, this logical argument about universities simply giving what they already give—degrees—was not only the easy way out, but it was not considerate of athletes and athletes' rights and choices, although it masqueraded as such. The athletic department is NOT:

> Just a PE department with "basketball" or "tennis" or "football" classes.

> Just a professional sports franchise.

> Just a talent scout or summer sports camp.

Intercollegiate athletics is a part of the educational and social mission of a college/university. Thus, the athletic department should not operate as a total institution, coordinating, managing, and regulating so much of a student athlete's time and life. In addition, it's not a professional franchise that has basically purchased the rights of selfhood. In short, athletics needs to come back home or open its doors more to the campus and community. It has gone out too far, and it soon may be untethered—like Sandra Bullock in the movie *Gravity*—and with very little chance of returning to higher education. Intercollegiate athletics could be a greater campus resource: providing facilities for more campus and community activities and augmenting academic programming by inviting prominent public figures (athletic, popular, and scholarly). It can be a catalyst for change on campus—sharing financial and support resources to build Title IV programs, providing counseling and health services for all students, and suggesting and hosting innovative courses and events. It could benefit from the training and research resources on campus—such as faculty and staff—to prepare coaches, administrators and staff for effectively leading today's students and student-athletes in the current collegiate and global environment.

The pendulum swings back and forth, and now is an important time to address, push for, and assert the rights of student-athletes to regain a balance with commercialism and institutional rights and authority.

Contributors

Eddie Comeaux is an associate professor of higher education at the University of California, Riverside. He maintains an active research agenda that examines the college student experience—with special attention on athletes and underrepresented students—and how those experiences influence their subsequent outcomes. Central to his work are issues of access and equity. Comeaux has authored two books and more than 50 peer-reviewed journal articles, book chapters, and other academic publications and reports. His research appears in *Educational Researcher, Journal of Higher Education, Journal of College Student Development, Journal of Intercollegiate Sport, Sociology of Sport Journal,* and several other well-regarded academic journals. As well, Comeaux has created and co-produced several narrative documentaries, delivered keynote addresses, and presented more than 150 research papers, workshops, and symposia at higher education institutions and national research conferences.

Comeaux teaches courses on college student development theories, intercollegiate athletics, foundations of research, and diversity issues in higher education. He is the cofounder and former chair of the Special Interest Group, Research Focus on Education and Sport for the American Educational Research Association. In addition, Comeaux serves on several editorial boards. Prior to earning his PhD at UCLA, he was drafted out of the University of California, Berkeley, in the amateur free draft by the Texas Rangers baseball organization and spent four years playing professionally.

J. P. Abercrumbie is a student-athlete engagement practitioner for Mississippi State University, responsible for the Bulldogs' personal and leadership development programs, professional and postgraduate preparation, and community outreach and engagement opportunities supported by the athletic department's Pay It Forward initiative. Serving as a member of the Mississippi State Athletics senior staff, Abercrumbie oversees all areas of the Life Skills program while assisting the senior women's administrator with daily operations and special projects. Prior to this role, she served as a student-athlete development coordinator for the California Golden Bears. A former Division I cross country/track and field competitor, Abercrumbie is a graduate of Temple University who also earned a Master of Arts in the Cultural Studies of Sport in Education from the University of California, Berkeley. Abercrumbie also serves as a member of various Mississippi State University, NCAA Leadership Development, and National Association of Collegiate Women Athletics Administrators (NACWAA) committees.

Jean Boyd serves as the senior associate athletic director for student-athlete development at Arizona State University (ASU). Boyd leads Sun Devil Athletics' commitment to graduating and preparing student-athletes to become high achievers in life. He also coordinates student-athlete well-being programs and leads the department's diversity and inclusion efforts. In 2012, Boyd was named the National Associate of Academic Advisors for Athletes' Lan Hewelett Award winner—given to the top academic professional as voted by his or her peers. Prior to this most recent appointment at ASU, Boyd served as coordinator then manager for life skills, manager for football academics, assistant then associate athletic director for student athlete development.

Boyd joined the ASU Athletic Department as a management intern in July 1995 after spending time with the New England Patriots in 1994 and the London Monarchs (NFL Europe) in spring of 1995.

Scott N. Brooks is an associate professor at the University of California, Riverside in the Graduate School of Education. He is primarily an ethnographer interested in equity, student engagement, coaching and leadership, and community-based learning. Dr. Brooks has published in academic journals and edited volumes and textbooks; he has been quoted and reviewed by the *Wall Street Journal, New York Times, Washington Post, Der Speigel,* and *SLAM* magazine. Additionally, Brooks has consulted for the NFL, MLB, and college and high school coaches and athletes. He is a senior fellow at the Wharton Sports Business Initiative and Yale Urban Ethnography Project. His book, *Black Men Can't Shoot* (University of Chicago, 2009), tells how young Black men in Philadelphia learn and utilize the importance of exposure, networks, and opportunities toward earning athletic scholarships. He is currently working on three manuscripts: one regarding coaching, a second that investigates high school basketball since 1950, and a third project on Black campus dating.

Mitchell J. Chang is professor of Higher Education and Organizational Change and Asian American Studies (by courtesy) at UCLA. Chang's research focuses on diversity-related issues and initiatives on college campuses. He has written over 90 publications, some of which have been cited in US Supreme Court rulings concerning the use of race-conscious admissions practices. Chang received a National Academy of Education/Spencer Fellowship in 2001 and was recognized for outstanding research in both 2000 and 2008 by the American College Personnel Association. In 2006, *Diverse: Issues in Higher Education* profiled him as one of the nation's top 10 scholars. Chang has also served in elected positions for both the American Educational Research Association, which inducted him as a Fellow in 2016, and the Association for the

Study of Higher Education, which awarded him the Founder's Service Award in 2014.

Joseph N. Cooper is an assistant professor in Sport Management within the Neag School of Education at the University of Connecticut (UConn). His research focuses on the intersection between sport, education, race, and culture with an emphasis on sport as a catalyst for holistic development and positive change in society. Cooper is also the founder of Collective Uplift (CU), an organization designed to educate, empower, inspire, and support individuals across racial and ethnic backgrounds to maximize their full potential as holistic individuals both within and beyond athletic contexts (CU video link: http://youtu.be/gIj9N_M_URI). Cooper is a native of Greensboro, North Carolina, and a proud graduate of the University of North Carolina at Chapel Hill (BA in Sociology and Recreation Administration and MA in Sport Administration) and the University of Georgia (PhD in Kinesiology with a concentration in Sport Management and Policy).

Jamel K. Donnor is an associate professor in the School of Education at the College of William and Mary. Professor Donnor's research focuses primarily on race and equity in education, the schooling experiences of Black male students, and college sports. *Teachers College Record, Race, Ethnicity and Education, Education and Urban Society,* and *Urban Education* are some peer-reviewed journals in which his research is published. His 2005 journal article, "Towards an Interest-Convergence in the Education of African American Football Student Athletes in Major College Sports," is one of the most widely cited publications on African American male student-athletes. Dr. Donnor earned his PhD from the University of Wisconsin at Madison. His dissertation was on the racialized experiences and outcomes of African American football players. His books include *The Resegregation of Schools: Education and Race in the Twenty-First Century* (Routledge, 2013), *The Education of Black Males in a "Post-Racial" World* (Routledge, 2012), and *The Charter*

School Solution: Distinguishing Fact from Rhetoric (Routledge, 2016).

Emmett Gill, Jr., currently serves as the founding president of the National Alliance of Social Workers in Sports (NASWIS), the national coordinator for the Student-Athletes Human Rights Project and as a consulting social worker for college athletes and athletic departments. Dr. Gill has worked at North Carolina Central University (NCCU), the US Military Academy Center for Enhanced Performance (where he supervised men's and women's basketball student-athletes' performance enhancement) as well as Rutgers University (as an assistant professor and faculty mentor for women's basketball). Dr. Gill began his career in athletics as a learning specialist for the University of Maryland football program, and he developed a Student-Athletes Wellness Center while at NCCU. Dr. Gill's scholarship focuses on the intersection between social work, athletics, scandals, and social justice in sports.

Whitney Griffin is a learning scientist from the Educational Psychology program at the University of Washington. Griffin completed postdoctoral work under Professor Eddie Comeaux in the Graduate School of Education at the University of California, Riverside before creating her own niche. Her research interests combine cognitive skills, compensatory strategies, and therapeutic yoga for retired athletes with histories of sport concussions and learning disabilities. She has authored several peer-reviewed articles in academic journals and has published chapters in two books. She continues her private work as a tutor for children with concussions, learning disabilities, and Attention-Deficit Hyperactive Disorder and as a caregiver for people with Alzheimer's and aphasia.

Gerald Gurney is an assistant professor of Adult and Higher Education at the University of Oklahoma, where he teaches in the subject areas of athletics in higher education, athletics academic reform, and ethics in athletics. He is an author and guest on a number of national media news shows. Dr. Gurney has been featured in popular documentaries on college sports including *Schooled, the Price of College Sports* and *HBO Real Sports* with Bryant Gumbel. Gurney previously served in senior-level athletic administration at four major NCAA Division I institutions, most recently at the University of Oklahoma as senior associate athletics director at for academics and student services. He also served in similar positions at the University of Maryland, Southern Methodist University and Iowa State University. He has served as president of the Drake Group and president of the National Association of Academic Advisers for Athletics.

C. Keith Harrison is associate chair and associate professor of Business Administration in the DeVos Sport Business Management Program. Dr. Harrison is a former NCAA scholar-athlete who played offensive center on the football team at West Texas A&M University. Harrison earned his MA degree in Physical Education from Cal State University, Dominguez Hills and his doctorate degree at the University of Southern California in Higher and Post-Secondary Education. Dr. Harrison has numerous peer-reviewed scholarly publications, presentations and book chapters. Harrison's brief list of clients past and present include the NFL, Oakland Raiders, Miami Dolphins, Minnesota Vikings, UCLA, University of Oregon, University of Florida, Emory University, UC-Boulder, Wharton Sport Business Initiative, and UMass Boston. Dr. Harrison is currently president and co-founder of scholarballer.org a non-profit organization dedicated to merging education with sport and entertainment where student-athletes embrace their academic identities in society.

Jennifer Lee Hoffman is an associate professor at the Center for Leadership in Athletics in the College of Education at the University of Washington. Hoffman's research examines educational policies and practices in intercollegiate athletics from a critical equity perspective. She has presented to the Knight Commission on Intercollegiate Athletics and to numerous academic conferences. Her scholarship appears in several books and publications, including the *Journal for the Study of Sports and Athletes in Education, Re/constructing Higher Education: Feminist Poststructural Perspectives and Policy Analysis,* and *Change Magazine: The Magazine of Higher Learning.*

Neal H. Hutchens is a professor of higher education at the University of Mississippi. Hutchens earned a PhD from the University of Maryland and a JD from the University of Alabama School of Law. His scholarship centers on law and policy issues in higher education. In the realm of college athletics, Hutchens has written on topics that include college athletes' speech rights and Title IX. He was the 2015 recipient of the William A. Kaplin Award from the Center for Excellence in Higher Education Law and Policy. His scholarship has appeared in publications that include the *University of Pennsylvania Journal of Constitutional Law, Journal of College and University Law, Kentucky Law Journal, West's Education Law Reporter,* and *Journal of Law and Education.* Dr. Hutchens is also a member of the author team for the upcoming sixth edition of *The Law of Higher Education.*

Angela J. Hattery, PhD, is professor and director of the Women and Gender Studies Program at George Mason University. She received her BA degree from Carleton College and PhD from the University of Wisconsin at Madison. Her research focuses on social stratification, gender, family, and race. She is the author of numerous articles, book chapters, and books, including *African American Families: Myths and Realities* (2nd ed., 2014), *The Social Dynamics of Family Violence* (2nd ed., 2016), *Prisoner Reentry and Social Capital* (2010), *Interracial Intimacies* (2009), *Interracial Relationships* (2009), *Intimate Partner Violence* (2008), *African American Families* (2007), and *Women, Work, and Family* (2001). She teaches classes in gender and sexuality; intersections of race, class and gender; gender-based violence; and feminist methods. She also has a research focus in the area of the Sociology of Sport. In addition to her academic work she administers the graduate programs (MAIS and certificate) in Women and Gender Studies.

Keali'i Troy Kukahiko received his BA and MA from the University of California at Los Angeles, where he is currently a PhD student in the Higher Education and Organizational Change Department, under the mentorship of Professor Mitchell Chang. Keali'i started the Pacific Islander Education and Retention (PIER) program at UCLA in 1998, he is a co-founding member of the AIGA Foundation (nonprofit that hosts the Polynesian All-American Bowl), and founder of Prodigy Athletes (an Olympic training program that supports the academic and athletic goals of college-scholarship and professional athletes). These nonprofit organizations have served the Pacific Islander diaspora to improve college access, transition, degree attainment, and professional development for the last 20 years. Keali'i focusses on research that can help inform programs and policies in higher education to create decolonized learning spaces and to develop cultural and racial identities (and its many intersectionalities), critical consciousness, praxis, and servant leadership through critical service learning curriculum.

Robert Scott Lemons graduated from Stanford University in 2015 with a Bachelor of Arts in Economics and a Master of Arts in Public Policy. Lemons played on the Stanford basketball team (2010–2014) and was awarded First Team PAC-12 All Academic Selection and the Pac-12 Leadership Award. Working with Professor John Cogan at the Hoover Institute, Lemons authored an honors thesis entitled "Amateurism and College Sports." While at Stanford, he worked with Carolyn Hoxby, researching tuition costs at American universities. Currently, he is completing a Masters in Banking and Finance from Newcastle University, UK. While in England, Lemons played for the Newcastle Knights, earning the team's MVP. He enjoyed the opportunity to compare and contrast college sports in the UK and USA. Lemons will be pursuing professional basketball opportunities.

Angela Lumpkin is a professor and department chair for Kinesiology and Sport Management at Texas Tech University. Lumpkin publishes in sport ethics, leadership, intercollegiate athletics, teaching effectiveness, and women in sport. Recent research projects range from the academic performance of high school athletes to ethical leadership in intercollegiate athletics to examining the career paths of athletic administrators and athletic directors in intercollegiate athletics. Her research has examined student perceptions of active learning, student-centered learning activities, and use of class time to increase student engagement. Dr. Lumpkin is the author of 25 books, including *Introduction to Physical Education, Exercise Science, and Sport* (10th ed.), *Modern Sports Ethics: A Reference Handbook* (2nd ed.), and *Practical Ethics in Sport Management* with two colleagues. She holds a BSE from the University of Arkansas, MA and PhD from The Ohio State University, and an MBA from the University of North Carolina at Chapel Hill.

Monica Morita is the executive assistant to the athletic director at the University of Southern California (USC). Morita earned her EdD with emphasis in Higher Education at USC while working as the director of student services. Her dissertation, in which she introduced the concept of athletic capital, was on the Pacific Islander scholarship football players' experiences in higher education. Morita has worked for over 28 years in an academic unit with admissions and advising and in the athletic departments of three different institutions of higher education. Her roles have included assistant to the head football coach, assistant athletic director, director of student services, compliance officer and senior woman administrator. Morita also was a Minority Opportunities Athletic Association grant recipient and NACDA attendee for 2016 and has a certificate for the Sports Management Institute grant sponsored by the Pac-10.

Leticia Oseguera is associate professor in Education Policy Studies and senior research associate in the Center for the Study of Higher Education at the Pennsylvania State University. Her research focuses on understanding college access and educational opportunities for historically underserved and underrepresented student populations. She has published a number of peer-reviewed journal articles and book chapters for top academic presses on student athletes, campus climate, and athletic success. She earned academic and athletic honors as a Division I student-athlete and was inducted to the athletic hall of fame at her former undergraduate institution, the University of California, Irvine. She has also served as a faculty representative for the student-athlete advisory committee.

Kaitlin A. Quigley is a PhD candidate in higher education at the Pennsylvania State University. She works as a graduate assistant for the Penn State Alumni Association. Quigley's research focuses on legal issues in higher education, and her dissertation examines the legal issues surrounding college students' online speech. For the past four years, she has worked as a mentor and tutor for student-athletes at Penn State through the Morgan Academic Center for Student Athletes. Quigley has provided academic support services to more than 30 college athletes from a variety of sports teams. She holds an MS in higher education administration from Marywood University and a BA in political science from Penn State. Upon completion of her PhD, Quigley hopes to lead an academic support center for student-athletes.

Valyncia C. Raphael, JD, is the director of diversity and compliance and the Title IX Coordinator at Cerritos College in Southern California. There, she coordinates the college's comprehensive equity, diversity, and inclusion initiatives for over 1,500 employees and 22,000 students. She also leads the college's prevention of and response to gender- and sex-based discrimination, which includes responses to sexual harassment, stalking, sexual assault, and dating/domestic violence. Prior to this role, Dr. Raphael played softball at the University of Wisconsin at Madison, where she earned her undergraduate, law, and doctorate degrees. She earned her doctorate from UW-Madison's School of Education in Educational Leadership and Policy Analysis, with research interests in equity issues in intercollegiate athletics. Earning dissertation of the year in her program, Dr. Raphael used intersectionality and critical qualitative methods to study the identity development and experiences of Black women competing in country club intercollegiate sports at a predominantly white institution.

Daniel A. Rascher (PhD in Economics, UC-Berkeley) is professor and co-director of Sport Management at the University of San Francisco, where he teaches and publishes research on sports economics, finance, management, and marketing topics. He has dozens of publications including a co-authored sport finance textbook (*Financial Management in the Sport Industry*) and analyses of college athletics. At SportsEconomics and OSKR, he has worked on over 100 sports business consulting projects. Dan has testified as an expert witness in federal and state courts, in arbitration proceedings, and provided public testimony numerous times to state and local governments. His work in college sports includes testifying in *O'Bannon v. NCAA, Rock v. NCAA,* and *In Re: NCAA GIA Cap Antitrust Litigation,* as well as working on *White v. NCAA,* Maryland's move to the Big Ten, business research on NCAA Final Fours, college football teams and bowl games, and athletics departments.

Steven J. Silver is a litigation associate at Pierce Atwood in Portland, Maine. In 2015, by arguing due process violations, he successfully obtained an injunction on behalf of a world-renowned Jamaican track star to block decisions by the University of Pennsylvania and the Pennsylvania Interscholastic Athletic Association barring his client from competing in the Penn Relays due to an alleged amateur eligibility infraction. Silver also testified in front of the South Carolina Senate Higher Education Subcommittee in support of a bill to create postgraduate trust funds for NCAA student-athletes. Prior to

becoming a lawyer, Silver, a Northwestern University Medill School of Journalism graduate, was a sports reporter for the *Tennessean* and *Las Vegas Sun*. His work on sports law and athlete advocacy issues has appeared on the Huffington Post, Deadspin, Above the Law, *Philadelphia Magazine, Dan Patrick Show, World Sports Law Report,* and *NCAA Journal of Compliance.*

Earl Smith, PhD, is emeritus professor of Sociology and the Rubin Distinguished Professor of American Ethnic Studies at Wake Forest University. He is the director of the Wake Forest University American Ethnic Studies Program. Dr. Smith is also the former chairperson of the Department of Sociology at Wake Forest. Prior to his appointment at Wake Forest, Professor Smith was the dean of the Division of Social Science at Pacific Lutheran University (PLU) in Tacoma, Washington. He also served as chairperson of the Department of Sociology at PLU. Professor Smith has numerous publications (books, articles, book chapters, etc.) in the area of professions, social stratification, family, and urban sociology and has published extensively in the area of the sociology of sport. His sport-focused books are *Sociology of Sport and Social Theory* (2010, Human Kinetics Publishers) and *Race, Sport and the American Dream* (3rd ed. 2014, Carolina Academic Press). He received his PhD and MA from the University of Connecticut at Storrs.

Ellen J. Staurowsky is a professor in the Department of Sport Management and interim associate director for the Center of Hospitality and Sport Management at Drexel University. She is internationally recognized as an expert on social justice issues in sport, including college athletes' rights and the exploitation of college athletes, gender equity and Title IX, and the misappropriation of American Indian imagery in sport. She is co-author of the book *College Athletes for Hire: The Evolution and Legacy of the NCAA Amateur Myth,* editor of the forthcoming *Women in Sport: Continuing a Journey of Liberation and Celebration,* and is working on a book entitled *Big Time*

Athletes, Labor, and the Academy. Dr. Staurowsky served as a witness on behalf of the plaintiff in *O'Bannon v. NCAA.* She is lead author on the Women's Sports Foundation's 2015 report *Her Life Depends on It III: Sport and Physical Activity in the Lives of American Girls and Women* and co-author of the 2016 WSF report entitled *Beyond Xs and Os: Gender Bias and Coaches in Women's College Sports.*

Andy Schwarz is an antitrust economist with a subspecialty in sports economics. Notably, Mr. Schwarz was the case manager for the NFL's economic expert in *L.A. Raiders v. NFL* and for the plaintiffs' economic experts in *O'Bannon v. NCAA* and the economic expert for the *Keller v. NCAA* settlement class. He has testified to the US House of Representatives' Committee on Education and the Workforce, participated on another US congressional panel on college sports, and has served as an economic expert in a wide variety of state and federal litigation. Schwarz has been featured on ESPN, in the *New York Times,* the *Wall Street Journal,* Bloomberg News, Sports on Earth, and *USA Today,* as well as in the book *Indentured: The Inside Story of the Rebellion against the NCAA.* He is a frequent contributor to Vice Sports and Deadspin and has written for Slate, Forbes.com, 538.com, and ESPN.com. Mr. Schwarz holds an MBA from the Anderson School of Management at UCLA (Class of '94) as well as an AB in History from Stanford University and an MA in History from Johns Hopkins.

John R. Thelin is a professor at the University of Kentucky who studies the history of higher education and public policy. He is the author of several books on higher education, including *Games Colleges Play,* about scandals and reforms in intercollegiate athletics, and *A History of American Higher Education*—both published by the Johns Hopkins University Press. John has received national research awards, including the Outstanding Research Award from ASHE and the outstanding research award in higher education from AERA. An alumnus of Brown University, he was elected to Phi Beta Kappa and was a varsity wrestler. He received his MA and PhD from the University of California, Berkeley. In 2006 he was selected to the Ivy League's 50th anniversary gallery of outstanding student-athlete alumni. He was a charter member of the NCAA's Research Advisory Board, appointed by the late Myles Brand, from 2008 through 2011.

Index